Decolonizing Democracy from Western Cognitive Imperialism

Tatah Mentan

Langaa Research & Publishing CIG
Mankon, Bamenda

Publisher:
Langaa RPCIG
Langaa Research & Publishing Common Initiative Group
P.O. Box 902 Mankon
Bamenda
North West Region
Cameroon
Langaagrp@gmail.com
www.langaa-rpcig.net

Distributed in and outside N. America by African Books Collective
orders@africanbookscollective.com
www.africanbookscollective.com

ISBN: 9956-762-16-4

Table of Contents

Acknowledgements

No one walks alone on the journey of life. Just where do you start to thank those that joined you, walked beside you, and helped you along the way continuously urged me to write a book, to put my thoughts down over the years, those that I have met and worked with, and to share my insights together with the secrets to my continual, positive approach to life and all that life throws at us. So at last, here it is. So, perhaps this book and its pages should be seen as "thanks" to the tens of thousands of you who have helped make my life what it is today.

This book would not have been possible without the support of many scholars. I wish to express my gratitude to the following scholars whose ideas have both inspired and enriched my book. My deepest gratitude therefore goes to: Francis Nyamnjoh (for pushing me on), Samir Amin, Walter Mignolo, Anibal Quijano, and Arturo Escobar. I would like to gratefully acknowledge the enthusiastic embrace of the timely struggle to theorize decolonization from Western coloniality of power in all forms such as Liberal Democracy as the New World Order.

Apart from my efforts and those of scholars mentioned above, the success of any project depends largely on the encouragement and guidelines of many others. I take this opportunity to express my gratitude to my friend Professor Jean-Germain Gros, University of Missouri- St. Louis, the person who has been instrumental in the successful completion of this book. I would like to show my greatest appreciation to him. I can't say thank you enough for his tremendous support and help. I feel motivated and encouraged every time I receive an unfriendly comment from him about my research work. Without his encouragement and guidance this book would not have materialized. Finally, I wish to thank Professor Bill F. Ndi immensely for his editorial cleaning and critical interventions, ideas, and ever-appreciated availability to get the book published.

Preface

Apparently, "Democracy" is in, and "development" is out as buzzwords for Africa nowadays. The very "development" idea and word are in apparently terminal crisis in the continent. The new idea to replacing it is "democracy." When Gandhi was asked what he thought of "Western Civilization," he answered "it would be a good idea." We can say as much of development and democracy as well. However, for Africa, "democracy" is likely to become no more real in the future than "development," or Western Civilization for that matter, did in the past. Instead, like the latter, "democracy" may well become a flag—or the fig leaf—for continued recolonization, exploitation and oppression of the continent by the West.

In Abraham Lincoln's words therefore, there can be little real and meaningful democratic government by the people, of the people, and for the people in any part of the world as long as their economic possibilities are limited and their policy options are controlled by their participation in the whole world economy, which is run from the West. Of course, there is no present claim or foreseeable hope of making decisions for the whole world economy on a democratic basis. As long as this lack of democracy remains for the world economy as a whole, political democracy in any "sovereign" African enclave called state thereof can be of limited scope and value at best.

This existential situation around the world explains why the word "democracy" is increasingly attached to an array of concepts, themes, political and social realities, and visions. Yet there are currently a number of groups, movements, interests and actors around the world that are contesting the normative, hegemonic meaning and manifestation of formal Western democracy being imposed on alien people in the South. Many people in the South do not see their interests served by formal Western electoral, representative democracy, that which concerns political parties, voting and tightly controlled electoral processes. Rather, there is visible concern in many quarters with not only the formal process of how elections are shaped and governments are formed but, also, with the political, economic, cultural, social and militaristic outcomes of such institutionalized configurations.

However, democracy remains a worthy and widespread goal, but it is important to distinguish the goal from the means used to attain it. There is a difference between assertive promotion and more gentle support of democratization. Avoiding coercion, premature elections, and hypocritical rhetoric should not preclude a patient policy that relies on economic assistance, behind-the-scenes diplomacy, and multilateral approaches to aid the development of civil society, the rule of law, and well-managed elections. Equally important to the foreign-policy methods used to support democracy abroad are the ways in which the West practices it at home. When they try to impose democracy, they tarnish it. When the West lives up to its own best traditions, it can stimulate emulation and create the soft power of attraction. This approach is what Ronald Reagan called the "shining city on the hill."

Another aspect of, say, America's domestic practice of liberal democracy that is currently being debated is how it deals with the threat of terrorism. In the climate of extreme fear that followed the attacks of September 11, 2001, the Bush administration engaged in tortured legal interpretations of international and domestic law that tarnished American democracy and diminished its soft power. Fortunately, a free press, an independent judiciary, and a pluralist legislature helped to hold for such practices up public debate.

Obama has proclaimed that he will close the Guantánamo Bay detention facility within a year, and he has declassified the legal memos that were used to justify what is now widely regarded as torture of detainees. But the problem of how to deal with terrorism is not just a matter of history. The threat remains alive, and it is important to remember that people in democracies want both liberty and security.

In moments of extreme fear, the pendulum of attitudes swings toward the security end of that spectrum. Abraham Lincoln suspended the right of habeas corpus – the principle that detainees are entitled to challenge their detention in a court of law – during the Civil War, and Franklin Roosevelt interned Japanese-American citizens during the early days of the Second World War.

When some of the Bush administration's more reasonable members are asked today how they could have taken the positions they did in 2002, they cite the anthrax attacks that followed 9/11, the intelligence reports of an impending attack with nuclear materials, and the widespread fear of a second attack against the American people. In such circumstances, liberal democracy and security are in tension.

Terrorists hope to create a climate of fear and insecurity that will provoke Westerners to harm themselves by undercutting the quality of their own liberal democracy. Preventing new terrorist attacks while understanding and avoiding the mistakes of the past will be essential if the US is to preserve and support liberal democracy both at home and abroad. That is the debate that the Obama administration is leading in the US today. However, this debate does not cancel the fact that democracy is being imposed by the West on non-Western societies as a system of recolonization.

Although democracy seems to have scored an historic victory over alternative forms of governance, a widespread commitment to democracy is a recent phenomenon and the creation and maintenance of democracy is a remarkably difficult form of government (as evidenced by serious threats to it such as fascism, Nazism, Stalinism). Liberal democracy has been championed as the agent of progress, and capitalism as the only viable economic system. People have even proclaimed the "end of history" (Fukuyama, for example) as ideological conflict is being steadily displaced by universal democratic reason and market-oriented thinking.

Theorists of democracy have assumed a "symmetrical" and "congruent" relationship between political decision makers and the recipients of political decisions. However, regional and global interconnectedness contests the traditional national resolutions of the key questions of democratic theory and practice. National communities by no means exclusively make and determine decisions and policies for themselves, and governments by no means determine what is appropriate exclusively for their own citizens. Decisions made by quasi-regional and quasi-supranational organizations (EU, NATO, IMF, etc.) diminish the range of decisions open to national "majorities." Given greater connectedness, one must ask questions. What is the relevant constituency? To whom should decision makers be accountable? Territorial boundaries demarcate the basis on which individuals are involved in and excluded from participation in decisions affecting their lives, but the outcomes of these decisions often "stretch" beyond national frontiers. The implications of this on democracy are considerable for consent, legitimacy, nature of constituency, meaning of representation, proper form and scope of political participation, relevance of the democratic nation-state, etc.

Globalization implies two phenomena. 1) Many chains of political, economic, and social activity are becoming world-wide in scope. 2) There has been an intensification of levels of interaction and interconnectedness within and between states and societies. There is a striking paradox about the contemporary era. More and more nations and groups are championing democracy just at the moment when the very efficacy of democracy as a national form of political organization appears open to question. As substantial areas of human activity are progressively organized on a global scale: the fate of democracy, and of the independent democratic nation-state in particular, is fraught with difficulty.

The meaning and place of democratic politics and of the contending models of democracy have to be rethought in relation to overlapping local, national, regional, and global structures and processes. A new agenda will have to be created for democratic theory and practice in order to rethink democracy in relation to the interconnectedness of states and societies in the global system. This new theory of democracy must offer an account of the changing meaning of democracy within the global order and of the impact of the global order on the development of democratic associations. In the modern age, there are many determinants of the distribution of power, many power centers, and authority systems within and across states and thus the bases of politics and of democratic theory must be recast and the meaning and nature of power, authority, and accountability reexamined.

The context of the modern polity has been altered in many important respects over time, raising questions about the validity and continuing relevance of some of the core concepts of modern political thought (such as sovereignty, liberty, representative democracy, etc.). Neither democratic theory nor international relations (IR) theory provide the conceptual resources necessary because democratic political theory of both the 19th and 20th centuries regarded the world beyond the state as a given and the "sovereignty" of the state was rarely questioned. Although the early modern theorists of "international society" (Grotius and Kant for example) did seek to develop an understanding of the state in the context of the "society of states", these contributions were often lost to political theory as a whole.

Much of the last century was dominated by the realist tradition (also referred to as "statist"). This tradition is almost exclusively concerned with how the global states system conditions the behavior of individual states. Within realist political theory, the interplay of internal and external forces remains largely unexplored. The state is conceived of as a sovereign, monolithic entity whose primary purpose is to promote and defend the national interest. The state is a means to secure national and international order through the exercise of national power. The state is taken for granted, with its goals assumed and little or no internal differentiation among its elements.

Some attempts to consider seriously the modern state within its web of global interconnectedness can be found in the rather diffuse literature which has its philosophical roots in the "liberal-idealist" tradition in international relations. The common thread of this tradition is the assumption that increasing global interconnectedness is transforming the nature and role of the state in the global system. This "transformationalist" literature portrays the modern state as trapped within an extensive web of global and complex interdependence, which has dramatic implications on sovereignty, autonomy, and accountability of the state. But this literature does not present a convincing or coherent account of the modern state - it tends to exaggerate the erosion of state power in the face of globalizing pressures and fails to recognize the enduring relevance of the modern state, both as an idea and as an institutional complex, in determining the direction of domestic and international politics.

Many of the same developments that gave rise to the "transformationalist" critique of realism also provided a stimulus to radical approaches to international relations, such as world systems theory and neo-Marxism, which have dealt with the globalization of capital. These approaches discuss the modern state's limited autonomy from the dictates of transnational capital or from the structural requirements of the global capitalist order. States are thus conceived as partially autonomous political entities. However, many neo-Marxist analyses fail to explore the independent dynamics of the state system and assess its relation to the operations of the world capitalist economy.

The traditional literature of democratic political theory and the existing frameworks of International Relations theory have complementary limitations – limitations which must be overcome if a satisfactory understanding of the nature and prospects of democratic political power is to be achieved. There cannot be an account of the modern democratic state any longer without an examination of the global system and there cannot be an examination of the global system without an account of the democratic state.

Today, the idea of "democracy" that was globalized through European imperial expansions is no longer the only way to conceive and organize harmonic and convivial societies. The crisis of "Western democracy" demands closer examination and invites us to seriously consider other conceptions to achieve peaceful futures. Indeed, there is widespread cynicism, decreasing voter participation, the general sentiment of disenfranchisement and marginalization, and increasing levels of resistance and mobilization in the form of alternatives to the formal Western "democratic" model, which could be characterized as "counter-hegemonic democracy." Counter-hegemonic democracy concerns lived realities inside of, as well as outside, the formal political vacuum, touching on how people seek to build a more resilient, deeper, thicker, more critically engaged and meaningful democracy. Some examples are presented by the mass anti-war, pro-environment, Occupy, World Social

Forum and other social movements that have sought to remove some governments and make others more accountable, or to make the world bodies that frame international politics more aligned with the needs of the masses that do not control the levers of power. Only de-westernization and de-coloniality are necessary to democratize societies in the original communal sense by delinking from Western epistemologies.

Delinking epistemology from globalizing capital is decolonization intended to produce de-colonial knowledge that will put Fanon's "wretched of the earth" in a different concept of life. But what is that concept of life? It is safe to note that society is modern; economy is capitalism but it is linked with racism which has a dispensability of human life. The massive enslavement of workers is an economic concept. Human life is dispensable because once a body does not produce profit, we throw it away and bring more bodies. The body becomes a commodity; human life becomes a commodity. They might have been free before, but once capitalist economy existed, their lives became commodities – the mercantilization of human life (children, women, organs).

What are the consequences of making human life dispensable? Economy is based on an extraction of gold and silver, coffee and cotton. But now because of technological advancement, there is a possibility of environmental catastrophe. Walter Mignolo says that there is a rhetoric of modernity—salvations, progress, triumph – that hides the logic of colonialism. You have to have both; there is no modernity without coloniality. The new technology and the rhetoric of modernity—save paper, save trees, put people in contact, no need to get into a car because you have the Internet— but how do you make technology? Mining! Where are the mines? What are the consequences of the mines and the technology that improves your life?

You need copper. So you need water to separate the copper from the stone; water which was a human right becomes a commodity. So when you are exploding mines to produce cell phones, you need to reduce costs to produce more and serve more using the rhetoric of modernity while using the logic of colonialism—that is the consequences of progress! They won't tell you what is behind modernity. The rhetoric of modernity always goes with colonialism—the problem is because knowledge is being controlled by those making decisions and building, so we criticize but we are always working at the level of the *annunciated*, a semiotic term for racism and patriarchy. It is the system of values in which life became dispensable in the 16th century. Indeed, it came from the logic of European enlightenment which was transformed into the US corporate world. That is, they had to classify a system of inferior people that was racist and use a system patriarchy to decide who was normal and who was not normal. This is where the control of knowledge is secured. The moment in which we start questioning the kind of issues that have been put in front of us to discuss is the moment of delinking. In other words, we should change the terms of the conversation and not the content of the conversation. This book is intended to provoke concerned scholars into changing the terms of the conversation on spreading Western democracy as a global messianic crusade.

Chapter I

Introduction: Framing the Global Democratic Dynamic

Overview

When demonstrations against the government start to take place even in such sleepy places as Swaziland, you know there is something afoot. People are not ready to take it any longer, and governments had better been aware. Absolute monarchies, like the Swazi and the Saudi ones, are especially vulnerable. Arab autocrats like Hosni Mubarak and late Muamar Gaddaffi are criticized for their alleged intention to perpetuate themselves in power through their offspring. Well, by definition, that is what monarchies do. And while constitutional monarchies have a place in today's world, it has become more and more difficult to justify the existence of absolute ones.

Background

Globalization, that is, the steady rise in trans-border flows of goods, services, capital, symbols and cultural products that we have seen over the past several decades or so, has gone hand in hand with an equally steady expansion of democratic ideas around the world. The notion that people ought to govern themselves and through their representatives—and not through some self-appointed masters—has percolated and stuck. Yet, while the central idea of democracy as self-rule, in its broad contours, is the same everywhere, the specific manifestations of it will vary from region to region and from country to country.

Democracy is spreading and it will be with us to stay. That is the good news. The bad news is that, through some sleight of hand, this powerful idea that has mobilized so many people and so much human energy around the world, has been turned by some into a highly parochial, procedural version of what self-rule is all about. It is the specific political practice of a few (ironically) self-appointed countries around the world, mostly in the North Atlantic, that have come to be defined as setting the tone and the parameters for what democracy is and is not.

Globalization, by spreading the idea of democracy, has helped to liberate people from many a dictatorial yoke. But globalization also embodies the danger that a 'one-size fits all' model of democracy be imposed from abroad and from above. As Manuel Castells (2000) has so eloquently demonstrated, we do live in the information society. The information society, in turn, is based on networks, a new, less hierarchical way of structuring organizations, and one in which the new currency of the realm is knowledge and the ability to handle it. This has also meant an upsurge in efforts to categorize, classify and rank countries around the world according to a variety of 'democracy indexes', which purport to tell us how democratic any given country is. And this is not a mere academic exercise. Real-life consequences flow from it. Funds are disbursed, loans are approved or rejected and countries are suspended from international organizations as a result of these rankings.

One of the great paradoxes of all this is that movements and governments that empower people and bring large numbers of the formerly disenfranchised into the political realm are often the targets of these self-appointed 'democracy policemen.' A number of countries in Latin America, like Bolivia, Ecuador, Venezuela and others have experienced this treatment. New leaders, new constitutions, new rights for the hitherto marginalized aboriginal peoples have brought about enormous changes in these countries in the course of the past decades. Bolivian President Evo Morales is the first Amerindian to be elected head of state in the Americas. Lula was the first trade union leader to become president of Brazil. Rafael Correa has brought political stability to Ecuador and a willingness to stand up against the oil majors to defend his country's rights. Yet, far from being welcome as major architects of the deepening of democracy in South America, some of these leaders are often demonized as populists by this fake international consensus about what democracy is and is not.

Democracy is the only game in town, and those that ignore this, like former president Blaise Compaoré in Burkina Faso, who overstayed his welcome, do so at their peril. But this cannot mean that the participatory, popular dimension of democracy is slighted for the sake of a narrowly procedural vision of this form of government. Throughout the Global South we are witnessing the rise of newly emerging powers that will set the tone for much of the twenty-first century. The fastest-growing and most dynamic economies today are not in the North, but in the South. Not all of them are democracies. But India is the largest democracy in the world. It is living proof that many of the standard verities about the so-called 'prerequisites for democracy' developed in the political science literature in the fifties and sixties, and largely inspired by the history of North Atlantic countries, have limited application elsewhere. Winston Churchill famously said that "India is no more a united nation than the Equator is", and assumed it would never hold.

Yet, sixty years and more after independence, India has proven to be much more resilient than many of its smaller, richer and more homogeneous neighbors, all of which were assumed to be more likely to develop strong and stable democratic institutions. A recent book by Juan Linz, Alfred Stepan and Yogendra Yadav, *Crafting State Nations: India and other Multinational Democracies*, elaborates on the fascinating reasons behind India's democratic success. The time has come to 'de-parochialize' the notion of democracy, to cease to believe that it has exclusively Western roots and forms, and to open the doors to the many ways in which the *demos*, that is, the people, organize themselves around the world to take charge of their own destiny.

The "White Man's Burden"?

Discourses on democracy and democratization are usually presented in the West as though they are entirely new notions and practices to the rest of the non-Northern world. The idea of democracy itself is viewed almost exclusively as a Western concept of which Southern societies now stand desperately in need of.

Similarly, the presumption has been that democratic values and practices are alien to the Southern continents, with the West posturing as their cultural flag bearers and defenders. This mindset considers "Others" as incapable of democratic thoughts and hence they should be infused with the "civilized" notion of Western democracy. What has been consistently ignored is that democratic values and processes have been as indigenous to, say, Africans as they were to the ancient Greeks. Non-Western traditional political cultures and organizations would give credence to this conclusion.

While the term *democracy,* now a Western buzzword for representative government, might have been borrowed from the Greeks, democratic thought and values have never been exclusively Greek or Euro-American preserve. Indeed, the desire for representation, inclusion, and participation in public affairs—essential elements of democracy—are universal to all humans; the difference rests in the methods of attaining these goals. To what extent a society "democratizes" is incontestably dependent on its sociocultural milieu, whether it is African, European, American, Asian, or even Islamic societies.

Efforts by the West to "introduce" and "spread" democracy to other parts of the world bear close semblance to the concept of the "civilizing mission" trumpeted by Europeans during the era of brutal and dehumanizing colonialism in the nineteenth century. In his now infamous poem "The White Man's Burden," Rudyard Kipling considers European colonization as a blessing to colonized but a huge burden for Europeans. Europeans sought to bring civilization to the colonized, whom Kipling saw as degenerate people, incapable of development and civilized behavior (Kipling,1995; Fredland, 2001). And, European cultural benchmarks were used in determining what civilization entailed, and who was or was not civilized. Since Europeans were themselves the judges, a civilized culture (whether social, political, or economic) was that which approximated the European model. Furthermore, since colonialism justified and legitimized itself on the assumption of the superiority of the "white race" (Europeans) over non-Europeans, it became quite logical for European colonizers to discredit the existing culture of the colonized non-Europeans no matter how comparable they were.

Consequently, in the case of Africa for example, the societies (including their indigenous democratic values) that were not necessarily "civilized" to the European mindset were portrayed as barbarous and, therefore, stood in need of "civilization." It was a unique union between cultural arrogance and dubious altruism. Thus, in reality, the supposed burden was an effort to replicate or reproduce European models and values in the non-European world—another form of neocolonialism so to speak. It was all about Western hegemony. The current obsession for spreading Western democracy, democratization and globalization in Africa and beyond is, then, a déjà vu. Reminiscent of European motives or justifications for colonialism, the current push for spreading democratization has little to do with the selfless notion of the "civilizing mission." Instead, the interests and well-being of the objects of "democratization" have been subordinated to those of the industrialized countries of the North.

Promoting Western Democracy

The spread of market economy and promotion of democracy are twin components of globalization. Both are generally positive phenomena that are taken by many to be something as obvious as God, motherhood and apple-pie. However, there is too much naivety and hypocrisy, especially in the process of promotion of democracy. In the case of societies that lack elementary preconditions for the introduction of democracy, the remedy may be worse than the illness. The end of the Cold War did not end the attempts to use concepts, such as democracy and human rights, as ideological tools to undermine other states. Attempts to change domestic social and political systems, especially those of great powers or their allies and neighbors, may lead to a new era of great power confrontation that would be especially dangerous because of common threats such as terrorism, spread of weapons of mass destruction, environmental crisis and so on.

The turn of the Millennium has brought about the acceleration of processes of globalization that for the first time have covered practically the whole world. Essential parts of these processes have been the spread of principles of market economy (often by means of "shock therapy" and in the form of free markets as expounded by the Chicago School of Milton Friedman) and ideas of democracy for which there has been both demand from the East and supply from the West. As articulated by Sachs (1994), the shock doctrine is a theory for explaining the way that force, stealth and crisis are used in implementing neoliberal economic policies such as privatization, deregulation and cuts to social services. In sum, pro-corporate neoliberals treat crises such as wars, coups, natural disasters and economic downturns as prime opportunities to impose an agenda of privatization, deregulation, and cuts to social services.

The end of the Cold War, indeed, signified a triumph of the Western style democracy and market economy over the Soviet version of communism. The Western world had shown not only that its values corresponded more to the aspirations of most people than the Soviet imposed value system, but also proved the much greater effectiveness of the market economy over centrally planned economy. Of course, the more pragmatic Chinese communists had understood it decades earlier when they under DENG Xiaoping had started to reform their economy. Therefore, it may have indeed seemed that at the end of the twentieth century, as Francis Fukuyama wrote, out of the two major competitors only one (the West) had stayed in the ring (Fukuyama,1999). It seemed that the world, while naturally remaining heterogeneous in many respects, is becoming in some important ways more and more homogeneous.

A liberal-democratic future of the world therefore seemed, for a while and for some, possible. Although new States of the former Soviet Empire were indeed in need of both free markets and democracy, there was a lot of idealism (even naivety) and hypocrisy (even cynicism) both at the export and import ends of the process. The introduction of markets, usually carried out by means of "shock therapy" prescribed by Friedmanite Chicago School of free marketeers, often clashed with the principles of democracy, and the latter always had to give way. Hard matter prevailed over soft values.

The spread of market economy and democracy—the concepts that are considered by many to be something as obvious as God, motherhood and apple-pie—in practice often turns out to be a mixed blessing. If planned economy of the Soviet type indeed left everybody and society as a whole poor and market economy may indeed be one of the preconditions of political freedoms, shock introduction of unbridled markets makes a few extremely rich while many become even poorer than they were under the old system. As one of the central planks of democracy, with some important qualifications of course, is that many count more than a few, it should be clear that economic "shock therapy" and democracy are incompatible. Cambridge economist Ha-Joon Chang (2008) goes even further, writing that "Free market and democracy are not natural partners", though it has to be emphasized that Professor Chang is not speaking of "market economy", but of "free market" or rather "unbridled market", as advocated by Milton Friedman and his followers.

Although nobody should ideally suffer from the spread of democracy, which even more than market economy seems to be a universal value, its promotion in practice does not always bring about general happiness. On the contrary, some societies may greatly suffer not only from inadequate methods of promotion of democracy, but also from the failure to understand that a remedy that cures one patient may kill another. The bombs that spread electoral democracy to Iraq and Libya best explain the irony of "democratic peace." Moreover, though only few of those who are involved in the business of exporting democracy are driven primarily by altruistic concerns (mixed motives should not necessarily discredit positive achievements, even if they come as side-effects), quite a few of the exporters of democracy have in mind rather different considerations such as oil, gas, war against terror and strategic advantages, and do not give a damn about democracy.

In parts of the former Soviet Empire (both the internal empire, i.e. the Union of the Soviet Socialist Republics (USSR) and the external one that included those nations that were *de jure* independent but *de facto* tightly controlled from the Kremlin), there was indeed quite a widespread desire to accept many Western values, despite the fact that there was not much understanding of what these values exactly meant. Some of the newly born countries had a short encounter with these values; they were also seen as being opposite to the imposed and hated Soviet ideals. Yet, soon quite a few started to miss the lack of the latter (e.g. free health care and education). However, when one changes the whole system, one is often forced to accept not only advantageous but also undesirable aspects of the new system; a choose-and-pick approach is not always possible.

Other parts of the former Soviet Empire initially also went along with the general trend of democratization, though in many cases there was more hypocrisy or naivety (sometimes a combination of both) than genuine desire or understanding of democratic values and institutions, though it is necessary to admit that in different proportions such a combination has been present in all post-communist countries. A mixture of idealism that often equals to naivety and hypocrisy that may sometimes even have positive consequences (due to the so-called hypocrisy trap) seems to be present in all societies undergoing radical reforms (the so-called "transitional societies"). Pressure of various international bodies, Western governments and non-governmental organizations (NGOs) often led to formal acceptance of concepts and legally binding obligations that did not correspond to local realities and therefore had few chances of being implemented.

Processes of globalization in the post-Cold War World, which were welcomed by most world leaders, interests of Western, especially American, capital and the popularity of democratic peace theories led to efforts to spread democracy not only to the fragments of the Soviet Empire, but to other parts of the world as well, including rather implausible places such as Afghanistan, Iraq and the Greater Middle East as a whole. Western countries, first of all Washington, but also the European Union (EU), its member-states and other European institutions such as the Organization on the Security and Co-operation in Europe (OSCE) started to implement programs of democracy promotion. It was done without any serious discussion of the readiness of different societies to accept these concepts; it would have been even politically incorrect to question the readiness of some societies for democracy. As with some "importers" of democracy, "exporters" too had mixed motives and sometimes rather naïve understanding of what democracy would mean in specific contexts of these far-away societies.

Idealism that often equals to naivety and hypocrisy that sometimes has to pay homage to virtue together with pragmatic approaches are all present in the export–import business of democracy. Naïve and hypocritical approaches to democracy promotion, especially when objectives of a naïve and a hypocrite coincide or when seemingly improbable combination of naivety and hypocrisy co-exist in a decision-maker, are not less dangerous than thoughtless experiments with markets and "shock therapy". Today, they are contributing, as an ideological cocoon of economic and strategic interests, to the emergence of a new great power confrontation where an "arc of democracies" may face a circle or some other configuration of authoritarian powers. For example, The *Economist* of 15–21 December 2007, p. 72 notes that the "hawkish" former Japanese Prime Minister Shinzo Abe "espoused a sweeping 'arc of freedom and prosperity' that was supposed to anchor Japan in a Eurasian community of democratic nations but was in practice a not particularly subtle attempt to throw a cordon around a rising China". Such a theme is a constant topic of American neocons today.

Today, it is clear that the Fukuyama "end of history" is not at the horizon. These are not only the so-called new and non-traditional threats such as global warming, religiously inspired terrorism or spread of weapons of mass destruction (WMDs) as well as the spread of weapons of mass deception that are challenging the world community of States. Unfortunately, at the horizon are already visible the contours of a new great power confrontation. The post-Cold War experience has shown that pushing aggressively for a change in other societies is as dangerous

9

and counterproductive as rejection of changes, whose time has come and which are demanded by people at home.

Outside pressure for democratization may indeed effect positive transformations, but usually in small countries, and even then only when there is a confluence of favorable conditions. In their foreign policy, such States practice bandwagonning, i.e. they are prone to join stronger and more prosperous actors, accepting to a great extent also their ways of life. Big countries that, due to their history, potential and size, have great power ambitions, on the contrary, resort to balancing, i.e. their response to outside pressure is usually defiance and internal consolidation against external challenges.

Conflicts of interests, especially between great powers, are inevitable in the world of limited resources. However, differently from the Cold War confrontation, there is much less ideology in today's great power disagreements, and in order not to aggravate emerging rivalry, it is necessary not to burden real and often inevitable conflicts of interests with ideological motives. What made the Cold War so special and also dangerous was its ideological component. Therefore, while continuing to promote values such as democracy and human rights, it is necessary, first, to avoid as far as possible discrediting these noble aims by using them as a cover for mundane economic, political or strategic interests (i.e. for politicians, not to be too hypocritical, and for the rest, to learn to look behind the words, not to be too naïve); secondly, not to think that democracy and human rights are like mechanical tools that work everywhere (to be realistic or pragmatic); and thirdly, not to have trust in those dictators and autocrats who either claim that they have already brought a haven of democracy to their people or refer to historical and religious traditions of their nations in order to delay responses to calls from their people for democracy and human rights. Not every Western politician who speaks of democracy in far-away places is necessarily a hypocrite; not every human right activist who claims to know a remedy for a dire human rights situation in another country is inevitably ignorant or naïve; not even every autocrat who claims to have the support of the population is automatically wrong. However, it is always safer to doubt and double-check. In matters where practical interests and ideology intermingle, one can never be sure.

A new era of great power confrontation—though quite probable—is neither desirable nor inevitable. To avoid slipping into a new Cold War, it is necessary to separate the wheat from the chaff. It is necessary to accept differences of domestic arrangements and values that usually result from long historical evolution of societies, levels of their development as well as diversity of pragmatic interests. Here, we need not only good faith but also good understanding of inevitability of diversity that, especially for a Western mind, schooled in the Enlightenment's idea of universality of reason and values, is especially difficult to accept (there are many who think: what works in America, should work everywhere; what is good for America, should be good for the world). At the same time, let us not forget that naivety and especially hypocrisy are the tools of not only exporters of democracy but also those who are at the importing end of the process. There are populist dictators who suppress popular demands for democracy, thereby destroying their countries. Although there is a lot of truth in the saying that people deserve their rulers, there are quite a few of them that no people should suffer from. It is necessary to confront such dictators, though even in such cases one has not to lose the sight of the necessity of choosing remedies that do not make the illness worse and kill the patient.

Thomas Friedman once put one of the most pertinent questions "The big question", in *The International Herald Tribune*, of 4–5 March 2006 (p. 6) concerning democratization of some societies, though he himself did not either know the answer or dare to formulate one. He asked: "Was Iraq the way Iraq was because Saddam was the way Saddam was, or was Saddam the way Saddam was because Iraq was the way Iraq was?" In some societies, unfortunately, a short- or even middle-term choice would be between a secular dictatorship, religious totalitarianism and anarchy or civil war. In such a case, the best scenario may well be an "enlightened dictatorship" (a rare breed indeed) that could gradually open up the way for democracy.

Finally, let us always try to see through the words. Words, be they concepts, doctrines or laws, may indeed reflect values that are universal or at least in principle universalizable, but they may also be used, either deliberately or mistakenly, to pass parochial ideas for universal values. Already in the 1920s, Carl Schmitt (1995, p.54) incisively wrote: "When a state fights its political enemy in the name of humanity, it is not a war for the sake of humanity, but a war wherein a particular state seeks to usurp a universal concept against its military opponent. ... The concept of humanity is an especially useful ideological instrument of imperialist expansion, and in its ethical-humanitarian form it is a specific vehicle of economic imperialism. Here, one is reminded of a somewhat modified expression of Proudhon's: whoever invokes humanity wants to cheat". Schmitt's controversial political affiliations should not diminish the topicality of his insights. If this all sounds too Machiavellian, it is only due to the subject-matter—politics, especially in its international dimension. In world politics, Machiavellian answers are preferable to Pollyannaish recipes because of the nature of the phenomena we are dealing with. Pragmatism enlightened by idealism (or idealism moderated by pragmatism) that sees through hypocrisy and naivety is the best tool for understanding our imperfect, but somewhat perfectible, world. Though, what is this export–import item that has become such a hot issue since the Cold War and the bi-polar world came to an end?

A family portrait of democracy

Although politicians, statesmen and academics continue to argue over the meaning, definition and models of democracy, very few of them would today proudly claim that they are not democrats or that they consider democracy unacceptable for their societies not only for the time being but also forever. Of course, there is often a lot of hypocrisy in pro-democratic declarations and statements as well as genuine misunderstanding of what democracy means, though the latter, due to the elusiveness of the subject matter, should not be so surprising. Nevertheless, today a few would

12

publicly agree with the greatest Greek philosopher who considered democracy as a corrupt and unjust form of government, as a rule of mob (Plato, Republic (1993), pp. 293–301). Therefore, today the issue is not so much whether democracy is, in principle, preferable to other forms of government.

One of the most serious practical as well as theoretical questions in this field is how to get there: how can a non-democratic society be transformed into a democratic one? This problem may be divided into sub-issues such as: are all societies indeed ready for democracy; are those who oppose dictators necessarily democrats (as is too often assumed); are not methods to promote democracy sometimes worse than the absence of democracy; and what may happen if democracy is brought, either through an internal popular demand or due to external pressure or by means of a combination of the both, to a society that is not ready for it? In this section, I will try to reflect on possible answers to these questions based, to a great extent, on recent developments in the former USSR and specifically in Central Asia, though I am naturally borrowing from the wisdom of other writers as well as drawing parallels with other regions.

When we speak of democracy, we must try not only to define what we are talking about, i.e. try to explain what we mean by democracy, but we also need to put this phenomenon into its proper context. This, among other things, requires us to compare democracy with other closely related phenomena, such as human rights, liberalism, the rule of law, good governance and development. In some cases, democracy may be part of these phenomena, in other cases it may be a precondition for their development, or, *vice versa*, it may be a result of the advance of these other phenomena. Although it is difficult to give one widely acceptable definition of democracy, it can be recognized using the concept of Wittgensteinian family resemblances. There are some traits that all democracies, though in different degrees, have in common. What are these features that allow us to include some States into the category of democracies, other States into the category of non-democracies, whereas there may be grey zones with some vaguely discernible family features while other features clearly do not fit in?

Democracy is such a political system, such an organization of a society, where those who govern do so for, with the consent of, and with regular consultation of the governed. It is governance by the people and for the people. David Held (2006) defines democracy as "a form of government in which, in contradistinction to monarchies and aristocracies, the people rule" (p.1). Charles Tilly (2007) considers that "a regime is democratic to the degree that political relations between the state and its citizens feature broad, equal, protected and mutually binding consultation" (p.14). Depending on various characteristics used by different writers, one may distinguish, for example, between direct and representative democracy. The notion of deliberative (or discursive, communicative) democracy is closely associated with works of Jürgen Habermas (1996, p.128), and even its partial implementation presumes high levels of institutional development of the State, and even more importantly, highly developed political culture of the population that has internalized liberal–democratic values. Today, this concept, or rather most of its elements, can be realized in practice only in highly developed societies. Although the term "liberal democracy" has been already used for long, only recently its logical opposite—"illiberal democracy"—has been introduced into academic discourse (Zakaria, 2003).

Sometimes democracy is not only understood as liberal democracy only, but even equated with liberalism. For example, when Hong Kong was handed over to China in 1997, *The Washington Post* of 8 September 1997, A16, published an editorial entitled *"Undoing Hong Kong's Democracy"*. However, there had been no democracy in Hong Kong under the British rule, though the population enjoyed considerable economic and even rather wide personal liberties all granted by London. The people of Hong Kong had all the bread and butter, but did not have any say (and until facing the hand-over to the People's Republic of China (PRC) did not even actively claim it) in how to arrange their life. This example shows that there may be quite wide liberties, especially economic and civil (personal) liberties, without political freedoms and democracy. As Jürgen Habermas notes, "only the rights of political participation ground the citizen's reflexive, self-referential legal standing. Negative liberties and social entitlements, on the contrary, can be paternalistically bestowed. In principle, the constitutional State and the welfare State can be implemented without democracy" (Op. Cit. n. 10, p. 78).

Although democracy and liberalism are not to be mixed (often they may indeed clash), they are nevertheless using the expression of Immanuel Wallerstein in the *frères–ennemis* relationship. They usually support each other and create conditions advantageous for each other's development, but at the same time, they also put limits to each other's flourishing. If we take the famous trinity of the French Revolution, *liberté, égalité and fraternité*, we may say that *liberté* is the essence of liberalism and as such it is in a relationship of *fraternité* with individualism. At the same time, *égalité* that is the essence of democracy very often comes into conflict with *liberté*. Wallerstein writes that "liberals give priority to liberty, meaning individual liberty, and that democrats (or socialists) give priority to equality. ... Liberals do not merely give priority to liberty; they are opposed to equality, because they are strongly opposed to any concept measured by outcome, which is the only way the concept of equality is meaningful", at www.fbc.binghampton.edu/iwfrenn.htm, accessed on 12/08/2014.

Jacques Barzun observes that "The strong current toward greater equality and the strong desire for greater freedom are more than ever in conflict. Freedom calls for a government that governs least; equality for a government that governs most" (1986, pp. 25–26). At the same time, Robert Dahl (1998) observes that "one of the most important reasons for preferring democratic government is that it can achieve political equality among citizens to a much greater extent than any feasible alternative" (p. 56). Does this mean that the more there is democracy, the less there are liberties? Not, of course. Only by absolutizing the importance of equality, or *vice versa* liberty, can one come to the conclusion that one negates the other.

The case of Hong Kong is, of course, a bit exceptional, but enlightened autocrats like Lee Kwan Yew or Mohamad Mahatir may indeed grant significant economic and personal liberties to their people, while leaders elected more or less democratically sometimes resort to repression against political opponents and stifle entrepreneurship (e.g. in Belarus under President Lukashenka). However, Zakaria's use of the term "illiberal democracy" somewhat misses the point since such "democracies" have not only deficits of liberalism, i.e. lack or severe limitation of personal freedoms, but also democracy deficit, though certain formal attributes of democracy such as regular elections are present. It may well be true that some societies may benefit from enlightened authoritarianism; in that respect Singapore and Malaysia may arguably serve as examples, and Kazakhstan in Central Asia has similar claims, though a caveat is necessary—reliance on autocrats, even if enlightened, is a risky business; moreover, for one Lee Kwan Yew or Mahatir there are usually dozens of "Sit Tightist" dictators like the Biyas, Compaorés, Mobutus or Mugabes.

Often, democracy is identified through elections. Some, what I would call, extreme formalistic or superficial approaches to democracy even claim that governments produced by elections may be inefficient, endemically corrupt, short-sighted, irresponsible, dominated by special interest and incapable of adopting policies demanded by the public good are nevertheless democracies. One can visit S. Huntington, *The Third Wave: Democratization in the Late Twentieth* Century (1993) and F. Zakaria, 'The Rise of Illiberal Democracy,' 76, 6, *Foreign Affairs* 1997, 56–73) for more on this issue. However, to equate democracy with one, though important but relatively technical, aspect of it would make a mockery of democracy.

Does democracy necessarily presume free and fair elections based on the one man, one vote principle? It certainly follows from Article 25 of the International Covenant on Civil and Political Rights (ICCPR), which provides for the right of every citizen "to vote and to be elected at genuine periodic elections which shall be by universal and equal suffrage and shall be held by secret ballot, guaranteeing the free expression of the will of the electors". It seems pretty certain that free and fair elections are one of the attributes or requirements of mature democracy in today's world, but this does not necessarily mean that they are the sufficient or even absolutely necessary condition. Other forms of consultation may be used to discover the public opinion, and the consent of the governed could also be expressed through other means. If the authorities in their policies do not ignore what the public wants and enjoy the consent of the governed, it is difficult to deny that there are elements of democracy in such a society even if their elections do not correspond to the Western standards, though in such cases we could hardly speak of mature or liberal democracy. Such governments are sometimes called populist regimes, but as Lord Dahrendorf has noted, "one man's populism is another's democracy and vice versa" (Acht Ammerkungen zum Populismus, 25 *Transit-Europäische Revue*, 2003, p.156).

Although elections, *per se*, do not make a country democratic and there may be elements of democracy in societies whose practices do not conform with requirements of Article 25 of the ICCPR, it is impossible in the twenty-first century to speak of democracy in the country that does not hold regular elections. For example, in an article entitled "No elections, no democracy", published in a local Beijing newspaper, WANG Changjiang, a scholar from the Central Party School in Beijing, writes that though we must not take elections as a miraculous cure for solving all problems of political democracy, they are "an indispensable part of democracy" (See his "No Elections, No Democracy, China Elections & Governance"). The General Comment of the Human Rights Committee on Article 25 also emphasizes that "genuine periodic elections in accordance with paragraph (b) are essential to ensure the accountability of representatives for the exercise of the legislative or executive powers vested in them" (See Para. 8 of General Comment 25 of the Human Rights Committee, at www.unhchr.ch/tbs/doc.nsf). Although the General Comment underlines that citizen's participation in the conduct of public affairs is "supported by ensuring freedom of expression, assembly and association", it does not require the existence of a multi-party system.

If we compare democracy with human rights, we see that the so-called political rights, as they are enshrined, for example, in the

17

Universal Declaration of Human Rights or the ICCPR, are rights close to the essence of democracy. Article 25 of the ICCPR provides that: "Every citizen shall have the right and *the opportunity* [sic, emphasis added], without any of the distinctions mentioned in Article 2 and without unreasonable restrictions: (a) To take part in the conduct of public affairs, directly or through freely chosen representatives; (b) To vote and to be elected at genuine periodic elections which shall be by universal and equal suffrage and shall be held by secret ballot, guaranteeing the free expression of the will of the electors; (c) To have access, on general terms of equality, to public service in his country". Therefore, Professor Thomas Franck (1992, pp. *46-9)* was not far from the truth (though this truth is normative, even a bit hypocritical, if there can be such a thing in parallel with absolute or relative truths) when in 1990 he wrote of the emerging right to democratic governance. However, as with some other human rights, this right seems hardly to be universal; its content is too general and its practical implementation not general enough.

As there are many models or forms of democracy, it is important to somehow limit the use of this term, i.e. it is necessary to say also what democracy certainly is not. That, however, is easier said than done. It is, of course, possible to use the old method and say that I know it when I see it. According to this method, say, the Democratic People's Republic of Korea (DPRK) would not be a democracy, however loose definition one may use. But what about the PRC or the Russian Federation? Are they democracies? Of course, there are those who have very clear, though obviously radically opposite, answers to these questions, but in an academic discourse that has to be as impartial as possible, I would prefer to follow the formula: the more I know, the less certain I am, and therefore I would not jump to hasty conclusions on such difficult matters. Rather than divide countries into clear categories as democratic and non-democratic (or even as the Freedom House does, into free, partially free and not free), it is better to see regimes on a scale between the absolute non-democracy (e.g. DPRK) and absolute democracy (only an ideal on which, moreover, there is no consensus).

18

Instrumental and intrinsic value of democracy

There are logical arguments favoring democracy over other forms of governance such as "a human being can be fully human only when he or she fully participates in the political life of his or her country", that democracy is "a fundamental mode of self-realization", or even that "only democratic governance can put an end to famines" and other similar arguments put forward by intellectual giants such as Jürgen Habermas and Amartya Sen. Nobel Prize winner for Economics Amartya Sen writes that "famines are easy to prevent if there is a serious effort to do so, and a democratic government, facing elections and criticisms from opposition parties and independent newspapers, cannot help but make such an effort. Not surprisingly, while India continued to have famines under British rule right up to independence (the last famine, which I witnessed as a child, was in 1943, four years before independence), they disappeared suddenly with the establishment of a multiparty democracy and a free press" (A. Sen, "Democracy as Universal Value", 3 *Journal of Democracy* (1999, p. 8).

However, such reasoning cannot persuade those who prefer pragmatic or emotional arguments to logical or rational reasoning, as many people do. One of such arguments in favor of democracy is best expressed by the Richard Rorty, the greatest pragmatist philosopher who passed away in 2007: "Followers of Dewey like myself would like to praise parliamentary democracy and the welfare State as very good things, but only on the basis of invidious comparison with suggested concrete alternatives, not on the basis of claims that these institutions are truer to human nature, or more rational, or in better accord with the universal moral law, than feudalism or totalitarianism" (.R. Rorty, *Philosophical Papers*, vol. 1 (2007), p. 211). As Cambridge philosopher Simon Blackburn writes, Rorty "opposes the tradition which descends from Locke or Kant to recent writers such as Jürgen Habermas and John Rawls, which seeks to prove that a democratic and liberal state is the only rational mode of social organization.

For such writers, someone who chose to live in an illiberal or undemocratic state would be trampling on his own reason. It is irrational to sell yourself into the mental servitude that a theocratic state demands. But for Rorty, this Enlightenment attitude with its talk of irrationality is useless. The right pragmatist observation is that theocratic states seem not to work very well, by comparison with liberal democracies – it is theocracies who lose refugees to us, and not *vice versa*. We can cope, and theocracies cannot" (S. Blackburn, Portrait (2003); Richard Rorty, 85 *Prospect Magazine* (2003). Rorty would have probably agreed with Winston Churchill who famously in the House of Commons of the British Parliament declared that "Democracy is the worst form of government, except for all those other forms that have been tried from time to time" (A House of Commons Speech on 11 November 1947).

There are certainly some strong points in Rorty's arguments, though most of those millions who leave their war-torn and poverty-ridden countries behind do not seek at all democracy in the West. Often they bring their highly undemocratic habits and traditions with them and even try to spread them in countries that have given them refuge. Of course, it is possible to argue that Western societies are prosperous because they are democratic, though it may well be the other way around—it is prosperity that leads to democracy. The truth is, probably, somewhere in between and where there is a chicken and where is an egg depends on concrete circumstances.

I enjoy living in a liberal-democratic country and I believe that notwithstanding all its imperfections it is best for me and for my family. However, it would be a mistake to make from this personal observation the following extrapolations. The first such invalid extrapolation would be the belief that everybody is like me. I would call it a "Bush fallacy" since it has been President George W. Bush who has most clearly and quite often expressed the belief that what are self-evident truths for the Americans are true for all and everywhere. The second is that even if democracy, especially liberal democracy, is in principle good for everybody (of which I am not so sure), the problem is when and how to get there.

American philosopher Daniel Dennett (2007, p.23), who believes that his sacred values are obvious and quite ecumenical, enlists them in alphabetical order as "democracy, justice, life, love, and truth". Is democracy really ecumenical and sacred? Does it have any intrinsic value at all or is its value wholly instrumental? David Held notes that "Within democratic thinking, a clear divide exists between those who value political participation for its own sake and understand it as a fundamental mode of self-realization, and those who take a more instrumental view and understand democratic politics as a means of protecting citizens from arbitrary rule and expressing (via mechanisms of aggregation) their preferences. ... According to this position, democracy is a means not an end" (D. Held, *Models of Democracy* (3rd Edn, 2006), p. 231).

Democracy, in my view, has indeed some intrinsic value, though I would not call it sacred. The gist of this value is that humans, at least most of them, and in principle, I believe, all adult and mentally non-handicapped persons, when their immediate needs for survival are met, are not content or happy if it is somebody else who decides what is good and what is bad for them, what they are allowed to do and what should be prohibited to do. Although one should not underestimate the human desire for emotional comfort that is provided by relieving people from the need to constantly take decisions. Somebody else—the parents, a party, the government, God represented by the clergy—takes over the burden. Many feel themselves comfortable only among their co-religionists or in the military (Jean-Francois Revel, 1976).

There have always been those who have not been satisfied with material well-being only. However, Dennett himself observes that "Biology insists on delving beneath the surface of 'intrinsic' values and asking why they exist, and any answer that is supported by the facts has the effect of showing that the value in question is—or once was—really instrumental, not intrinsic, even if we don't see it that way" (Dennett, Op. Cit., p.69). Although democracy has also this intrinsic value because only under democracy—as if by definition—human beings obtain their adulthood, become citizens instead of subjects, its primary value is instrumental—it has to contribute, and usually it does, to the realization of other values, such as material prosperity, social stability, personal freedoms and security, scientific or artistic creativity. However, this is not what always happens since even the road to hell is also paved with good

21

intentions. Moreover, if we speak of those who are involved in democracy promotion, we have to remember that according to the Bible, a Good Samaritan is rather an exception than a rule.

On absolute and relative universality of the concept of democracy

In 1770s, a Royal physician Johann Friedrich Struensee (2003), who by a strange and fatal confluence of circumstances, became so close to the physically feeble and mentally unstable King Christian VII of Denmark that soon he was the most influential person and *de facto* prime minister of the country, issuing laws that, among other interesting and wonderful things like abolition of serfdom and secession of subsidies to unprofitable industries owned by the nobility, also included unrestricted freedom of expression and religious freedoms. Unfortunately, though quite predictably, such laws had little effect in the eighteenth-century Danish Kingdom, and the only tangible result of the freedom of expression was that shortly everybody started to talk about Struensee's love affair with the Queen. Soon the man who was well ahead of his time was executed and the Queen was sent into exile.

This case is interesting and topical also because it allows one to distinguish between pretexts and reasons. The love affair served as a pretext, while Struensee's reform attempts were the reason for his downfall. Today's politics is full of such examples (e.g. the attempts of US Republicans to impeach President Clinton over his affair with Monica Lewinsky or the Khodorkovsky criminal case in Russia). As a reaction to Struensee's reform attempts, Denmark became even less tolerant and free than it had been before the Royal physician had tried to put into practice some radical ideas of the Enlightenment. It took centuries before these noble ideas become the reality in Europe, including the Kingdom of Denmark.

Now, let us move more than 200 years and from Scandinavia to the Middle East. In 2003, the Bush Administration in America, enlightened *inter alia* by the neo-conservative (neo-con) ideology, which too may have some one-sided links with the Enlightenment heritage, undertook an attempt to export democracy to Iraq. Two years earlier, the same export item was sent to Afghanistan. Of course, neither Afghanistan nor Iraq can be considered as pure testing grounds for the export of democracy, though some neo-cons probably sincerely believed that by overthrowing the bloody regime of Saddam and democratizing Iraq, it would be possible to bring democracy also to the wider Middle East. However, pragmatic reasons were prevalent in both of these cases. Al Qaida terrorists had found refuge in the Taliban's Afghanistan, and Iraq had invaded oil-rich Kuwait and Saddam's regime was indeed constantly in breach of UN Security Council resolutions. A reminder: there is a lot of oil in Iraq and in the Middle East as a whole, and whenever somebody talks about democracy and human rights in regions with rich energy and other mineral resources, one should be especially on guard when hearing lofty words.

Both the Struensee case and the current attempts to promote democracy in Afghanistan and Iraq show that it is not enough to have a burning desire to bring about democracy; quite a lot of more is needed if one were to succeed. At the same time, there are big differences between today's Iraq and Afghanistan, on the one hand, and the 1770s Denmark, on the other. One of such differences is especially important for our discussion on democracy promotion. Two hundred and thirty years ago, Enlightenment ideas concerning personal freedoms and democracy were nowhere realized in practice and therefore may have been considered by many, probably by most of the people at that time, not only utopian but also simply mad and dangerous.

The editors of a book on democracy promotion write: "Certainly, in most countries, even that celebrated home of constitutional liberty, Great Britain, democracy was not something that gradually evolved and matured sometime after the Napoleonic Wars, but was rather a political aspiration that had to be fought for against those who sought to control, manipulate and often retard what they saw as this most dangerous of political deviations. Regarded by its enemies – included most nineteenth-century liberals – as a threat to stable order and the institution of private property, democracy had few friends in high places" (Ikenburry, p.1). Anthony Dworkin, for example, questions: "Is it right to see the neoconservative project of exporting democracy as itself utopian, sharing some kind of essential flaw with other utopian projects, despite obvious differences?" (A. Dworkin, The Case for Minor Utopias, *Prospect Magazine,* 2007, p. 42). Today this cannot be the case.

Democracy and freedom of expression exist in reality in many countries. However, if, today, these ideas cannot be considered as utopian in an absolute sense, i.e. in the sense that they can never and nowhere be put into practice since they, say, go against the human nature (whatever this may mean), maybe they are nevertheless utopian in relative sense, i.e. in the sense that they are not acceptable in some places and at least for the time being? One of the differences between concepts such as communism and democracy is that democracy, even if always far from the ideal (but ideal is always utopian and utopia can exist only as an ideal since in Thomas Moore's coinage the very term "utopia" means "no place"), does exist in practice. In the case of democracy, we could speak of utopia only in the sense whether it can exist everywhere (whether this is a universal or in principle a universalizable concept); if the answer to the previous question is positive, then whether certain economic, social and other preconditions are nevertheless needed for democracy to emerge and take root; and closely related to the last point, whether it can be exported or promoted from outside or whether it has always to be home-grown? It has to be emphasized that an approach expressed in President George W. Bush's words about freedoms in the United States and the world, that if "the self-evident truths of our founding are true for us, they are true for all" is not only simplistic; it is simply wrong and dangerous (See President G. W. Bush, Commencement Address to the United States Coast Guard Academy, 21 May 2003).

There are societies, some of them, say, in Central Asia, that prioritize many things higher than personal freedoms, though this does not mean that for them such freedoms do not have any value at all. There are many peoples in the world who put stability first and value strong, even authoritarian-style, leadership over individual liberties. These are not always just the leaders of such countries and their closest entourage who directly benefit from authoritarian regimes. Many people who may even suffer from such regimes nevertheless believe that strong, that is to say authoritarian, leadership is preferable to chaos that may (or will) follow if the reins of power are loosened. Therefore, President George W. Bush is wrong when he believes that everybody in the world cherishes individual liberties to the same extent as most Americans do. People who have gone through wars, be they international or civil, or revolutionary turmoil in which thousands perish, usually value stability and order more highly than individual liberties. Besides, historical traditions often support and magnify value ladders that may significantly differ from Western priorities.

Randall Peerenboom (*China Modernises: Threat to the West or Model for the Rest* (2007), pp. 124–25) for example, writes that "not everyone assigns the same value to civil and political freedoms relative to social order. Social order ranks much higher in the normative hierarchy of most Chinese than it does in the normative hierarchy of many Westerners, in part because stability is precarious in China. The consequences of instability for China, the region and the world would be severe. Adopting this measure virtually assures a wide margin of deference to restrictions in the name of public order". This is not to say that there are not people in China or in Central Asian societies who highly value individual freedoms; this is not even to say that such societies will never start valuing individual freedoms more highly than an order that limits these freedoms; this is to say that because of different histories, both ancient and recent, as well as differences in their current situations, societies have different value priorities.

At the same time, in the world, which is rapidly becoming smaller and smaller as well as more and more "networked", pipelined and crisscrossed by various communication means, twenty-first century ideas and practices, including democracy and human rights, are spreading around even without purposeful efforts of governments, inter-governmental bodies or civil society organizations (Non-Governmental Organizations). The combination of such "automatic" spread of democracy and focused efforts of various institutions is certainly changing societies much faster than had they evolved in sovereign isolation. Yet, this role of external examples and efforts, though mostly positive, is not without problems. Of course, this means that it is not necessary for every society to invent its own "social wheels"; others show what they have achieved and may even help take over many things. However, this also means that borrowed may be ideas and practices that either do not work everywhere (that are not universalizable) or for introduction of which certain important preconditions are needed (that are in principle universalizable, but not yet universal).

On idealism, hypocrisy and pragmatism in promoting democracy

So, we have seen that democracy is indeed a high-value good, though not seen as such by everybody and everywhere. Its value is also relative to the time and place. Now, what about motives of those who are involved in the business of its promotion? The "exporters" of democracy have been led by three categories of motivations that, though *in abstracto* completely incompatible, in practice may nevertheless become bedfellows, albeit uncomfortable. These motivations are idealism, hypocrisy and pragmatism.

Idealists want to better the world, and as democracy, as they know it, is preferable, notwithstanding all its deficiencies, to all other existing social and political arrangements, they believe that by helping less fortunate or less developed nations to achieve what they habitually enjoy in their home countries they make other peoples happier, the world more prosperous and peaceful and their own societies safer. They often claim that democracies do not fight each other and those who resort to terror do it because of their discontent and frustration caused by oppressive and undemocratic regimes.

Hypocrites do not give a damn about democracy, especially in faraway places, but today it is more difficult than ever, and politically incorrect and almost suicidal to reveal what the real interests behind lofty words are (remember Ferenc Gyurcsany, the Prime Minister of Hungary, who admitted that his Government had constantly lied; instead of welcoming such frankness most people were appalled, though only the most naïve person does not know that governments are often economical with the truth). Oil, gas,

26

directions of pipelines and safety of tanker navigation are their values, but these interests have to be expressed in terms of democracy, human rights and development. A more general strategic goal, for hypocrites, allowing to reach various more specific known as well as even unknown objectives, is the maintenance and consolidation of existing hegemonic domination, the change of the existing unfavorable for them *status quo* or *vice versa*.

If the United States today is a status quo power in the sense that it seeks to maintain and consolidate its dominant position in the world (notwithstanding that by exporting "democracy", say, to the Middle East Washington may seem to change the region), China in that respect may be indeed seen as a revisionist power. Of interest in that respect is an article by Chinese scholar FENG Yongping entitled "The Peaceful Transition of Power from the UK to the US", 1 Chinese JIP (2006), 83–108, who ends his historical study with the unmistakable conclusion that: "[f]rom the perspective of China, which can be considered in a similar state to the United States at that time [i.e. when Washington peacefully took over from London the reins of world politics], the example of successful transition undoubtedly holds deep implications and provides a source for inspiration". One can be sure that such ideas do not inspire people in Washington. That is why, among other issues such as Taiwan, Tibet, Xinjiang and the trade imbalance, references to China's democracy deficit and human rights violations may be used as an instrument to stop or slow down the coming transition of power. Democratic, i.e. peaceful, transfer of power in the balance of power world is somewhat really exceptional. The US national security strategies of 2002 and 2006 are both based on the premise of American economic and military superiority that should help the United States shape the world and not to be shaped by it; no strategic competitor is allowed to rise.

Commenting on the drafting of the Universal Declaration of Human Rights in the UN Human Rights Commission, headed at that time by Eleanor Roosevelt, and the Soviet attempts to derail the work on an international bill of human rights, Mary Ann Glendon writes that "Washington and London may not have been

27

displeased [though Mrs. Eleanor Roosevelt certainly was] at Soviet obstructionism in the Human Rights Commission. As historian Brian Simpson has demonstrated, the Foreign Office viewed human rights as basically for export and as a weapon to be used against the Soviet Union". Unfortunately, things have not changed much since the rise of the human rights movement after World War II.

As one of the strongest advocates of promotion of democracy, Thomas Carothers correctly writes, "where democratic change in a particular country or region aligns with Western economic or security interests, it receives support. In many places, however, the United States and Europe have been and continue to be quite happy to support or get along with autocratic governments for a host of reasons" (T. Carothers, The "Sequencing" Fallacy, 18 *J. Democracy* (2007), p. 21). What he does not mention is the fact that Washington has more than any other State in the world helped overthrow democratically elected governments, such as Mossadeq's government in Iran 1953, Arbenz's government in Guatemala in 1954 and Alliende's in Chile in 1973, when their policies threatened American economic or strategic interests. (Lumumba, Gbagbo, and Laurent Désiré Kabila may join this list as an example from Africa)

Then, there are pragmatics who may even be fond of the goals of idealists but who think that these goals are utopian and therefore attempts to put them into practice will be counterproductive or who believe that before one enters a brawl, one should have a clear exit strategy, i.e. who often concentrate on the means so much that they lose the sight of the ends. Therefore, pragmatists are cautious, sometimes overcautious, when facing prospects of radical change (they may be suffering from a Burkean complex). They recognize the importance of oil and gas in the real world and see the inevitability of competition, if not conflicts, over the access to these and other resources. Pragmatists are often cynical when dealing with issues of international politics not necessarily because they are cynical by nature, but because such is the character of the subject matter they are dealing with. As private persons, not as professional statesmen, politicians or diplomats, they may be most moral persons, yet one would not invite a good number of professional idealists for dinner.

If the hypocritical approach to world politics, which uses lofty words such as democracy and human rights to conceal economic and military-strategic interests, is always to be deplored, idealism—even if often naïve and sometimes indeed dangerous—may serve as an engine of progress. Anthony Dworkin (The Case for Minor Utopias, Prospect (Issue 136, 2007—a review of J. Gray's Black Mass), p. 44), in response to John Gray's attempt to outlaw all utopian projects as dangerous, writes in defense of minor utopias, "If realism is a necessary corrective to utopian idealism, it is equally true that unchecked realism is likely to lead to a narrowing political possibility.

Without some appeal to universal values, there is no standpoint to challenge unjust practices that are widely taken for granted. To take two examples from the Enlightenment era, the slave trade would not have been abolished when it was, nor the use of torture banned in criminal investigations, if William Wilberforce, Cesare Beccaria, John Woolman and their followers had not clung to grand visions of human advance". Although there is a so-called hypocrisy trap, which means that accepting or recognizing hypocritically some obligations or values, one may later be forced to act upon them. Today too, idealism remains a tool of progress. However, in social affairs generally and in international relations specifically, idealism has to be tempered by realism. Social experiments are not carried out in laboratories; they directly affect lives of millions. Failures of such experiments may be fatal and their consequences are usually irreversible.

The current process of promotion of democracy is, like its predecessor the *mission civilisatrice* or white man's burden of the nineteenth century, though in different degrees and forms hypocritical and idealistically humanitarian. Both of these aspects have their roots in the Enlightenment's dual legacy: desire for freedom and tendency for domination. Within Europe, at least initially, Enlightenment ideas, to a great extent, served the liberating purpose, while it created material as well as intellectual and psychological conditions, for the colonial domination outside Europe. Dan Hind observes that "we can certainly trace one history of Enlightenment from Bacon to the British Empire and to the modern global administration. The insurgent European powers of the period after 1700 depended heavily on the 'enlightened' institutions for a technological base that in turn empowered global domination. The desire for total knowledge, in the service of total power that we find in the Department of Defense and the Ministry of Defense is an expression of Enlightenment.

But this history must ignore the sense of Enlightenment as freedom of inquiry and freedom to publish. For the Enlightenment could not be contained within those institutions and their equivalents in the Soviet Russia and Nazi Germany. Enlightenment informed the movements of national and social liberation within and outside Europe as surely as it informed the colonial powers' war-making technology" (2007, p. 104) Swedish writer Per Olov Enquist (2004, p. 92) observes that "if the Enlightenment has a rational and hard face, which is the belief in reason and empiricism within mathematics, physics and astronomy, it has also a soft face, which is the Enlightenment as freedom of thought, tolerance and liberty". This "hard face", which is morally neutral, has been indeed used not only to liberate men and women from oppression but also for the purposes of domination. As one of the profoundest thinkers of the past century John Kenneth Galbraith famously said: "Under capitalism man exploits man: under communism, it is just the opposite" (Chang, Op. Cit. n. 3, p. 103).

John Gray (2007, p. 97) explains that former British Prime Minister Tony Blair's vision of the world was a simplistic one-dimensional vision where the world is moving towards a specific final destination since he "never doubted that globalization was creating a worldwide market economy that must eventually be complemented by global democracy". Therefore, he also believed in the power of force to ensure the triumph of the good (*Passim.*). Gray is right when he is warning against the dangers of utopian visionaries who have acquired political power. The Bush–Blair axis did indeed lead to some disasters, among which the Iraqi invasion of 2003 stands up as a warning for future generations.

However, Gray, like his predecessor at the London School of Economics and Political Science (LSE) Karl Popper, who introduced the concept of "piecemeal engineering" into philosophy of politics, is himself too absolutist when he denies any positive role for social utopias and visionary politicians. Gray is also too harsh towards the Enlightenment legacy seeing it as a monolithic whole. The so-called "war against terror" is not a war of reason against religiously justified violence. It is rather a war of a faith against a faith. It is the faith in the supremacy of Western values, including free market, globalization and spread of democracy against the faith in the ability of Islam to bring justice and well-being to the whole mankind. It is not by chance that Tony Blair is one of the most, if not the most, religious British Prime Minister for years and President George W. Bush is not only a newly-re-born Christian but he has also been very close to American religious conservatives most of whom believe in literal interpretation of the Bible. If idealism has to be tempered by pragmatism, faith has to be moderated by doubt, at least for a politician.

Globalization and spread of Democracy

Globalization is a complex and controversial process. It has changed the world in many ways and has brought several countries together. Its global manifestations are unmistakable. Madonna images in Botswana, computers produced in Bangladesh, Burger King in Beijing, exchanging yen in Chile have now become standard experiences. Those who try to explain these recent developments look to a change in the production, consumption and exchange of commodities and money since the early 1970s (Barnet and Cavanagh, 1994). Though the world market for commodities, capital and money has existed for centuries before, the "globalization" theorists argue that until recently most production, consumption and exchange took place within national (or at least national-imperial) frameworks. This has now changed. Transnational corporations and banks and supranational agencies like the World Bank (WB), the International Monetary Fund (IMF) and the World Trade Organization (WTO) are "delinking" themselves from political attachments to nation-state "homes." They have "deterritorialized" and "globalized" themselves and as a consequence have the capacity to move capital, money and expertise at will to the places of highest return. They can produce, market, borrow on a global level while the legal and financial framework for this global capacity for movement and integration has been slowly but definitively put into place.

Consequently, nation states, provincial governments, municipalities, local officials, and labor unions are now increasingly helpless in controlling the movement of capital, money, and jobs. "Corporations rule the world," in David Korten's phrase, along with their allies in the supranational level (the IMF, WB, WTO, UN) (Korten, 1995). The main consequence of this globalization of corporations has been a widening gap between "North" and "South," which are the operative conflictual terms for this perspective. The globalizing corporations are "integrating only about one-third of humanity (most of those in the rich countries plus the elite of the poor countries) into complex chains of production, shopping, culture, and finance" (Broad and Cavanagh 1995-96). However, as well as bringing countries together in some ways, globalization has also driven them apart. One of the most controversial changes it has made is to the political culture of many countries around the world. Many scholars such as David Held would agree that democracy is commonly being regarded as the best form of government. However, is globalization solely responsible for the spread of democracy around the world?

The concept of democracy is derived from the Ancient Greek term *dēmokratía* which means "rule of the people" and it defines "a form of government in which the supreme power is vested in the people and exercised directly by them or by their elected agents under a free electoral system" (Dictionary.com Unabridged. Random House n.d.). This form of government, however, has become increasingly popular since the demise of communism in the late 1980's. Hence, it is widely regarded that "*Democracy is a cornerstone of human dignity and the good society. A public should shape its own destiny, even if some might doubt the wisdom of certain of democratic decisions taken. A society that is not striving after democracy tends to be a less worthy and also more dangerous place.*" (Scholte, 2005).

Similarly, globalization has also become an increasingly popular process that countries are opening themselves to. The concept was created in the late 1800's by American entrepreneur Charles Russell, but was only popularized in the 1960's by economists and social scientists. Pro-globalists would argue it is inevitable for countries to open themselves up to globalization. There are too many benefits and the ones that do not, become isolated from the rest of the world. Hence, this essay will examine if globalization has led these countries to opt for a democratic form of government and if so, what reasons underlie it?

Many scholars such as Jens Bartelson would agree with the idea that globalization poses a threat to the democratic state instead of aiding its expansion. It is believed that it undermines the essential requirements of state autonomy, patriotism and national identity (Bartelson 2004). For this reason, one could argue that political globalization could be a contradiction in terms. One of the anti-globalist theories is that globalization is causing the decline of the nation state, as governments no longer have control over their economy, their trade and their borders. Nation states may have in the past been in complete control of their markets, exchange rates and capital. Now, trans-national companies are becoming increasingly imperative to the economy, and the state is becoming obsolete. This supports the argument that globalization is reducing the power of democracy and the state, resulting in hollow democracy.

Sceptics believe that while globalization promotes opportunity for growth and increase in wealth, it has also increased the socio-economic disparity between people, making nations less democratic and progressively more ruled by the wealthy multi nationals. This means that "governments now try and compete for foreign capital and design their policies to please global investors and firms, who may not act in the best interest of, nor be held accountable to, the voters. It follows that the level of democracy declines." (Quan & Reuveny, 2003). Also, scholars such as Peter Drucker argue that globalization cripples even more those who are less fortunate, as previously stated. Companies which are unable to compete with multi nationals on an international scale lose from more economic openness. The results of this loss cause a weakening in the country's democracy (Drucker, 1994).

The unfortunate losers in the globalization battle thus, tend to seek support and unity with their identities, usually based on religion or ethnicity. This encourages the prosperous economic winners to maintain their edge over the poorer and reduce their competition. These actions intensify social inequality and undermine the progress democracy has made (Robertson, 1992). This inequality, however, is not only carried out on a national scale. Even in the international community, globalization has increased the cleavage between the developed countries from the north and the developing countries from the south. In international organizations such as the United Nations it is commonly witnessed that the elite wealthy countries always have the final say in conflicts or important issues that are discussed, which ends up swaying the domestic politics of less developed countries to their favor (Amin, 1996).

Another argument made by many such as O'Donnell is that in order for a stable and functioning democracy to work, the concept of citizenship and participation must be active and embedded in the population. Globalization has transformed the common citizen into an individual who is more willing to pursue its own economic interest than to be concerned with the content of public policy (O'Donnell, 1993). As observed, there are many reasons as to how globalization has weakened democracy around the world. However, like any controversial issue, it is important to evaluate the two sides of the argument to fully comprehend the implications of the statement. For this reason, there are several claims of notable scholars that defend the idea that globalization has spread democracy around the world.

According to Schumpeter's *Capitalism, Socialism and Democracy* globalization has helped promote economic development which has augmented the number of educated and well-trained citizens. This has resulted, contrastingly to previous statements, in a decrease in economic inequality. This illustrates the freedom and development of the people in allowing them to prosper from the benefits of globalization. As previously stated, globalization has increased the power of multi-nationals. However, differently to what has been stated, international businesses demand an increase in democracy.

34

In order for businesses to grow, peace and stability must be entrenched in all potential investment countries.

Subsequently, as democratic countries scarcely ever fight with each other, there is an increase in the demand for a democratic form of government. As economic links among states expand, authoritarian countries experience an increase in pressure from trans-national companies for political liberalization. These authoritarian states, as a result of globalization have fewer incentives to cling to power or proceed with their radical policies. Globalization encourages authoritarian states to decentralize power as they hand over their control to make progress for the market, which is fundamentally democratic. This concept of allowing the economy to fluctuate is known as laissez-faire, a French expression meaning "let it be" which allows industries to be free from state involvement in restrictions such as taxes and state monopolies.

Many other advantages of globalization also help promote democracy. The reduction in information and travelling costs mean that people have access to a lot more information not only from their government but from all over the world. This means democracies can now promote their values and ideals to autocratic countries a lot more freely, as autocracies have diminishing control over information. (Hanen, 1990) Other advantages of globalization reducing borders is that is strengthens the distribution of democratic values over borders. The more democracies border non-democratic countries, the more the chances that country has of becoming democratic.

In addition, with the increase in the demand for human rights and humanitarian interventions in countries which abuse power, democracy is progressively becoming the only alternative to autocratic regimes.

As the preponderance of states withholds democratic values, it is expected that any other state that is non-democratic is in violation of human rights as they are not allowing their citizens to voice their opinion and have a say in the way their government is run. Hence, interventions have contributed to the democratization of numerous countries such as Iraq and several other countries in Sub-Saharan Africa. Currently, international organizations such as the IMF and the World Bank have reformed numerous of these authoritarian countries so that they become potential investment opportunities for multi-nationals, and this is only due to the result of the expansion of globalization to such nations (Kura 2005).

This, however, is one of the main causes of rising military conflict and tensions amongst nations in the international community. Many sceptics and especially countries with alternative values believe that the process of globalization has pressured them into becoming liberal democracies and believing in western capitalist values. Since the beginning of the cold war, there has always been a great tension between the western democracies and the rest of the world. Now, the few countries that do not withhold western values feel threatened and ever more forced into opening their economies and becoming a democratic system.

Globalization encourages democratic institutions which promote democracy. As the global market relies on capitalist democratic values, it is inevitable that organizations that reinforce these values are rewarded. This means that they can expand into countries with other forms of government and promote these ideals. Hence, the increase involvement of INGO's and other businesses furthers the transparency and liability of institutions that reduce state intervention, all of which facilitate democracy. *"Western policymakers and nongovernmental groups trying to promote greater political liberalization have placed their faith in the indirect effects of globalization. An authoritarian government agrees to a global regime to gain benefits of one sort but is forced to accept the political consequences that follow."* (Dalpino 2001).

In conclusion, the question of globalization and the spread of democracy is a complex one. On the one hand, it may be considered a threat to democracy as it is believed that it undermines the essential requirements of state autonomy, of patriotism and of national identity. Many argue that globalization is the sole reason for the decline of the nation state, as governments do not have control over their economy, their trade and their borders anymore. Now, trans-national companies are becoming increasingly imperative to the economy, and the state is becoming obsolete. Even though globalization has many advantages, one of them is the opportunity for economic growth both at an individual and a national level. This means that governments now try and compete for foreign capital and design their policies to please global investors and firms, which results in them not necessarily acting in the best interest of its citizens and this disregards its primary purpose (Quan & Reuveny 2003). Many people, however, cannot benefit from the advantages of globalization. Small companies which are unable to compete with multi nationals on an international scale lose from more economic openness. The results of this loss cause a weakening in the country's democracy.

Hence, globalization has transformed the common citizen into an individual who is much more willing to pursue his own economic interest than to be concerned with the content of public policy. On the other hand, however, globalization has expanded greatly the values of the democratic state. According to Schumpeter globalization has helped promote economic development which has increased the number of educated and well-trained citizens, which has resulted, in a decrease in economic inequality. Also, international businesses demand an increase in democracy. In order for businesses to prosper, peace and stability must be established in all potential investment countries.

As economic links among states expand, authoritarian countries experience an increase in pressure from trans-national companies for political liberalization. Globalization encourages authoritarian states to decentralize power as they hand over their control to make progress for the market, which is essentially democratic. Another proof that globalization has expanded democracy is through the reduction in information and travelling costs. People have access to a lot more information not only from their government but from around the globe. This means democracies can promote their values and ideals to autocratic countries, as autocracies have less and less control over information (Hanen, 1990). It is because of these and other reasons like globalization encouraging democratic institutions and INGO's which promote democracy, that democracy had expanded so drastically over the past decades. Hence, if one were to analyze carefully how globalization had reduced democracy and how it has expanded it, one could safely affirm that even though it has somewhat decreased the power of the nation state, on the whole, the process has in fact spread democracy around the world.

In a nutshell, the triumph of the Western social order was widely heralded in the closing decades of the twentieth century. "The end of ideology" was proclaimed and an age of global prosperity anticipated, driven by the twinned forces of global free-market capitalism and liberal democracy (Bell, 1988). In the ensuing years, the vacuum left by the collapse of the Soviet Union, along with new tensions created by a perceived "clash of civilizations," (Huntington, 1996) has propelled advocates of free-market capitalism and Western liberal democracy to step up their efforts to export or impose these models around the world in former communist states, Muslim nations, and elsewhere.

To date, the global free-market capitalism aspect of this project has been the subject of considerable critique in both the popular and academic press (Stiglitz, 2002; Frieden, 2006; Cavanagh, 2002; Korten, 1995; Naomi, 2002) . It has also spawned a network of global justice organizations and activists who have become ever more visible and vocal through various strategies, including mass protests and internet organizing. Concerns have been raised about the increasing global disparities of wealth and poverty; the absence of environmental and labor standards and enforcement mechanisms in the global marketplace; the devastating impacts of currency speculation and trans-national capital flight; the rising and largely unregulated power of multi-national corporations; the undemocratic nature of global financial institutions and trade organizations; and a host of other issues.

Significantly, these critiques of the global free-market capitalism project have frequently come from authors and activists within the Western world itself. The same cannot be said, however, of the project to export liberal democracy. Throughout the West, it is still generally assumed that the Western democratic model is the natural and inevitable way to organize free and enlightened societies.

However, there is an alternative perspective. Could it be said that Western liberal democracy—or what might more accurately be called *competitive democracy*—has become anachronistic, unjust, and unsustainable in an age of increasing global interdependence?

(Karlberg,2004). "The signs of impending convulsions and chaos can now be discerned," wrote Bahá'u'lláh, "inasmuch as the prevailing order appeareth to be lamentably defective" (Bahá'u'lláh, 2005, p. 216).

Competitive Western Democracy

Western liberal democracy, at its core, is based on the premise that democratic governance requires individuals and groups to compete for political power. The most recognizable form that this takes is the party system. Political competition also occurs without formal political parties in many local elections, and when independent candidates run in provincial (or state) and national elections. In all of these cases, however, the underlying competitive structure is the same, and it is this underlying structure that has become anachronistic, unjust, and unsustainable.

Granted, competitive democracy represents a significant and valuable historical accomplishment. It has proven a more just form of government than the aristocratic, authoritarian, or sacerdotal forms of governance it has generally replaced. It also represents a reasonable adaptation to the social and ecological conditions prevailing at the time of its emergence. But the theory and practice of political competition emerged in the earliest days of the West's Industrial Revolution, when human populations were still relatively small and isolated. It predates the invention of electricity, the internal combustion engine, air travel, broadcast media, computers, the internet, weapons of mass destruction, appetites of mass consumption, and global free-market capitalism. In the past three centuries, our success as a species has transformed the conditions of our existence in these and many other ways.

Competitive democracies, for reasons that will be discussed here, appear to be incapable of dealing with these new realities. Yet, Western populations are, by and large, living in a state of denial regarding the anachronistic nature of competitive political systems. When concerns are raised about the condition of these systems they tend to focus on surface expressions rather than underlying structural causes. For instance, in many Western countries it has become commonplace to bemoan the increased negativity of partisan political rhetoric. Political discourse, some commentators suggest, is suffering from a breakdown in civility and a rise of mean-spiritedness. As a result, politicians are mired in a gridlock and cannot address the complex issues that face them (Tannen, 1998). Even many elected politicians have raised these concerns. In a collection of essays by retiring U.S. Senators at the close of the twentieth century, one was moved to "lament the increasing level of vituperation and partisanship that has permeated the atmosphere and debate in the Senate" (Orstein, 1997, p. xi). One observed that "bipartisanship… has been abandoned for quick fixes, sound bites, and, most harmfully, the frequent demonization of those with whom we disagree" (Heflin, 1997, p.79). Another claimed that "there is much more partisanship than when I came to Washington two decades ago, and most of it serves the nation poorly" (Simon, 1997, p. 172). Yet another wrote that "our political process must be re-civilized" due to the "ever-increasing vicious polarization of the electorate, the us-against-them mentality" that "has all but swept aside the former preponderance of reasonable discussion" (Exon , 1997), p. 57).

Statements such as these raise legitimate concerns about the state of partisan discourse, but they obscure the underlying problem of political competition. According to these views, political competition and political parties are the natural, normal, and inevitable way to organize democratic governance; the problem arises only when partisan rhetoric becomes too adversarial or mean-spirited. As the socio-linguist Deborah Tannen states: "a kind of agonistic inflation has set in whereby opposition has become more extreme, and the adversarial nature of the system is routinely being abused" (Tannen, Op. Cit., p. 96). Tannen (Ibid. pp.96-100) attributes this "more general atmosphere of contention," or this "new mood" in partisan politics, to a wider combative culture that is corrupting the partisan system and socializing politicians into more conflictual patterns of interaction, resulting in gridlock, the spread of corruption, and the breakdown of unwritten rules of civility, cooperation, and compromise.

Western model of 'Liberal Democracy' as The 'New World Order'?

Currently, the liberal international order is not just a collection of liberal democratic states but an international 'mutual-aid' society—a sort of global political club that provides members with tools for economic and political advancement. Participants in the order are claimed to gain trading opportunities, dispute-resolution mechanisms, frameworks for collective action, regulatory agreements, allied security guarantees, and resources in times of crisis. And just as there are a variety of reasons why rising states will embrace the liberal international order, there are powerful obstacles to opponents who would seek to overturn it. What then is this New World Order bearing such enticing promises?

New World Order Definition

The term New World Order (NWO) has been used by numerous politicians through the ages, and is a generic term used to refer to a worldwide conspiracy being orchestrated by an extremely powerful and influential group of genetically-related individuals (at least at the highest echelons) which include many of the world's wealthiest people, top political leaders, and corporate elite, as well as members of the so-called Black Nobility of Europe (dominated by the British Crown) whose goal is to create a One World (fascist) Government, stripped of nationalistic and regional boundaries, that is obedient to their agenda (See Ken Adachi at educate-yourself.org, accessed on 03/03.15). As Paul Warburg insists:

"We will have a world government whether you like it or not. The only question is whether that government will be achieved by conquest or consent" (February 17, 1950, as he testified before the US Senate). Their intention is to effect complete and total control over every human being on the planet and to dramatically reduce the world's population by two thirds. While the name *New World Order* is the term most frequently used today to loosely refer to anyone involved in this conspiracy, the study of exactly who makes up this group is a complex and intricate one. For further research sources, please see the side bar on the left."

41

In 1992, Dr John Coleman published *Conspirators Hierarchy: The Story of the Committee of 300*. With laudable scholarship and meticulous research, Dr Coleman identifies the players and carefully details the New World Order agenda of worldwide domination and control. On page 161 of the *Conspirators Hierarchy*, Dr Coleman accurately summarizes the intent and purpose of the Committee of 300 as follows:

"A One World Government and one-unit monetary system, under permanent non-elected hereditary oligarchs who self-select from among their numbers in the form of a feudal system as it was in the Middle Ages. In this One World entity, population will be limited by restrictions on the number of children per family, diseases, wars, famines, until 1 billion people who are useful to the ruling class, in areas which will be strictly and clearly defined, remain as the total world population."

"There will be no middle class, only rulers and the servants. All laws will be uniform under a legal system of world courts practicing the same unified code of laws, backed up by a One World Government police force and a One World unified military to enforce laws in all former countries where no national boundaries shall exist. The system will be on the basis of a welfare state; those who are obedient and subservient to the One World Government will be rewarded with the means to live; those who are rebellious will simply be starved to death or be declared outlaws, thus a target for anyone who wishes to kill them. Privately owned firearms or weapons of any kind will be prohibited."

Why the Conspiracy is Unknown

The sheer magnitude and complex web of deceit surrounding the individuals and organizations involved in this conspiracy is mind boggling, even for the most astute among us. Most people react with disbelief and skepticism towards the topic, unaware that they have been conditioned (brainwashed) to react with skepticism by institutional and media influences. Author and de-programmer Fritz Springmeier (*The Top 13 Illuminati Bloodlines*) says that most people have built in "slides" that short circuit the mind's critical examination process when it comes to certain sensitive topics.

"Slides," Springmeier reports, is a CIA term for a conditioned type of response which dead ends a person's thinking and terminates debate or examination of the topic at hand. For example, the mention of the word "conspiracy" often solicits a slide response with many people.

What most people believe to be "Public Opinion" is in reality *carefully crafted and scripted propaganda* designed to elicit a *desired behavioral response* from the public. Public opinion polls are really taken with the intent of gauging the public's acceptance of the New World Order's planned programs. A strong showing in the polls tells them that the programming is "taking," while a poor showing tells the NWO manipulators that they have to recast or "tweak" the programming until the desired response is achieved.

The NWO Modus Operandi

The NWO global conspirators manifest their agenda through the skillful manipulation of human emotions, especially fear. In the past centuries, they have repeatedly utilized a contrivance that NWO researcher and author David Icke has characterized in his latest book, *The Biggest Secret*, as Problem, Reaction, and Solution. The technique is as follows: NWO strategists create the Problem - by funding , assembling, and training an "opposition" group to stimulate turmoil in an established political power (sovereign country, region, continent, etc.) that they wish to impinge upon and thus create opposing factions in a conflict that the NWO themselves maneuvered into existence. In recent decades, so called opposition groups are usually identified in the media as 'freedom fighters' or 'liberators.'

At the same time, the leader of the established political power where the conflict is being orchestrated is demonized and, on cue, referred to as 'another Hitler' (take your pick: Saddam Hussein, Milosevic, Kaddafi, etc.). The 'freedom fighters' are not infrequently assembled from a local criminal element (i.e. KLA, drug traffickers). In the spirit of true Machiavellian deceit, the same NWO strategists are equally involved in covertly arming and advising the leader of the established power as well (the NWO always profits from any armed conflict by loaning money, arming, and supplying all parties involved in a war). The conflict is drawn to the world stage by the controlled media outlets with a barrage of photos and video tape reports of horrific and bloody atrocities suffered by innocent civilians. The cry goes up "Something has to be done!" And that is the desired Reaction.

The NWO puppeteers then provide the Solution by sending in UN 'Peace Keepers' (Bosnia) or a UN 'Coalition Force' (Gulf War) or NATO Bombers and then ground troops (Kosovo), or the military to 'search for Weapons of Mass Destruction,' which of course are never found. Once installed, the 'peace keepers' never leave. The idea is to have NWO controlled ground troops in all major countries or strategic areas where significant resistance to the New World Order takeover is likely to be encountered.

Who is the NWO?

The corporate portion of the NWO is dominated by international bankers, oil barons and pharmaceutical cartels, as well as other major multinational corporations. The Royal Family of England, namely Queen Elizabeth II and the House of Windsor, (who are, in fact, descendants of the German arm of European Royalty – the Saxe-Coburg-Gotha family – changed the name to Windsor in 1914), are high level players in the oligarchy which controls the upper strata of the NWO. The decision making nerve centers of this effort are in London (especially the City of London), Basel Switzerland, and Brussels (NATO headquarters). The United Nations, along with all the agencies working under the UN umbrella, such as the World Health Organization (WHO), are full time players in this scheme. Similarly, NATO is a military tool of the NWO.

The leaders of all major industrial countries like the United States, England, Germany, Italy, Australia, New Zealand, etc. (members of the "G7/G8") are active and fully cooperative participants in this conspiracy. In this century, the degree of control exerted by the NWO has advanced to the point that only certain hand-picked individuals, who are groomed and selected, are even eligible to become the prime minister or president of countries like England, Germany, or The United States. It didn't matter whether

Bill Clinton or Bob Dole won the Presidency in 1996, the results would have been the same. Both men are playing on the same team for the same ball club. Anyone who isn't a team player is taken out: i.e. President Kennedy, Ali Bhutto (Pakistan) and Aldo Moro (Italy). More recently, Admiral Borda and William Colby were also killed because they were either unwilling to go along with the conspiracy to destroy America, weren't cooperating in some capacity, or were attempting to expose/ thwart the takeover agenda.

The NWO's Role in Shaping History

Most of the major wars, political upheavals, and economic depression/recessions of the past 100 years (and earlier) were carefully planned and instigated by the machinations of these elites. They include The Spanish-American War (1898), World War I and World War II; The Great Depression; the Bolshevik Revolution of 1917; the Rise of Nazi Germany; the Korean War; the Vietnam War; the 1989-91 "fall" of Soviet Communism; the 1991 Gulf War; the War in Kosovo; and the two Iraq wars. Even the French Revolution was orchestrated into existence by elements of the NWO. The instigation of a trumped-up war as a cover for amassing fortunes which can be dated back to at least the 12th Century when only a core group of nine members of the Knights Templar, kicked off The Crusades that lasted for over a century and a half. The core group mentioned above have been reported as being the military arm of a secret society known as the Priory of Sion, but this has been proven to be a hoax,

In 1307, the king of France, Philippe the Fair, coveted the wealth and was jealous of the Templars' power. The French king set out to arrest all the Templars in France on October 13. While many Templars were seized and tortured, including their Grand Master, Jacques de Molay, many other Templars (who had been tipped off) escaped. They eventually resurfaced in Portugal, in Malta (as the Knights of Malta) and later in Scotland as The Scottish Rites of Freemasonry, with Albert Pike playing a key role in defining a plan for establishing a world government. The acquisition and consolidation of ever greater wealth, natural resources, total political power, and control over others are the motivating forces which drive the decisions of the NWO leaders. The toll in human suffering and the loss of innocent lives are non-issues for these individuals.

'New World Order' for the Third World Too?

The development of Third World societies is of utmost importance to the well-being of millions of individuals. This is because many developing and under-developed societies are a product of decades, and in some cases centuries, of colonial rule. The question of political order is thus of profound pertinence to the future of the international system. European societies have historically been dependent on colonialism for national expansion, during an epoch of inter-state conflict in an attempt to establish territorial integrity and comparative advantage. This Westphalian model of governance and political order, with its emphasis on sovereignty, has been appropriated in the West and replicated a posteriori in Third World developing nation-states (Barkawi & Laffey, 2002). This has, however, been challenged by the contemporary age of globalization and its vicissitudes, namely its effect on liberal democracy.

Let us critically assess the extent to which liberal democracy is a desirable goal for developing Third World societies, by way of analyzing the relationship between liberal democracy and development on the one hand, and its intrinsic characteristics on the other. The essay will first offer a critique of mainstream discourse on liberal democracy. It will then move onto a discussion around the preconditions for liberal democracy to flourish, and lastly analyze the extent to which it could be not only feasible but also desirable to see its implementation in developing societies. It will acknowledge and take into consideration the role of culture in judging the extent to which cultural differences affect the feasibility of its implementation. Liberal democracy has been termed the finality of history and the universal modality of political order, for its claimed success in standardizing international relations.

This narrative follows the liberal democratic conceptualization of the human condition, namely that human beings are by their very nature egotistic and that government control is necessary, but that it should be limited by a system of checks and balances (Saul, 1997). It follows that such control should be exercised by elected representatives with the aim of forming constitutional governance. However, this system is not without its flaws and does not signify that it should therefore be a desirable goal for developing Third World societies. To claim such would be to argue that it cannot be improved upon and that it remains the 'least bad' system out of all the others. Whilst this may hold true on reflection of contemporary history, it would essentially signify a profound determinism which should be avoided in normative discourse.

Globalization is re-shaping the international system. Since the end of the Cold War twenty years ago, the bipolarity engendered by the two mainstream ideologies, liberal capitalism on the one hand and communism on the other, provoked alterations in the organization of the international system. The collapse of the Soviet Union signaled for some the 'end of history', namely that one ideology had trumped all others and that such ideology calcified the ultimate end-point for civilization (Fukuyama, 1989). Nonetheless, given the failure of liberal democracies to satisfy its populations in terms of economic and social stability, it has recently come under pressure by sections of civil society. For example, the 'Indignados' movement in southern Europe and 'Occupy' around the globe.

These movements argue that whilst liberal democracy has assisted in certain democratic processes such as representation and in the introduction of the rule of law, it has devolved too much power to unaccountable and unrepresentative entities, such as financial markets (Hardt & Negri, 2000). This will be discussed further in the final section. As a reminder, the concept of liberal democracy was borne out of Western philosophy, deeply influenced by key figures of the Age of Enlightenment (Pausewang et al, 2002). Growing liberal Enlightenment thinkers at the time believed that monarchs had no right to rule because 'all men are created equal' but monarchs held onto the belief that they had been ordained by God to such position of nobility, thus any attempt to question their legitimacy would constitute blasphemy. The debate surrounding the liberal democracy ideal is situated within multiple strands. Much talk surrounding the discourse on liberal democracy ignores the role of colonialism in accounting for the economic, social and cultural position of Western nation-states that adopted the liberal democratic model a posteriori, one that entails representation via free and fair elections (Hobson, 2009).

The liberal narrative translates into the support of liberal tenets, particularly in economics, which in turn are argued to create the foundations for the emergence of democratic institutions. Advocates of liberal democracy point to Western liberal democracies as examples of its ideological capacity to instill development, in a manner suggesting that liberalism brought about the endured supremacy of European nations in the international system (Edigheji, 2005). This narrative, as dependency theorists argue, undermines the role of colonialism in accounting for the development of the 'North'. Since the collapse of the Soviet Union in the late 1980's, suggestions have been made of the need to export liberal democracy to other parts of the world (Dirks, 2004). It is now widely regarded as the best system of political and societal order in mainstream academia. Much research has been carried out on the link between democracy and economic growth and whilst these two concepts were believed to positively correlate, it is now no longer the case.

The rise of 'capitalism with Asian values', problematic as it may be, signifies and illustrates that economic growth is not by inherence dependent on democratic values. Any attempt to export a specific model of governance to societies whose culture is not adjusted or particularly used to such principles, is an attempt that ultimately fails to materialize. The success of liberal democracy lies in its profound ability to advance Western interests. The push for the democratization of Africa, that is to say the entrenchment of capitalism rather than the adoption of an alternative political and economic model; hegemonic class rule, namely the empowerment of wealthy elites as opposed to the dislodgment of dominant ruling classes, and the hollow symbolism based on citizen rule that in reality is, however, more akin to the insulation of the populace from democratic involvement, suggest that liberal democracy in the African context appears to translate into virtual democracy (Tar, 2010, p.84).

Prior to engendering an argument that purports to endorse the desirability of liberal democracy in the dominion of the Third World, it is imperative to reflect on the extent to which liberal democracy is responsible for the well-being and economic growth of Western nation-states. It would be inappropriate to encourage the democratization of the Third World in the same fashion as it occurred in the West if there are fundamental structural flaws in the Western model. Liberalism is a political philosophy that concerns itself with ideas of liberty, tolerance and equality.

In its classical format, liberalism represented an empiricist approach to individual liberty by condemning the illegitimate application and use of authority. Liberal classics like Humboldt's 'Limits of State Action' which later influenced John Stuart Mill was deliberated in a post-feudal but pre-capitalist society where the power of the state was significant and where civil liberties and individual freedoms were restricted. Thus, in Humboldt's view the disparity between individuals and the state was too great and thus necessitated to be addressed by way of limiting state power. Liberalism has since been appropriated in the context of contemporary globalization to mean what political elites wish it to mean. Classical liberals did not conceive of a society where corporations would be categorized as individuals, and thus able to hold virtually the same rights and freedoms. This concept and its appropriation are an essential aspect of contemporary liberal democracies, encompassing economic liberalism as well as political liberalism. In reality, the present liberal democracies are hampered by an economic model justified under the premise of liberal philosophy.

Moreover, there exist diverse centers of authority, and in economic terms the agglomeration of private power that regards individuals as cogs in a machine. As a result, liberal democracy embraces neo-liberal fundamentals about how best to live. Bryan Hughes (2005, p. 50) observes that the neo-liberal democratic social order relies on the following commitments, "...a) rights conceived at the individual rather than group level; b) a preference for competition (both political and economic) over cooperation; c) the belief in minimalist government intervention into the social realm

49

and commodification contrasted to extensive public sector guidance", as well as the capitalist obsession for production, consumption and endless conquering of markets, and finally that all the above commitments illustrate, from the perspective of liberal democrats, the best way to live. Moreover, Tully (1999, p. 172), refers to 'structures of domination' to demonstrate that the (neo) liberal democratic structure gives minorities very little room for dissent. Liberal democracies are heavily dependent on market mechanisms and reliance on unelected bureaucrats in addition to hedge fund managers and other non-accountable bodies.

The notion of tolerance is also central to liberal democracies. Zizek (2010) refers to tolerance as a 'notion of disorientation' insofar as it naturalizes/neutralizes real structural grievances and labels them as cultural problems. This, he claims, represents the 'decaffeinated other', namely a profound moral relativism that, in liberal democratic terms, must be 'respected'. When Martin Luther King Jr. was involved in the Civil Rights movement in the 60's in America, he never used the term 'tolerance' as a way to defend his cause against overt racism. It would make little sense to witness such a proclamation because the problem was not related to culture, but rather reflected the deeply entrenched social divisions in American society.

Liberal democracies obfuscate the root of problems by mystifying them as issues of tolerance thus often excusing behaviors, even if overtly problematic to the well-being of individuals. It embodies the fear of imposing one set of principles and values over another; it relativizes difference. Yet the notion of tolerance as he argues "…is more and more a kind of intolerance. What it means is 'Leave me alone; don't harass me; I'm intolerant towards your over-proximity" (Zizek, 2010). For example, the Hispanic society in the Southwest U.S was founded on notions of communal access and ownership of land, contrary to the neo-liberal democratic preference for individually owned private property (Hughes, 2005, p. 54). In the 1970's the society's identity was drastically affected by this growing intolerance manifested by the neo-liberal democratic system. In other words, the 'other' in liberal democracies is good as long as it does not interfere with the dominant way of life or political model. Here lies a fundamental paradox of liberal democracy.

In the context of developing African countries, for example, liberal democracy appears to be undermined by the post-colonial political culture and the nature of social and economic processes (Diamond, 1997, p. 19). Less developed countries possess weaker structures and are therefore unable to apply the Western concept of democracy to fit their own needs. Yet, as has been pointed out, this may not be a desirable goal in any case. In Nigeria, for example, the evidence from the 2007 and 2011 general elections suggests that not only were the elections marred by imperfections and charges of corruption, the results remained largely unchallenged domestically and internationally. According to Tar and Shettima "...as African countries continue in their march towards neo-liberal democracy, elite power politics has assumed new but macabre heights. The continent's governing class is demonstrating dramatic behaviour[sic] in achieving and sustaining power by all means possible" (Tar and Shettima, 2010).

Whilst it is not academically sound to make continent-wide generalizations based on one example, it appears worthwhile presenting an example that illustrates the difficulty of liberal democracy institution in the region. The challenges faced by the third world in building liberal democratic societies are as follows: lack of credible opposition, namely the lack of organized political parties that could stand for election ; weak civil society, fragmented and partitioned society due to the lack of a strong middle class; weak economies, little productive capacity to supply national populations; no separation between state and ruling party, constitutions are often amended to the benefit of ruling parties in order to retain power; ethnicity, religion and nepotism, namely the vast level of sectarian divisions which affect state policies; potential for military intervention, given the democratic deficit and sectarian divisions, the chance of military intervention to resolve any deadlock is elevated; weak democratic political culture, lack of institutional respect for democratic values such as rule of law and human rights culminating in the lack of regime change, meaning an incumbency continuum.

If a principal tenet of liberal democracy is the legitimate negotiation for power, then Nigeria is a case which reflects its failure. In Nigeria, elites have appropriated "...ethnicity, wealth and religion to outwit one another and remain in power" (Tar, 2010, p. 89). Pressures for democratization have usually tended to be engulfed by donor double standards, insofar as pressures for democratization in one region have been remarkably different from another (Pace, 2009). For example, in Africa the pressure for democratization has been foisted but in the Middle East it has hardly been a point of great interest for Western liberal democracies.

The events of September 11th 2001 resulted in external and domestic pressures for democratization. The event has been used as a pretext to widen the applicability of the Middle Eastern stereotype of 'Islamic fundamentalism' with the intent of forcing democratization and eliminating the biggest threat to the 'free world'. In Iraq for example, the West sought military intervention to institutionalize democracy by way of deposing the despotic regime (Von Hippel, 2000). Nonetheless the pressures for democratization, as asserted previously, also have domestic roots signaling that whilst the populations of developing societies may not wish to replicate the Western model, they are not satisfied with the current model of power that sees tribal rule or overt authoritarianism. As such, the Middle East has not made significant progress toward liberal democracy. The Arab Spring brought about renewed commitment toward change in the region but geopolitical interests, consequence of a battle for resources like oil, have greatly decreased the chance of change.

Academics have written about a special kind of African democracy, namely one that according to post-independence Africa leaders such as Nyerere, Nkrumah and Kenyatta, dismisses multiparty democracy as not congruent with African traditions. The arguments propose that a system of one-party government is an essential aspect of the African tradition (Ahluwalia, 2001). Another argument proposed by post-independence African leaders used in an attempt to dismiss liberal democracy is that African societies depend on notions of consensus as opposed to competition, a principle which appears to correlate with liberal democracy insofar as parties compete for power (Ake, 1993). Nonetheless, this consensus in reality was and is achieved by the ruling elites rather than the populations, thus constituting an act of democratic deception. Arguments such as these have been used by nationalist post-independence leaders to justify claims to power. In essence, post-colonial African leaders envisioned a type of democracy that was heavily reliant on curbing dissent and institutionalizing hierarchy (Uwizeyimana, 2012, p. 140).

Moreover, one of the prerequisites for sustainable liberal democracy is the holding of regular elections. However as Obama, Clinton and others have stated, liberal democracy is about "...more than just holding elections" (Obama as cited in Cyllah, 2010). However, this requires the formation of political parties. Schattschneider argues that "...political parties created democracy and one cannot imagine modern democracy except in terms of political parties" (Schattschneider, 1942). In the same light, Clapham suggests that democracy cannot be measured by the simple contestation of elections (Clapham, 1999). Obeng reinforces this apparent maxim, namely that "...multi-party elections are today about the only internationally acceptable route to power" (Obeng, 2011). It is always worth bearing in mind that any arguments one may advocate must be contextualized within the context of post-colonial reality.

Colonial rule, for the most part, was brutal and inhumane. Whilst European colonizers may have had formal liberal democracies back 'home', the process of colonization was all but democratic. Firstly, it represented the appropriation of resources via the use of force for the purposes of extracting wealth. Secondly, it was externally imposed, meaning that it did not have the consent of the populations (a key tenet of liberal democracies in national border contexts). Thirdly, it unmercifully encouraged the arbitrary use of power and it disregarded civil liberties of the local populations (Bratton & van de Walle, 1992). For the reasons above, it is imperative to state that the logic and rationale of post-independence leaders, however problematic it may be for the future of the continent, can be understood even if judged as unjust and worrisome. There was also the belief that the post-independence years would result in *uhuru* (freedom in ki-Swahili) (Mafeje, 2002). This, however, has not materialized to the extent that it was expected.

Liberal democracy, as understood in the 21st century, entails neo-liberal economics. IMF and World Bank programs were implemented in the 1980's in order to encourage democratization, not purely in Africa but also in other considered Third World developing countries in Latin America (Smith & Ziegler, 2008, p.45). Some of the implemented measures included the establishment of financial aid as well as economic sanctions for countries that did not conform to the Western model of 'good governance' (Chan, 2002, p.17). However, free market solutions have not resolved the structural problems of the post-colonial set-up. In effect, these programs contributed to the destruction of the social fabric in countries like Rwanda and Zimbabwe, exemplified by the emergence of "intra-elite power circulation" (Ahliwalia, 2011).

To conclude, Third World developing societies particularly in Africa, have been continuously marginalized by Western mentality. This became more evident after the 1970's, following the decades of financial liberalization protracted by Margaret Thatcher and Ronald Reagan. Robert Pinkney (2004) is right to assert that liberal democracy, as an ideal or 'staging post', offers Third World countries something which is different from what most have experienced as political reality, however that does not mean as this essay has hopefully clarified, that it signifies the 'end of history' nor that it is what developing societies should aim to achieve.

The mere replication of the Western concept of liberal democracy is thus not only practically difficult to implement, given the structure of Third World societies that value communalism over individualism, but more importantly that it is not desirable for the reasons outlined in this book. As Sankatsing posits, "...the consistently bad record and failure of liberal democracy to offer a viable political system in the vast majority of the countries of the globe and the unacceptably high social cost it demanded and still has in store for humanity, poses an urgent challenge to governance and politics at a global scale, in the twenty first century" (Sankatsing, 2004, p.4). The extent to which the 2008 global crisis undermined faith in democracy around the world— including the Euro-Atlantic world—will become clearer with time. But can anyone still argue that liberal democracy is the only model that is both democratic and promotes the public good? The liberal model is likely to face challenges from so-called hybrid models combining features of democracy and authoritarianism. These mixed systems springing up in Latin America, Asia, Africa and Eastern Europe incorporate formal institutions of democracy into a country's existing historical, societal and cultural milieu, pragmatically combining efficiency and stability. Their success is what legitimizes them in the eyes in citizens.

Chapter II

Western Liberal Democracy as Cognitive Imperialism: A Theoretical Exploration

Overview

One of the devastating consequences of modernity is a consistent cultivation and maintaining of the economic, social, cultural, ethical, epistemic and ontological bondage – in de-colonial terms, a global coloniality of Western power, of being and last but not least, of knowledge evidenced by the spread of democracy from the North to the South. Therefore decolonizing knowledge and learning to unlearn in order to relearn other than modern/colonial grounds is the central task for border thinking. The argument is that border thinking is marked by a shift in the established geography of reason, a shift from its Western place contaminated by the hubris of the zero point to various intersecting liminal and exterior positions marked by the color of skin (and hence the color of reason). Border thinking is also characterized by gender, sexuality, religion, by the geopolitics and body-politics of knowledge, of being, and of perception. Today's world more and more openly celebrates and endorses its universal pluriversality in which the principle of many intersecting and interacting worlds, cosmologies and visions comes forward. The more important it becomes to master the tools of decolonization and setting our minds and bodies free from the constraints of modernity/coloniality, the better for our common humanity.

Introduction

> *The "West's" hegemonic desire is made plain by the grandiose claim that liberal capitalist democratic society would be "the end of history".* (Haut, 2010:200)

Liberalism on its own is not a tool for anything; however, it is promoted by the "West" to maintain and reinforce its status as global hegemon. Gramsci's (1971) conception of "hegemony" is used to describe the "West's" influence in the global community. That is why Gramsci states that consent, not coercion, must be at the forefront of the hegemon's influence. Thus if consent is present, then hegemony is legitimate. This essay argues that the "West" uses liberalism as a tool to maintain its status as a global hegemon in knowledge since liberalism relies on consent and is therefore self-legitimizing. There are three key channels that the "West" uses to reinforce and extend its hegemony. These channels mirror Kant's (1970) three variables of democracy and liberalism, international institutions, and international trade, which make up a self-perpetuating triangle. This essay also critiques the legitimacy of the Western liberal regime. As it has become too expansionist, the regime no longer relies on the consent of states to join. They now have no other option, if they want to gain political or economic power, to go through the Western regime, as is the case with China and Russia. This essay argues that this is a form of concealed coercion which thus delegitimizes Western hegemony. It will define the concepts of liberalism, the "West" and hegemony, going on to analyzing and critiquing the three Kantian variables: international institutions, international trade, and democracy in succession.

Towards a Definition of Cognitive Imperialism

Cognitive imperialism is a form of cognitive manipulation used to discredit other knowledge bases and values, and seeks to validate one source of knowledge and empower it through public education (Battiste, 1986). It has been the means by which the rich diversity of peoples have been denied inclusion while only a privileged group have defined themselves as inclusive, normative, and ideal. Cognitive imperialism denies many groups of people their language and cultural integrity and maintains legitimacy of only one language, one culture, and one frame of reference. This has been singularly achieved through education into the democratic process. Minnick (1990) notes, according to the same logic that "It is in and through

58

education that a culture and polity, not only tries to perpetuate but enacts the kinds of thinking it welcomes, discards and/or discredits the kind it fears" (pp.11-12).

As a result, disconnected from their own knowledge, voices, and historical experiences, cultural minorities in the South have been led by the North to believe that their poverty and powerlessness are the result of their cultural and racial status and origins. In effect, their difference is the cause of their impoverished state. As Albert Memmi (1969) explains, "Racism is the generalized and final assigning of values to real or imaginary differences, to the accuser's benefit and at his victim's expense, in order to justify the former's own privileges or aggression" (p.185). Memmi has identified four related racist strategies used to maintain colonial power over Indigenous people: (a) stressing real or imaginary differences between the racist and the victim (b) assigning values to these differences to the advantage of the racist and the detriment of the victim (c) trying to make these values absolutes by generalizing from them and claiming that they are final; and (d) using these values to justify any present or possible aggression or privileges (p.186). All these four strategies have been the staple of Eurocentric research of Indigenous peoples that frames much of the discourse on Aboriginal peoples in school textbooks as well as democratic processes. Through these strategies Eurocentric research has manufactured the physical and cultural inferiority of Indigenous peoples.

Indigenous knowledge, embraced in Southern aboriginal languages, values and institutions, is thus being supplanted in First Nations schools with Eurocentric knowledge supported by policies that mandate provincial curriculum. Instead of an education that draws from the ecological context of the people, their social and cultural frames of reference, embodying their philosophical foundations of spiritual interconnected realities, and building on the enriched experiences and gifts of their people and their current needs for economic development and change, education has been framed as a secular experience with fragmented knowledge imported from other societies and cultures, specifically from the West.

This fragmented accumulation of knowledge builds on Eurocentric strategies that maintain their knowledge as universal, that it derives from standards of good that are universally appropriate, that the ideas and ideals are so familiar they need not be questioned, and that all questions can be posed and resolved within it (Minnick, 1990). In effect, Eurocentric knowledge, drawn from a limited patriarchal sample remains as distant today to women, Indigenous peoples, and cultural minorities as did the assimilationist curricula of the boarding school days. For Indigenous peoples, our invisibility continues, while Eurocentric education perpetuates our psychic disequilibrium.

But mainstream knowledge has rarely been questioned or reconsidered; rather the *other* is acknowledged as *a* knowledge, not *the* knowledge, as in the case of academia's special case studies such as Democratic Studies, Women's Studies, Native Studies, or Black Studies. The "add-and-stir" model of education, however, does not help disempowered students to reconcile their position in society or find the awareness or means to overcome the root problems of their oppression (Cummins, 1989). As Minnick (1990) argues, education is liberating "only when the works and lives of the few are regularly discussed in the curricular canon within their own contexts, such that the meanings that emerge from analyses of intertextuality are coherent and illuminating" (p.43). What a willing apologist for Eurocentric education patriarchal hegemony?

Indigenous Democratic Knowledge and Eurocentrism

Few academic contexts exist in which to talk about Indigenous democratic knowledge, as most literature dealing with aboriginal knowledge would like to categorize it as being peculiarly local and not connected to the normative knowledge. The fact that public schools do not offer any real examination of democratic knowledge bases or ways of knowing is a reflection of what the universities offer as well. As a result, most teachers in public schools have neither taken courses about and from Indigenous peoples nor developed awareness of cross-cultural realities.

To put before them the issue of inclusion in the curriculum takes inclusion to the lowest common denominator. As such they do not think of Aboriginal peoples as having anything more than anthropological "culture" in its limited sense of concrete objects like beads, buffalo, and bannock. The negative innuendoes in the identification of the peculiarities of Indigenous knowledge are the result of European ethnocentrism based on the theory of diffusionism (Blaut, 1993) in which knowledge is thought to be diffused from a European center to its periphery.

This theory postulates the superiority of Europeans and their descendants over non-Europeans, founded on a false polarity between "civilized" and "savage", and "center" and "marginalized" peoples. This theory is currently labeled as Eurocentrism or Eurocentric thought (Amin, 1988). An understanding of this theory and its negative caricature of Indigenous people and their knowledge is vital to the current reconceptualization of Indigenous peoples and their knowledge, as well as understanding the limitations of law and policy built on this false polarity. Eurocentrism is not like a prejudice from which informed peoples can elevate themselves. In schools and universities, traditional academic studies support and reinforce the Eurocentric contexts and consequences, ignoring Indigenous world views, knowledge, and thought, while claiming to have superior grounding in Eurohistory, Euroliterature, and Europhilosophy.

The universality of Eurocentrism creates a strategy of difference that leads to racism, which allows Europeans and colonials to assert their privileges while exploiting Indigenous people and their knowledge. Eurocentrism must be analyzed and challenged at every instance it appears, just as Indigenous peoples must come to understand the socio-historical context that was created by Eurocentrism and how it continues to affect their daily lives as well as their negotiated, often manufactured, identities.

Historian No&eumll (1994) has dramatically captured the consequences of this cognitive reality of Eurocentrism: "Alienation is to the oppressed what self-righteousness is to the oppressor. Each really believes that their unequal relationship is part of the natural order of things or desires by some higher power. The

61

dominator does not feel that he is exercising unjust power, and the dominated do not feel the need to withdraw from his tutelage. The dominator will even believe in all good faith, that he is looking out for the good of the dominated, while the latter will insist that they want an authority more enlightened than their own to determine their fate" (p.79).

A strong critique of Eurocentrism is underway in all fields of social thought. These critiques, such as postcolonial and postmodern thought, reveal that the assumptions and beliefs that constructed and maintained Eurocentrism are not universal. These givens are derived from locally and socially constructed knowledge. Under postcolonial and postmodern thought, many beliefs and assumptions of Eurocentrism are being exposed as false (Rosaldo, 1989; Said, 1992; Blaut, 1993; No&eumll, 1994). These critiques raise anguished discourse about knowledge and truth. As questions are raised about alternative ways of knowing and diversity, the discussion quickly slips into paradigm maintenance by supporters of the Eurocentric canon. Thus Eurocentrism resists change while it continues to retain a persuasive intellectual power in academic and political realms.

The modern intolerance in Eurocentric consciousness has had profound implications for schooling, curriculum, and in particular for Aboriginal people who are seeking through education to liberate themselves. In terms of knowledge and research, where are Indigenous people to find experts who can rise above the value contamination of their own education, much less find those who speak their language? Where are they being trained? By what faculty are they being taught? Because of the persuasiveness of colonial Eurocentric knowledge, Indigenous peoples are deemed not to have at our disposal today any valid, undistorted search for truth. Almost all constantive structures of university research or performative discourse in university disciplines have a political and institutional stake in Eurocentric diffusion and knowledge that is, perpetuating colonization. Almost all universities have preserved Eurocentric knowledge in the name of universal truth. Drawing on this limiting knowledge base, schools and curriculum texts have maintained the legacy of cultural and linguistic imperialism.

Definitions: Liberalism, the West and Hegemony

Liberalism is a political doctrine that takes protecting and enhancing the freedom of the individual to be the central problem of politics. Liberals typically believe that government is necessary to protect individuals from being harmed by others; but they also recognize that government itself can pose a threat to liberty. Firstly, we must define "Liberalism". Panke and Risse note that 'there is no such thing as a single theory of "classical liberalism" in International Relations' (2007:91). Furthermore, Doyle states that '[w]hat we tend to call liberal resembles a family portrait of principles and institutions, recognizable by certain characteristics' (1986:1152). Liberalism 'champions [the] scientific rationality, freedom and inevitability of human progress. It is an approach to government which emphasizes individual rights, constitutionalism, democracy and limitations on the powers of the state' (Burchill, 2005:57), seen in a manipulated form within the Washington Consensus (GTN, 2003). Liberalism is distinctly Western. It 'amalgamates Greek rationalism, Roman Stocism, Christianity, Newtonian physics, and the critique of the European ancien regime' (Gress, 1998, as cited in Puchala, 2005:580). Genealogically, liberalism has historical roots in the "West", thus the "West" sees liberalism and its extension as natural and legitimate. The result of such extension is that the "West" extends its hegemony with imposed liberalism.

Secondly, the "West" is defined by Hurrell (2006) as the "great power club". Pachala (2005) defines the "West", in economic terms, as a group of capitalist countries, committed to open markets; in political terms, as a 'club of democracies; ideologically, the source and center of liberal internationalism; hegemonically, a transnational coalition of elites sharing interests, aims and aspirations stemming from similar institutions and common ideology' (2005:577). These shared ideas and ideals unite the elites of the "West" into a Gramscian "Blocco Storico". In the post-Cold War era, the "West" is as yet unchallenged and will probably remain so for some time. This is because no single state or coalition of states in the near future will outperform the collective power of the Organization for Economic Cooperation and Development (OECD). 'The celebration of liberalism defines the West; the universalization of liberalism is the West's project; employing Western power to construct a liberal world is the purpose of Western hegemony today' (Puchala, 2005, p.580).

Thirdly, Gramsci's (1971) concept of hegemony is used as a signpost. The Gramscian turn offers a way to conceptualize world order free from the confines of state-centric approaches without discarding their importance. Using a historicist framework, they focus upon the emerging subject of global civil society as the ground over which the struggle for hegemony takes place (Germain and Kenny, 1998). 'The richly textured and suggestive deployment of this concept in the Gramscian IPE literature provides insights into the social basis of hegemony' (Germain and Kenny, 1998, p.6). This leads to an enlarged definition of the state, into the base and the superstructure constituting a "Historic Bloc", or "Blocco Storico". A historic bloc cannot exist without a hegemonic social class, which in this case is the Western liberal class.

The state maintains cohesion and identity within the bloc through the propagation of a common culture, ergo liberalism and market openness. He 'took over from Machiavelli the image of power as a centaur: a necessary combination of consent and coercion. To the extent that the consensual aspect of power is in the forefront, hegemony prevails' (Cox, 1983:52). This is how the hegemon retains legitimacy.

Western hegemony is made up of the liberal values and culture that the dominant classes possess. It is communicated and exported to the rest of the world through Kant's three variables of liberal institutionalism: international institutions, international trade and democracy; therefore, the "West" uses liberalism as a tool to maintain its hegemony. In addition, there is no need to use coercion as liberalism is self-reinforcing, self-legitimizing and self-perpetuating. It absorbs counter-hegemony via its international institutions, economic interdependence and democracy. The prolific export of liberalism has compelled other states to establish international institutions, liberalize their economies and strengthen their Western endorsed democracies. The façade of legitimacy built on perceived consent has eroded into concealed coercion.

International Institutions

Western international institutions include, but are not limited to, the Bretton Woods Institutions, the World Bank (WB) and the International Monetary Fund (IMF), the World Trade Organization (WTO) and United Nations (UN), the European Union (EU) and the North Atlantic Treaty Organization (NATO). Cox states five universal norms of hegemony as expressed through international institutions. In the case of the "West", liberal international organization are characterized by the fact that: (1) They embody the rules which facilitate the expansion of hegemonic world orders; (2) they are themselves the product of the hegemonic world order; (3) they ideologically legitimate the norms of the world order; (4) they co-opt the elites from peripheral countries and (5) they absorb counter-hegemonic ideas (1983:62).

These five characteristics are used to maintain the "West's" hegemonic legitimacy. The first function institutions have is the maintenance of hegemony. They achieve this hegemony through rules that encourage the expansion of the dominant economic forces; the IMF's Poverty Reduction Strategy Papers (PRSPs), which have an extreme likeness to the terms originally implemented in the Washington Consensus, are a manipulated form of liberal ideology (Jones and Hardstaff, 2005, Stiglitz, 2002). The second function is true of the IMF and WB, set up by the US – the metaphorical center of the "West". In addition, participation is most often weighted in favor of the dominant powers to maintain this strangle-hold; however, as of November 2010, this hegemonic control was reduced as the IMF agreed to reforms of its governance to ensure that developing countries preserve their influence.

'[T]he 2010 reform will produce a combined shift of 9 percent of quota shares to dynamic emerging market and developing countries' (IMF, 2012), and a move to an all elected Executive Board, with two fewer European chairs (IMF, 2010), as the soothing claim goes. There is an informal political structure within these institutions reflecting the real political and economic power of each participating state, performing an ideological role, reaffirming the hegemonic hierarchy. At the same time, however, they do allow alterations to be made by subordinated interests with minimum pain as a way of legitimizing their actions. For example, the Bretton Woods Institutions provided more safeguards for domestic social concerns like unemployment than did the Gold Standard. However, this was on the condition that national policies were consistent with the goal of liberal world economy, thus extending Western influence (Cox, 1983). This arrangement seemingly legitimizes the "West's" hegemony; however, it is actually fulfilling Cox's (1983) fourth function of institutions, to co-op elites from peripheral countries.

In addition to the Bretton Woods Institutions the effect of Western hegemony can be seen within the UN. It institutionalizes and regulates liberal internationalist world order (Puchala, 2005:571). During the Cold War, for example, the UN was a frequently used instrument of US foreign policy, especially in the condemnation of Iran in 1979. US goals are pursued at the threat of vetoes in the Security Council, preponderant influence over the selection of successive Secretaries Generals and overrepresentation in the Secretariat. This was demonstrated in the denial of China's membership until Washington acceded.

This UN veto power has not gone without criticism mostly from the Group of 77 who perceive the US as using the UN to further the spread of economic liberalism and democratization, even using bombs, air strikes and military tanks. 'The primary role of the UN under the hegemony of the West is to validate the liberal world order' (Puchala, 2005:581), therefore fulfilling Cox's (1983) third function of international institutions created in order to retain hegemony. It is no surprise, therefore, that aspiring powers devote so much attention to these institutions. The Chinese have a fixation with the UN and resist any reform of the Security Council to permit new members (Hurrell, 2006), which would decrease its power. As such, the UN, as a product of Western liberal hegemony, is used as a tool by the US to retain its global hegemonic position. These institutions are imperative for states to gain legitimacy in the international arena.

International institutions employ processes that eliminate counter-hegemonic movements. Gramsci (1971) termed this "transformismo". It absorbs potentially counter-hegemonic ideas and aligns them with the hegemonic doctrine (Cox, 1983). Thus, one method for changing the structure of liberal world order can be ruled out in toto. A war of movement needed to challenge Western hegemony is not probable. Radicals, having to acquire control of the superstructure of international institutions, could do nothing with it as the superstructure is connected to the national hegemonic classes of the core states. 'Hegemony is like a pillow: it absorbs blows and sooner or later the would-be assailant will find it comfortable to rest upon' (Cox, 1983:63). International institutions, such as the ones mentioned above fulfil Cox's (1983) fifth function. This does not stop forms of counter-hegemony from emerging however; i.e., the Shanghai Cooperation Organisation (SCO) (SCO, 2012) Sino-Russian military exercises.

'[S]uch developments are picked up with alacrity by those looking for signs of a coordinated willingness to challenge Washington, or for evidence of emerging multi-polarity and a renewed potential for systemic revisionism' (Hurrell, 2006:3). These international institutions act as conduits through which liberal values and economic openness are transmitted. The above section shows how the "West" uses liberalism as a tool to maintain hegemony via international institutions. They were born of the "West" in its own image after the Second World War. They are self-legitimizing and absorb counter-hegemonic moves: to resist the liberal order is to risk being categorized together with rogue regimes and with the enemies of economic and political freedom, thus receiving a question mark above their legitimacy and authority as a sovereign state. The "West" now dictates what constitutes legitimacy.

International Trade/ Economic Interdependence

International trade acts as a medium of communication and depends on the expectations of peace with the trading partner (Russet, 2010). The economic interdependence of the EU underpins democracy and makes war between member states economically irrational. The principles of liberal international trade are built upon Western capitalism, namely, competition and free trade. It first united the "West" and now the "West" seeks to unite the world using the tool of economic liberalism. We can see historically how economic liberalization organization spread: for example, the Organization for European Economic Cooperation has become known globally as the Organization for Economic Cooperation and Development, spreading Western liberal hegemony. (Russet, 2010). It is widely recognized that the prevalence of capitalist economies is a major feature of the Western order. The "West" tries to entice new states into its liberal system via the absolute and relative gains argument. Advanced capitalism creates higher than average prospects for absolute gains so states want to embrace economic interdependence to avoid the need to pursue relative gains.

Lindert and Williamson (2003) 'find clear convergence among countries that integrate more fully into the [liberal] world economy, but divergence between those who elect to remain insulated from global markets'. The relative versus absolute gains argument points to a power explanation of why states will try to mitigate anarchy. Here the absolute gains produced by economic openness are so ample that states have a large incentive to abridge anarchy. The increase of international trade fourteen-fold (1950-1994) can be attributed to the spread of liberal economic policies (WTO, 1995). There are also political reasons that Western states seek to maintain economic openness, for example, 'free trade spreads and strengthens liberal democracy. The expansion of capitalism that free trade stimulates tends to alter the preferences and character of other states in a liberal and democratic direction, thus producing a more strategically and politically hospitable system' (Deudney and Ikenberry, 1999:192) for the "West" to import liberal ideology, thus demonstrating the reciprocal nature of Kant's variables.

The strategy of economic openness, used by the architects of the post-World War II liberal order, acts as a buffer to 'regional blocs, trade wars, illiberal regimes, and ruinous rivalry': would-be counter-hegemonies (Deudney and Ikenberry, 1999:192). 'Roosevelt sought to create a one-world system managed by cooperative great powers that would rebuild war-ravaged Europe, integrate the defeated states, and establish mechanisms for security cooperation and expansive economic growth' (Ikenberry, 2008:28). Barriers to economic participation are low, and the potential benefits are high to encourage other states to integrate. For example, China has already discovered the substantial economic returns that are possible by operating within the Western open-market system.

One of the ways Western hegemony absorbs counter-hegemonic attempts is through international institutions such as the World Trade Organization (WTO). It rests on the presumption that it is normatively valuable and beneficial to participate in the global activity of capitalist free trade (Sterling- Folker, 2010); because state power is built upon sustained economic growth, China is aware that it cannot gain this without integration into the Western capitalist system, and thereby joining the WTO. 'The road to global power, in effect, runs through the Western order and its multilateral economic institutions' (Ikenberry, 2008:32).

The challenge now is to make China so institutionalized that it has no choice but to become a full-fledged member of it. The US cannot thwart China's rise, but it can help ensure that China's power is exercised within the institutions that the "West" has crafted, institutions that will protect the interests of liberal states in the crowded global economy. (Ikenberry, 2008) However, Wade (2007) argues that the WTO, under the banner of "free trade and a level playing field", has in fact tipped the playing field decisively in favor of the "West" as seen in agreements about textiles, agriculture and intellectual property. Therefore, trade, investment and technological flows are increasingly concentrated in the OECD. This pattern of international economic activity reinforces historical structures of dominance and dependence, liberalization and Western power. As a result, Western hegemony is also delegitimized as there is no other option for China to gain political power without economic prowess. In order to gain economic power, they are forced to conform to the "West's" liberal ideology; therefore, Western hegemony is not relying on consent, but a form of concealed coercion.

However, Chorev (2005) identifies contradictions between the WTO to Western hegemony. For example, it has become increasingly difficult for the US, in spite of its economic resources, with the legalization of trade disputes to pursue goals not compatible with the legal logic of the WTO. Under GATT, the US could impose liberal trade rules on others while retaining protectionist measures at home; conversely, with the inception of the WTO, the US could no longer effectively maintain its protectionist policies. Although this has detrimental effects for the US, it does work to legitimize Western hegemony and encourages other states to join the WTO. Furthermore, the structural transformation of the WTO means that the political influence of member-states has been reshaped. Now decisions reflect the liberal internal logic of the WTO meaning member-states have actually lost authority to the organization itself. 'Paradoxically, now that states have better capacity to take advantage of what the system offers, the system only offers a one-sided benefit: liberal goals can be successfully achieved, but protectionist goals are effectively silenced' (Chorev, 2005, p.344). Again this means that liberal world order and Western hegemony is maintained. However, it does disadvantage weaker states that need to protect laborers in their own country because their economy is not yet strong enough to embrace economic openness.

Additionally, the "West" pushes states to liberalize their economies, believing that this is beneficial for all, especially the liberal world, yet in few countries does the liberalization of their economies actually improve the wealth of the mass public. Mexico is just one example where WB and IMF involvement has been more destructive than beneficial. Most Mexicans would have been better off in 1998, had their government kept policy autonomy by not imposing economic liberalization, and supported jobs for people in the population's bottom 80 per cent who saw their income steadily declining after 1982 (Pieper and Taylor, 1998). Moreover, not only have the liberalizing policies of the IMF and WB had detrimental effects for under-developed countries, but Stiglitz (2002) states that today even the IMF agrees that they have pushed liberalization too far, destabilizing Western hegemony and contributing to the global financial crisis of the 1990s. It was pushed to the breaking point, and experienced resistance. Here one can see how the liberal policies of the "West" have even failed itself, and raise questions of legitimacy.

Democracy or Recolonization?

This section discusses the effects of Kant's third variable, democracy and how it is used in conjunction with his first and second variables by the "West" to maintain liberal hegemony or recolonization. Some supporters of the recolonization analysis like Nyerere and major thinkers in the Third World Network like Raghavan take a statist approach and call for a new era of Third World nation-state unity in response to recolonization (Raghavan 1990). They envision the revival of efforts like the Non-Aligned Movement of the 1960s and the New International Economic Order movement of the 1970s that would make the notion of "the South" not just a geographical but political reality in the fora of international negotiation. A large spectrum of other thinkers, from Esteva, to Latouche, to Mies, view the revival of the project of development in the South with suspicion. They argue that perhaps the greatest (though least likely) calamity of the 21st century would be a successful capitalist development of the South. Their hope for a post-capitalist life lies not in the Third World Nation state but in the "the archipelago of the informal," "the new commons," and the revival of "subsistence" that lies beyond the reach of both the recolonizing supra-national organizations and their nation-state minions (Latouche 1993); (Esteva, 1992); (Mies, 1986).

Morozov (2010) states how democracy itself is Western in origin. Its promotion in Eastern Europe, Latin America, and East Asia together form 'a complex layer cake of integrative initiatives that bind the democratic industrial world together' (Ikenberry, 2004, p.622). It is not surprising that the "West" has become infatuated with preserving and extending its control over institutions, markets and world politics, given that liberalism has produced such asymmetrical rewards for the "West" and the rest. Consequentially, non-western countries are under continuous pressure to liberalize politically and economically, and import policies from Western Europe and the US (Morozov, 2010) and the standards are set by comparison to the US and the EU as par excellence. A key factor for explaining democratization is East Asia in the 1970s and 1980s. Economic liberalization here led to the rapid growth of the middle classes and in turn the rise of social movements concerned with labor exploitation. This is the Lipset (1959) hypothesis; thereby there is a causal relationship between economic development and democracy, which has been the basis of US foreign policy for the last twenty five years. Because the "West" has become so infatuated with the exportation of democracy, so much so that it will resort to military intervention, it has in fact delegitimized its role as global hegemon.

Nevertheless, China, and its counter-hegemonic ideology, bucks this trend, showing that economic advances and increasing openness have actually contributed to the stability of authoritarian rule (Gallagher, 2002). On the other hand, Gallagher (2002) does make an important qualification that the reforms and economic openness in China have resulted in delaying political change, not an end to political change. As a part-result of this, Kagan (as cited in Deudney and Ikenberry, 2009), insists that the "West" should abandon its expectations of global democratic hegemony. They should instead look to strengthen internal ties among liberal democracies through a form of a "league of democracies". He suggests a realist notion: "balance of power rather than concert of power". However, Deudney and Ikenberry (2009) disagree with this statement. They argue that the success of autocratic regimes such as those in China and Russia are not a denunciation of the liberal way; their recent success has depended on their access to the international liberal order, and they remain dependent on its success. Therefore, they are not true counter-hegemonies: as stated above, they must go through the liberal (Western hegemonic) system, for example the WTO and the UN Security Council, to gain any real political power.

Moreover, 'given the powerful logic that connects modernization and liberalization; autocratic regimes face strong incentives to liberalize' (Deudney and Ikenberry, 2009, p.79). As a result, Western hegemony absorbs these counter-hegemonic ideas by making the liberal path more accommodating and appealing.

Because of this, 'the near-universal eagerness of peoples and states to join the expanding capitalist international system gives further credibility to this liberal vision' (2009, p.80). Hence, the "West" should seek to integrate China and Russia further, thus encouraging them to convert to democracy. 'Proposals to "draw up the gates" of the democratic world and exclude non-democratic states- with measures such as exclusion of Russia from the G8- promise to worsen relations and reinforce authoritarian rule'(2009, p.93). Therefore, via the liberal system of increased integration of autocratic regimes thus predisposing them to cooperation, pacifying them as a potential threat, and eventually converting them to democracy, Western hegemony is maintained.

This is not to say that the democratic crusade of the "West" has not come under criticism. Morozov (2010) states how non-western leaders criticize the "West" for being undemocratic, for usurping power and promoting their "civilisational" interest in the name of democracy, and being undemocratic themselves. For example Putin, at the Munich Conference on Security Policy (February, 2007, as cited in Morozov, 2010), asserted that the "unipolar world" promoted by the "West" is "a world of one master, one sovereign", with "nearly the entire legal system of one state, first of all, of course, of the US, has transgressed its national boundaries and… is being imposed on other states". He goes on to argue that the unilateral actions of the "West" are illegitimate, because no state can find refuge in international law (Putin, 2007, as cited in Morozov, 2010).

This form of Western interventionism 'delegitimizes the political process of the state intervened in' (Chandler, 2006:485), hence denying any non-Western standards of democracy of any credibility. 'Democracy (imposed from the outside) is often presented as a solution to the problems of the political sphere rather than as a process of determining and giving content to the good life' (Chandler, 2006:483). However, when the "West" needs to impose democracy from the outside it calls into question the issue of consent. Rather the "West" is exporting democracy via concealed coercion. This is true both in the case of the US's "democratic crusade" and its "with us or against us" logic, and in the case of the EU policy of conditionality, which strives to remodel the neighbors, from Montenegro to Russia to Libya, in its own image and likeness. In Richard Cheney's (2006) statement in Vilnius, the "return to democratic reform in Russia" is synonymous to Russia's "aligning with the West".

Denial of Capitalist Democratic Hegemony and Contesting Concepts of Class

One way that capitalism maintains its hegemony in imposing its democratic values is by repressing discussion or even awareness of Marx's particular concept of class – the one he invented and added to the tradition of class analyses before him. Marx's new concept focused on the exploitation of a surplus from workers, replacing the old concepts that defined class chiefly in terms of property and power. Conservatives, liberals, and radicals all contribute to the repression of Marx's class analysis, albeit in different ways. Some simply remove *all* class concepts from their discourses on society from their analyses as well as from their policy proposals. Others admit and use concepts of class, but insist on defining class in the ways that preceded Marx. By returning to those concepts of class, they exclude Marx's contribution and thereby lose the theoretical insights and political strategies made possible by his particular concept of class. My argument is that an effective socialist counterhegemonic strategy requires us (1) to expose this exclusion of Marx's breakthrough (to undo its repression), and (2) to recover and integrate Marx's original concept into socialist strategies for the twenty-first century. The bibliography lists works with detailed elaborations of Marx's class analytics.

Expunging Class Altogether

In popular discourses – such as those in the mass media – various overlapping propositions express the perspective that class simply does not exist. In this view, class is an irrelevant category for social analysis. Hence, "class" disappears from the language or else appears fleetingly as a straw man to be quickly and decisively dismissed. Historical arguments of this kind suggest that while classes may once have existed, they have been superseded in modern times. Society is now comprised of individuals, rather than classes. Cultural production becomes the work of individual genius, not collective movement. Political rhetoric defines democracy and equality, for example, as pertaining exclusively to individuals. Economic commentary proposes that "we are all in the middle class now," a standpoint that quickly removes class difference and hence class analysis from discussion.

In the more formal academic versions of the same arguments – epitomized in the dominant neo-classical economics tradition – classes likewise virtually disappear. No entry on "class" appears in most contemporary economics textbooks. Economic outcomes – prices, incomes, growth, and so on – are theorized as products of the maximizing strategies of individual consumers and individual enterprises. The values of all commodities depend on supply and demand, and they emerge from the desires of individual consumers and producers. Incomes flow to each individual according to what each individually contributes to commodity production. Neoclassical economic theory not only proves to its own satisfaction that such an economy is optimal in all respects. It also demonstrates that if and when individuals act other than individually – say in monopolistic groupings to coordinate with others for extra advantages – the economic results are necessarily sub-optimal.

When proponents of such "classless" analyses engage in political struggles for social change, their agendas do not include class change. Expunging class from their thinking and their programs thus serves to secure the hegemony of the existing class structure. It has become invisible in and for their goals and strategies. Social problems are not approached as having class components; therefore, social solutions do not entail or require class changes. A society's class structures sit above the fray, out of sight and out of mind. Its citizens struggle over their problems with the unrecognized and unspoken commitment to leave those class structures intact. Any class changes that do occur become unintended byproducts.

Admitting Some Concepts of Class While Excluding those of Marx

Then there are the conservatives, liberals, and radicals who do admit concepts of class into their analyses and prescriptions. Partly this is because concepts of class have figured prominently in countless literatures for thousands of years. From the ancient Greeks and Romans to Adam Smith, Robespierre, and David Ricardo, and from populist radicalisms to the Marxist challenge to modern capitalism, class categories proved central to many arguments on all sides of contested issues. For those aware of the history of class analysis, simply to dismiss the category of class out of hand has seemed indefensible. Even those unaware of the history of class analyses have often been sensitive to the use of class in contemporary social criticism. Such thinkers make class appear in their arguments. However, they do so in several conceptualizations *other than* Marx's surplus concept. The latter they ignore or, in a few cases, reject.

When admitted into their arguments, classes exist as simple aggregates of individuals sharing some common characteristic. Thus there might be the "class" of the poor, of property-owners, of immigrants, of wage-earners, of ethnic minorities, of the powerful, of the dominated and oppressed, and so on. Class functions as a synonym for "social group" or "social stratum" or "elite" in parallel usages. Like such synonyms, class exists as a derivative category: a social theory, although premised on individuals and their individual characteristics, recognizes groupings of such individuals as classes. The latter are logically derived or aggregated from what their component individuals are and do. Classes are here nouns, whereas, for Marx, as we shall see, class was an adjective modifying a particular social process unrecognized by those who preceded him.

Two particular characteristics have most often been used, since at least the ancient Greeks, to aggregate the individuals sharing them into classes. The first of these is property ownership. Individuals who do own property confront individuals without property: hence a class of rich over and against a class of poor. Conservative, liberal, and radical theorists who recognize such property-defined classes usually disagree about their significance.

Conservatives tend to see them as reflections of the more or less inherent different capacities and contributions among individuals – perhaps even necessary as socially productive incentives. Liberals tend to worry lest extreme inequalities of wealth destabilize society. They fear the possibilities and consequences of "class struggles" which they define/understand as conflicts between the greedy and the needy. Radicals define social stability as ultimately dependent on social justice, which they equate with an equality of property ownership (likely requiring and embodied within some kind of socialization of productive property). Marx was clearly a radical, but his new theory of class was overwhelmingly focused on surplus production and distribution, not on property ownership.

Power is the second common characteristic defining the social aggregates called "classes" for those who admit that concept into their analyses. Individuals who possess and wield power over others confront those controlled by that power: classes of the powerful and the powerless, of the rulers and ruled, of the order-givers and order-takers. Once again, the relatively more conservative see power as either inherent in or else won legitimately by the more capable individuals; perhaps human nature distributes it unequally in all societies. For many conservatives, an unequal distribution of power – i.e. class difference so defined – serves as an ordering mechanism necessary for social cohesion. Liberals, in contrast, worry about the social distribution of power. They fear that conflict between the powerful and the powerless – which some define as class conflict – can destabilize society. They prefer more equal power distributions and seek to constrain the extent of class differences understood as differential powers wielded by social groups.

Radicals often take unequal power distributions to be the foundation of the dominating-dominated dichotomy intrinsic to all social evils. Some view class differences as simply one (economic) kind or form of power inequality alongside such others as gender, racial, ethnic, and religious juxtapositions of dominators and dominated. For radicals, democracy has become, on the one hand, the central slogan expressing their hostility to unequally distributed authority. On the other, democracy is both their goal and their strategy for overcoming every society's flaws and injustices.

The vast majority of social discourses that admit class concepts (conservative, liberal, radical, and the various mixtures among them) define them in terms of social groups with different quantities of property and/or power. Sometimes they insist on definitions in terms of either property or power; more typically they combine the definitions into a composite: the class(es) of the rich and powerful arrayed against the class(es) of the poor and powerless. When they find mere dualistic approaches inadequate, they specify intermediary groups: for example, middle classes who have less property and/or power than some but more than others, and so on. However nuanced, all these admissions of class treat the term as a noun, an aggregate of individuals sharing some common possession or characteristic.

The debates among conservatives, liberals, and radicals turn on their allegations about the necessity for more or less equality in the social distributions of property and power. Each side seeks to argue that stability, prosperity, happiness, and justice —all of which — depend on its preferred class structure understood as its preferred distribution of property and power among individuals. Political parties, movements, and revolutions informed by such concepts of class aim at preserving or overthrowing particular social distributions of property and power.

Given that such conservatives, liberals, and radicals define classes in terms that exclude Marx's new and different concept of class, their analyses, debates, policy proposals, and social actions ignore what Marx meant by class structure. In this way, they contribute to a broad social blindness to class structures in Marx's sense. The invisibility of class supports the hegemony of contemporary capitalism by keeping class off the agendas for social change advocated by social critics.

Marx's Concept as Counterhegemonic

Marx's work clearly shows his sympathetic knowledge of the property and power concepts of class that long predated him. His

78

contribution was a new and different concept enabling him to supplement all previous class analyses in a revolutionary way. Marx's new class concept referred to the way a society organized the production and distribution of a surplus. Class was an adjective, the label for the particular set of processes whereby a surplus gets produced and distributed. In all societies, some of its members use their brains and muscles to transform nature into useful objects. They always produce more of those objects than they themselves consume; that *more* is the surplus.

Marx then asked the questions directly implied by the existence of such a surplus: (1) who produces such surpluses, (2) who gets the surpluses, and (3) to whom are these surpluses distributed by those who first get them and for what purposes are these distributions made? The answers that Marx only began to construct in his work led him to recognize that societies exhibit different ways of organizing their class processes. The producers of surpluses can be rich or poor, powerful or powerless, male or female, and so on, depending on the varying social contexts of surplus production. The same applies to the appropriators and distributors and to the recipients of distributed shares of the produced surplus. Property and power distributions (class in its pre-Marxian senses) are simply different aspects of society from surplus production and distribution (class in Marx's new sense).

The unique culture, natural endowments, politics, and economics of each society combine to determine the specific qualities and quantities of its class processes. From one time and place to another, societies vary in terms of who produces and appropriates surpluses (of what size and in what ways) and who distributes surpluses (in what portions) to whom, for what purposes, and in what ways. Marx's attention to historical detail led him to identify five qualitatively different kinds of class processes (or "class structures"): communist, slave, ancient, feudal, and capitalist. He concentrated overwhelmingly upon the last given his judgment that it constituted the hegemonic class structure within modern society, However, he sketched some initial lines of the analysis of the other class structures (especially the feudal which preceded the capitalist in Europe) and recognized that multiple class structures typically coexist within most societies.

The counterhegemonic thrust of Marx's new concept of class was this: capitalism's injustices (including its unequal distributions of property and power) and its wastes and inefficiencies (business cycles, unemployment, natural despoliation, etc.) *were connected to its particular set of class structures.* To remedy those systemic problems likely required changing more than property and power distributions; it likely also required changing its class structures. The progressive criticisms previously addressed to inequitable property and power distributions had now to be supplemented. Marx provided that supplement by his exposure of class structures as particular organizations of surplus production, appropriation, and distribution and by his demonstrations of their multiple, complex effects on the societies in which they existed.

Marx's *Capital* demonstrates the existence and social effects of one kind of class structure, the specifically capitalist mode of organizing the production, appropriation, and distribution of surplus. Surplus is the book's main topic and focus across the three volumes. Property and power are ancillary considerations. Marx's punch line is that previous progressive social movements, including revolutionary upheavals, had often fallen short of their goals because they had lacked an awareness of the interdependence of property and power distributions with the very different – and hitherto untheorized – matter of class structures *in their surplus definition.*

Marx's political objective was to improve the prospects for radical social movements aimed at justice, democracy, solidarity, and equality by adding to their arsenal the class analysis he had produced. No longer would revolutionary demands limit themselves, for example, to equalizing property and power without adding the demand for the class changes needed to accompany and support such equalizations. Marx's poetics also drove home the point that class changes were not just necessary means to other ends; they were moral issues in themselves. Marx's focus on the notion of *exploitation* – defined as the circumstance where the workers who produced the surplus were excluded from its appropriation and distribution – rendered it as morally objectionable, in itself, as slavery, child abuse, or autocracy (reference influence of Quakerism here: cf. http://ijbssnet.com/journals/Vol_3_No_11_June_2012/17.pdf). He chose pointedly to refer to the exploited workers in capitalist enterprises as "wage-slaves."

The Repression of Marx's Concept of Class (Just like the Quakers in the 17th, 18th, 19th century)

For many reasons, Marx's new conceptualization of class in terms of surplus was repressed over the last hundred years. Revolutionary movements steeped in the property and power concepts of class could not easily accommodate Marx's class-qua-surplus arguments beyond formulaic invocations of his powerful writings. Masses and leaders long used to defining their problems and solutions essentially in terms of redistributing wealth and power did not quickly demand as well the transformation of their societies' organization of surplus. The devotees of exploitative class structures, when threatened by Marx's work, deflected its thrust by accepting some equalization of property and power as, for them, a lesser evil than revolutionary class change. In the later nineteenth and across the twentieth centuries, social democracy emerged national movements toward relatively less unequal distributions of property and power than had existed before. In some places and for some times, they enjoyed limited successes, but these were never secure.

In a sense, Marx's new surplus labor concept of class was lost. It faded back into the older property and power concepts as if it were simply a restatement or elaboration of them. No conspiracy achieved this result, nor was there any explicit project toward that end. A complex of social conditions repressed Marx's concept. Thereby, modern capitalism's distinctive class – i.e. surplus – structure and its specific effects remained invisible. This served to keep progressive social movements – even when led by Marxists sincerely invoking his name and work – limited to the fight for less inequality of property and power distributions as the meaning and content of class struggles. In this way, the repression of Marx's class analytical insights functioned to support capitalist hegemony. It kept capitalism's distinctive mode of producing, appropriating, and distributing surplus out of radical sights and radical minds. When surplus was even mentioned, it was seen as derivative of property or power; attending to the latter would then suffice to deal effectively with the former.

Thus both socialist and communist movements of the last century have focused virtually exclusively on utilizing state power to equalize property and/or power. Moderate socialists seek these ends by mild and partial state regulation of private capitalist enterprises. Left socialists favor less mild and more comprehensive regulations in the interest of fuller equalizations. Communists often go further still: a workers' party committed to state ownership and state planning should take power toward the end of dispossessing the private capitalists and superseding the market. That alone, they argue, will secure the democratization/equalization of property and power presumably sought by all on the left. Lost in all these degrees of leftism is the issue of displacing the existing set of class structures (modes of organizing the surplus) with a different set.

Thus, when the Bolsheviks took power in Russia, they transformed property and power relations in countless ways, many in the direction of far greater equality than had ever existed there before. But in the factories and offices seized by the workers and turned over to their new workers' state, the same system of surplus production, appropriation, and distribution remained largely in place. The private capitalists on the boards of directors gave way to state officials, but the workers remained producers of a surplus they did not appropriate. They remained within an exploitative class structure in Marx's precise sense. The resulting position of the state as an exploiter had disastrous consequences – all the worse because that reality could not be admitted, debated, or addressed. The Soviets were blind to their class situation in its surplus sense, having been caught up fully in the loss of Marx's class concept and the failure to grow beyond the older property and power concepts.

The social democrats across the world fared no better. Often in critical reaction against the communists – accusing them of not delivering on the promise of greater equality of property or power – they pursued parliamentary strategies within predominantly private capitalist societies. Progressive tax structures, free mass education, government employment programs, social service provisions, and so forth became the incremental steps toward that equalization of property and power that defined their socialism just as exclusively as it defined the communists'. They differed on the means, not the end, although their ferocious debates found each denouncing the other as corrupted renegade in the quest for that end. The social democrats too left intact the exploitative capitalist structure of surplus production, appropriation, and distribution. They too focused their supporters' attention on the quests for greater property and power equalization (increasingly combined under their banner of "democracy"). They too suffered and also fostered the blindness to Marx's surplus concept of class. The absence from their political programs of any demand for an end to exploitative class structures in Marx's sense did not disturb them. Thus, they too secured the hegemony of the capitalist class structure by limiting their struggles – even when called class struggles – to issues of property and power, thus reducing democracy to the mere commodification of bourgeois privilege.

Seeds of Competitive Western Democracy

The infectious danger lies in the breakdown in civility, the rise of mean-spiritedness, the problem of gridlock, and the spread of political corruption—assuming these things have indeed deteriorated over time—are not abuses or corruptions of the partisan system. Such developments are the culmination—the "perfection"—of a system that political scientist Jane Mansbridge (1980) refers to as "adversary democracy." They are the sour fruit inherent in the seeds of competitive democracy. "No two men can be found who may be said to be outwardly and inwardly united," wrote Bahá'u'lláh (Op. Cit., p. 218).

These seeds, to be more precise, are the deepest assumptions about human nature and social order that underlie political competition. The first of these assumptions is that human nature is essentially selfish and competitive. The second assumption is that different groups of people will naturally develop different interests, needs, values, and desires, and these interests will invariably conflict. The third assumption is that, given the selfish human nature and the problem of conflicting interests, the fairest and most efficient way to govern a society is to harness these dynamics through an open process of interest-group competition.

Based on these assumptions, it should come as no surprise that the fruits of competitive democracy include the aforementioned breakdown in civility, rise of mean-spiritedness, problem of gridlock and spread of political corruption. These are to be expected if we accept, and enact such assumptions. In fact, this is the reason why some competitive democracies have set up complex systems of checks and balances in an effort to limit the excessive accumulation of power in the hands of any given interest group. It is also why some competitive democracies have tried to cultivate, within their political systems, codes of civility and ethics intended to restrain the basest expressions of political competition. And this is the reason that most competitive democracies struggle, to this day, to reign in the worst excesses of political competition by experimenting with term limits, campaign finance reforms, and other stop-gap measures. Yet none of these efforts fundamentally changes the nature or the fruit of the system, because the fruit is inherent in the system's internal assumptions—its seeds.

To grasp this inherent relationship, consider the market metaphor that is often invoked as a model for political competition. Competitive democracy is generally conceived as a political marketplace within which political entrepreneurs and the parties they incorporate try to advance their interests through open competition (Schumpeter, 1976; Downs, 1965). The "invisible hand" of the market allegedly works to direct this competition toward the maximum public benefit. As Lyon explains, supporters of party government argue that if one looks at the larger picture and sees the "political market" in which several parties, the media, interest groups, and individuals all interact, democratic needs are served in a kind of mysterious way as though another "invisible hand" is at work (Lyon, 1992, p.129).

Within this market model, political parties incorporate around aggregated sets of interests in order to pool their political capital. Contests then determine leadership and control within and between parties—as politicians and parties organize to fight and win elections. The logic of competitive elections, however, ensures that the goal of winning trumps all other values. As Held explains:

'Parties may aim to realize a programme[sic] of 'ideal' political principles, but unless their activities are based on systematic strategies for achieving electoral success they will be doomed to insignificance. Accordingly, parties become transformed, above all else, into means for fighting and winning elections.' (Held, 1996, p. 170).

Once political leadership and control is determined through electoral contests, processes of public decision-making are structured in a similar manner. Decision-making is organized as an oppositional process of debate. In theory, political debate functions as an open "market-place of ideas" in which the best ideas prevail—again through the operation of some hypothetical invisible hand. In practice, the logic of the competitive system transforms debate into a struggle over political capital. Victory results in a gain of political capital, defeat results in a loss. Debate thus becomes an extension of the electoral process itself, providing a stage for "permanent campaigns," or never-ending contests over political capital, in anticipation of the next round of elections (Blumenthal,1980).

Much political decision-making also occurs outside of formal public debates. Indeed, these debates often serve as little more than a dramatic veneer on complex behind-the-scenes processes of political bargaining and negotiation. Yet these behind-the-scenes processes tend to be characterized by similar competitive dynamics (Clift and Brazaitis,1997). Blumenthal,1980). These processes involve not only elected officials but also lobbyists, think tanks, media strategists, and numerous species of political action groups—all of whom are vying with one another to pressure politicians, shape media coverage, and influence public opinion in ways that advance their own agendas and interests.

Social Injustice and Unsustainability of Western Democracy

Interest-group competition has no necessary relationship to the goals of social justice and environmental sustainability. On the contrary, the track record of competitive democracy is clear. It is a record of growing disparities between rich and poor (Ackerman 2000). It is also a record of accelerating ecological destruction (Brown *et al.*, 2000; Suzuki and Dressel 2004). Therefore the problems of competitive democracy, a few of which are discussed here, go well beyond the breakdown of civility and the rise of mean-spiritedness.

a) Corrupting Influence of Money

In theory, when there are excesses and deficiencies in the operation of the market economy, a democratic government should be able to regulate and remedy these. The practice of political competition, however, makes this virtually impossible. The reasons for this are not difficult to understand. Political competition is an expensive activity—and growing more expensive with every generation. Successful campaigns are waged by those who have the financial support, both direct and indirect, of the most affluent market actors (i.e., those who have profited the most from market excesses and deficiencies).

The problem of money in politics is widely recognized and it largely explains the cynicism and apathy reflected in low voter turnout at the polls. The underlying cause of this problem, however, is seldom examined and never seriously addressed. We hear occasional calls for campaign finance reform and similar regulatory measures. Yet the root of the problem is political competition itself. From the moment we structure elections as contests, which inevitably require money to win, we invert the proper relationship between government and the market. Rather than our market existing within the envelope of responsible government regulation, our government is held captive within the envelope of market regulation.

As long as governance is organized in a competitive manner, this relationship cannot be fully corrected. Any scheme to tweak the rules here and there will merely cause money to flow through new paths. This is what occurs, for instance, with attempts to reform campaign financing. New forms of contribution merely eclipse the old. Even if societies could eliminate campaign financing entirely, money would simply flow through other points of political influence such as the constantly evolving species of political action groups that exert strategic influences over media coverage of issues, public opinion formation, electoral outcomes, and many other political processes. In a competitive political system, where candidates are vying for favorable coverage, public opinion, and votes, money will always flow to the most effective points of political influence just as water always flows to the point of lowest elevation. We can alter the path of that flow, but we cannot stop it.

This problem is a primary cause of the growing disparities of wealth and poverty that are now witnessed throughout the world, including within the Western world. The expanding income gap is not simply a result of the market economy itself. It is a result of the competitive political economy that is coupled with it. Through this political economy, the wealthiest market actors define the market framework within which they accumulate wealth. This framework comprises systems of property law, contract law, labor law, tax law, and all other forms of legislation, public infrastructure, and public subsidies that shape market outcomes. In competitive democracies this framework is defined, over time, by the wealthiest market actors, owing to the influence of money on political competition. The result is a political-economy feedback loop that serves the swelling interests of the wealthiest segments of society.

The subordination of governance to market forces also has implications for the environment. In unregulated markets, production and consumption decisions are based solely on the internal costs of manufacturing, which include labor, materials, manufacturing equipment and energy. These internal costs determine the retail prices that consumers pay for products, which influence how much people consume. These costs do not, however, always reflect the true social or ecological costs of a product. Many industries generate external costs, or externalities, that are never factored into the price of a product because they are not actual production costs (Caporaso, and Levine,1992, pp. 89–92. For instance, industries that pollute the environment create substantial public health and environmental remediation costs that are seldom factored into the actual costs of production. Rather, these costs are borne by the entire society, by future generations, and even by other species. Because an unregulated market does not account for these external costs, the prices of products with high external costs are kept artificially low. These artificially low prices inflate consumption of the most socially and ecologically damaging products. For these reasons, market economies are ecologically unsustainable unless carefully regulated by governments that factor such costs back into the prices of goods through "green taxes" and other means (Folmer, 2001, Aronsson and Löfgren, 1997). As discussed above, however, markets are not responsibly regulated within a competitive political system because the system subordinates political decision-making to market influences. Markets regulate competitive democracies rather than the other way around.

Finally, the social and environmental costs of political competition converge in the case of "environmental racism" and related environmental injustices (Heiman, 1996). The poor, ethnic minorities, and women tend to suffer the most from the effects of environmental degradation because they are more likely to live or work in areas of increased environmental health risks and degradation. These segments of the population are least able to influence political decision-making due to their economic disenfranchisement. As a result, environmental practices that are seldom tolerated in the backyards of more affluent groups are displaced onto groups that are politically and economically marginalized. These are the people who pay most of the costs of such environmental externalities.

b) Perspective on Exclusion and Issue Reduction

In addition to the problem of money, political competition does not provide an effective way to understand and solve complex problems because it reduces the diversity of perspectives and voices in decision-making processes. There are a number of reasons for this. First, political competition yields an adversarial model of debate which generally defaults to the premise that if one perspective is right then another perspective must be wrong. In theory, the most enlightened or informed perspective prevails. This assumes that complex issues can adequately be understood from a single perspective. However, an adequate grasp of most complex issues requires consideration of multiple, often complementary, perspectives. Complex issues tend to be multifaceted—like many-sided objects that must be viewed from different angles in order to be fully seen and understood. Different perspectives therefore reveal different facets of complex issues. Maximum understanding emerges through the careful consideration of as many facets as possible.

Political competition militates against this process because it assumes the oppositional rather than the potentially complementary character of diverse views. One cannot gain political capital at the expense of one's opponent unless there is a winner and a loser. As a result, political competition reduces complex issues into binary oppositions in which only one perspective can prevail. This is what Blondel calls "the curse of oversimplification" (Blondel, 1978, pp. 19–21).

This problem is exacerbated by the hyper-commercialized media sectors that are emerging in most Western societies—products of the political economy discussed above. These are driven by the logic of manufacturing mass audiences in order to sell them to advertisers. The cheapest, and therefore most profitable, way to manufacture a mass audience is through the construction of spectacle—including partisan political spectacle. Political coverage is thus reduced to a formula of sound-bite politics in which emotionally charged sloganeering becomes the ticket into the public sphere. As a result, simplistic political mantras echo throughout the public sphere, distorting the complex nature of the issues at hand, constraining public perceptions, and aggravating partisan divisions. In such a climate, it is virtually impossible to solve complex, multi-dimensional, social, and environmental problems.

A closely related consequence of this competitive model is the exclusion and inhibition of diverse voices of those who avoid or withdraw from the arena of public service because of its simplistic and hostile atmosphere. Such an atmosphere does not attract individuals who, by nature or nurture or some combination of the two, are neither inclined toward nor comfortable with simplistic adversarial debate—even though they may have important contributions to offer. Partisan mudslinging aside, adversarial debate does not elicit the best reasoning even among the most confident individuals. Such conditions can entirely silence less confident and less aggressive—or simply more thoughtful and caring—individuals.

By extension, adversarial contests also tend to privilege males who, again by nature or nurture or some combination of the two, tend to be more aggressive than women and thus gain the advantage within an adversarial arena (Moulton, 1983). The resulting disadvantage experienced by many women may also be experienced by some minority groups who, in order to survive, have learned to adopt cautious and guarded postures in relation to dominant social groups. Moreover, women and minorities may be further disadvantaged because even though male or dominant-group expressions of aggression are often considered natural and appropriate, the same kinds of expressions, when employed by women or subordinated minorities, are often viewed as unnatural and inappropriate. Thus the same rewards do not necessarily accrue to women and minorities for the same adversarial behaviors (Lakoff, 1975). By inhibiting and excluding various social groups in these ways, political competition and adversarial debate tends to impoverish public discourse and undermine the resolution of complex problems.

c) Time-Space Problem

Partisan politics is also inherently incapable of addressing problems across time and space. Complex social and environmental issues generally require long-term planning and commitment. Competitive political systems, however, are inherently constrained by short-term planning horizons. In order to gain and maintain power, political entrepreneurs must cater to the immediate interests of their constituents so that visible results can be realized within relatively frequent election cycles. Even when long-term political commitments are made out of principle by one candidate or party, continuity is often compromised by succeeding candidates or parties who dismantle or fail to enforce the programs of their predecessors in order to distance themselves from policies they were previously compelled to oppose on the campaign trail or as the voice of opposition. The focus of campaigns and political parties on constituencies-in-the-present therefore undermines commitment to the interests of future generations. Prominent among the interests of future generations is environmental sustainability. As we degrade our environment today, we impoverish future generations.

Many social problems, from poverty to crime to drug dependency to domestic abuse, also require long-term strategies and commitments. Sustained investments in education, the strengthening of families, the creation of economic opportunities, the cultivation of ethical codes and moral values, and other approaches that yield results across generations, are required. Yet the competitive pressure to demonstrate visible actions within frequent election cycles tends to lead instead toward investments in things like new prisons and detention centers to hide the growing social underclass in many countries; new mega-schools to warehouse increasingly alienated and anonymous children and youth; and new shopping malls to distract citizens with short-term material enticements.

Furthermore, just as competitive political systems are responsive to constituents-in-the-present at the exclusion of future generations, they are also responsive to the interests of constituents-within-electoral-boundaries at the exclusion of others. This is the problem of space—or territoriality—which is especially the case at the level of the nation state owing to the absence of an effective system of global governance. Again, this has significant social and ecological implications. The supra-national nature of modern environmental issues—such as ozone depletion, global warming, acid rain, water pollution, and the management of migratory species—signals the need for unprecedented levels of global cooperation and coordination.(World Commission on Environment and Development,1987). Competitive notions of national sovereignty, however, render the existing international system incapable of responding to these ecological imperatives. Today, cross-border coordination is sacrificed to the pursuit of national self-interests because political entrepreneurs have no choice but to cater to the interests of their own voting citizens. The consequence is an anarchic system of nation states vying with one another in their rush to convert long-term ecological capital into short-term political capital.

The problem of territoriality is equally significant when it comes to social issues. Challenges such as poverty, crime, the exploitation of women and children, human trafficking, terrorism, ethnic conflict, illegal immigration and refugee flows do not respect national boundaries any more than most ecological problems do. These problems cannot be solved by national governments alone. Yet political competition within nation states undermines effective commitment and coordination between them. Political competitors are responsive to the interests of voting constituents-within-electoral-boundaries to the exclusion of non-voters outside of those boundaries. This creates an irresistible incentive for political competitors in wealthy nations to externalize the worst manifestations of these social problems on poorer nations. Consequently, in the long run all of these problems tend to fester and spread until they again threaten the interests of the wealthiest nations. Competitive politics is not about planning for the long term; it is about securing electoral victories in the short term. Hence the problem of space is inseparable from the problem of time in competitive democracies.

d) Spiritual Problem

Other challenges associated with competitive politics are less tangible, but no less important. These are the spiritual costs of partisanship and political competition. Again, these problems stem directly from the assumptions that underlie the model: that human nature is essentially selfish and competitive; that different people tend to develop conflicting interests; and that the best way to organize democratic governance is therefore through a process of interest-group competition. By organizing human affairs according to these assumptions we are institutionally cultivating our basest instincts. In the process, we become what we expect of ourselves. The Universal House of Justice has observed that,

it is in the glorification of material pursuits, at once the progenitor and common feature of all such ideologies, that we find the roots which nourish the falsehood that human beings are incorrigibly selfish and aggressive. It is here that the ground must be cleared for the building of a new world fit for our descendants. (The Universal House of Justice, 1985, p. 6).

These culturally-formed expectations, however, have no solid basis in the social and behavioral sciences. In these fields, the emerging new consensus is that human beings have the developmental potential for both egoism and altruism, competition and cooperation—and which of these potentials is more fully realized is a function of our cultural environment (Zamagni, 1995). This insight is also familiar to many of the world's philosophical and religious traditions. Metaphors that allude to humanity's "lower" and "higher" nature, or "material" and "spiritual" nature, convey this insight, as does the eastern concept of "enlightenment." However, contrary to the theory and practice of political competition, the primary impulse behind these philosophical and religious traditions has been to cultivate these more cooperative and altruistic dimensions of human nature.

The uncivil nature of much partisan discourse, alluded to at the beginning of this essay, is an inevitable outgrowth of this inversion of material and spiritual priorities. When the pursuit of self-interest comes to be understood as a virtue, and selflessness is dismissed as naïve idealism, it is not surprising that politics becomes an uncivil arena. In this regard, the reality of partisan politics is better captured by war metaphors than by the market metaphors discussed earlier in this essay. A campaign, after all, is a military term, not a market term. Like military campaigns, political campaigns are expensive. Candidates amass "campaign war chests" as they prepare to "fight" election "battles." In an age of mass-media spectacle and sound-bite politics, this translates into an escalating cycle of negative advertising, insults, and mudslinging, as political campaigns and debates become a "war of words" conducted from "entrenched positions."

In the abstract, debate is about ideas rather than people. In practice, however, the competitive structure of the system erases the line between ideas and people, because if your ideas do not prevail, neither does your political career. Hence political debate slides easily into the quagmire of egoism and incivility. On the sidelines, meanwhile, the public grows increasingly cynical and disaffected—yet another spiritual cost of this system.

Finally, competitive democracies exact high costs as they divide rather than unite susceptible segments of the public. Any process that routinely produces winners and losers within a population will be divisive. When governance is structured as a process of interest-group competition, the pursuit of material interests becomes more important than the cultivation of mutualistic social relationships.

Furthermore, the formation of political parties, which requires the arbitrary aggregation of distinct and widely varied interests, results in the artificial construction of oppositional identity camps that become increasingly entrenched—and reified—over time. Consider, for instance, the American two-party system with its "left vs. right" or "liberal vs. conservative" camps. In reality, American collective life is characterized by countless complex issues, each of which may be viewed from multiple perspectives.

However, to construct a manageable political contest, the two dominant political parties reduce all possible issues down to simple binary conflicts and then aggregate conflicting positions on every different issue into two opposing super-camps. Over time, this artificial aggregation has begun to appear natural to many people. Moreover, segments of the population that initially identified strongly with one or two salient positions in any given camp have begun to embrace other aggregated positions through simple association. The result is that diverse people, who do not naturally fall into simple oppositional camps, come over time to separate themselves into such camps—a process that can be accelerated by astute politicians who make emotionally charged "wedge issues" the centerpieces of their campaigns in an effort to create and enforce partisan loyalties. The social divisions that result are further spiritual costs of competitive Western democracy.

Conclusion

In sum, capitalist hegemony arose from and has been sustained by many overdetermining factors. The anti-capitalist left cannot control all of those factors. But we can undertake the self-criticism proposed in this book, to the end of controlling the concepts of class informing our politics. We can interrogate the differences among alternative concepts of class. We can recognize the stakes for our political practice in deciding how the contesting concepts of class will inform our agendas for social change. Our desire to achieve greater successes in the twenty-first century than those we achieved in the twentieth requires no less. We need not pick among the different concepts of class. Rather we need to integrate them all into our social criticism and the alternatives we propose.

This perspective is practical. The left's historic quest for greater equality in the distribution of property and power is noble and valuable, but it needs extending. For this, the left must overcome its blindness to Marx's new concept of class. Analytically, this means determining which of Marx's five basic organizations of surplus production, appropriation, and distributions coexist in our society. Politically, the left must take an explicit political position against our society's exploitative and for the non-exploitative (the communitarian or, in Marx's phrase, the communist) class structures. We must show the public how non-exploitative class structures support as well as complement the greater equalities of property and power central to our programs for progressive social change. In short, we can contribute to undermining capitalism's hegemony if we expose its distinctive class qua surplus structure and make the transformation of that structure into an explicit component of our revolutionary objectives. This is long overdue.

Western hegemony uses liberalism as a tool for its maintenance, via the self-perpetuating triangle of international institutions, international trade and democracy. Once a state is integrated into one via its all-encompassing nature, the state will be gradually integrated into the other areas of the liberal world order. Furthermore, the triangle absorbs any attempts at counter-hegemony, which reinforces its own legitimacy. However, this book has also highlighted the cracks in Western hegemony. It argues that the increasing aggressive nature of exportation the "West" employs with regard to liberalism actually works to delegitimize its hegemony. As legitimate hegemony, as Machiavelli (as cited in Cox, 1983) states, rests upon consent, the "West's" need to employ concealed coercion to align emerging states with regard to gaining political and economic power, such as China, actually delegitimizes the hegemonic status of the "West". As such, the "West's" position is under threat as a result of their own actions – shattering their own perceived legitimacy.

Chapter III

Globalization and Democratization as Rewesternization

Overview

Western civilization is not just an ordinary civilization. It is characterized by supremacy and it is called Western supremacy. Western supremacy comes into existence as a result of imposing its will upon unsuspecting numbers of people throughout the world, violating them to produce wealth for the coffers of imperialism. When people accept this sort of thing (and it takes a long time to happen, years and years, it doesn't happen overnight), what tends to happen is that people begin to suffer from various forms of psychic anguish, psychic torture. People begin to feel, without any explanation, that they're somehow inferior, that they're somehow incomplete and incompetent. You see, unlike many people, I am reluctant to subscribe to the idea that colonization has ended. I want to see the evidence. It is the spread of white supremacist control characterized by Western civilization's notion of its own supremacy and its economic organization, capitalism. This consortium is in fact working towards the totalitarian control of every inch of earth and every person on earth. But it is euphemistically called "globalization." Globalization is the incessant chant of white (male) supremacy today. In fact, "democracy" is a white supremacist conceit that we have to be careful of. So many people use this word as though it is a wonderful word, a saviorism. It is elitist to begin with. It is a phallocentric representation based on state order over people. The acceptance of democracy is in fact the acceptance of a particular method of manipulating the public to facilitate their insertion into the capitalist order of the day. It is not about any kind of significant democratic change in the South or former colonies of the West.

Introduction

The administration of George W. Bush made democracy promotion a central aim of U.S. foreign policy. The president devoted his second inaugural address to the subject, the 2006 National Security Strategy focused on spreading democracy abroad, and the White House then launched a series of initiatives designed to foster democracy across the globe, not least the military engagements in Afghanistan and Iraq. However, in Afghanistan, Iraq, and other parts of the Arab world where the prospects for democracy once seemed promising—Lebanon, the Palestinian territories, and Egypt—U.S. efforts have not succeeded. In none of these places, as the Bush administration entered its final 18 months in office, was the much vaunted democracy even close to being securely established. This is a familiar pattern. Virtually every president since the founding of the republic has embraced the idea of spreading the American form of government beyond the borders of the United States. The Clinton administration conducted several military interventions with the stated aim of establishing democracy. Where it did so—in Somalia, Haiti, Bosnia, and Kosovo— democracy also failed to take root.

Yet the failure to promote Washington's democracy has not meant the failure of democracy itself. To the contrary, in the last quarter of the twentieth century this form of government enjoyed a remarkable rise. Once confined to a handful of wealthy countries, it became, in a short period of time, the most popular political system in the world. In 1900, only ten countries were democracies; by mid-century, the number had increased to 30, and 25 years later the count remained the same. By 2005, fully 119 of the world's 190 countries had become democracies.

The seemingly paradoxical combination of the failure of U.S. democracy promotion and the successful expansion of democracy raises several questions: Why have the deliberate efforts of the world's most powerful country to export its form of government proved ineffective? Why and how has democracy enjoyed such extraordinary worldwide success despite the failure of these efforts? And what are the prospects for democracy in other key areas—the

Arab countries, Russia, and China—where it is still not present? Answering these questions requires a proper understanding of the concept of democracy itself.

We are thus at present engaged in what purports to be a planned reordering of the world by the powerful Northern states. The wars in Iraq and Afghanistan are but one part of a supposedly universal effort to create world order by 'spreading democracy.' This idea is not merely quixotic – it is dangerous. The rhetoric surrounding this crusade implies that the system is applicable in a standardized (Western) form, that it can succeed everywhere, that it can remedy today's transnational dilemmas, and that it can bring peace, rather than sow disorder. It cannot. Democracy is rightly popular. In 1647, the English Levellers broadcast the powerful idea that 'all government is in the free consent of the people.' They meant votes for all. Of course, universal suffrage does not guarantee any particular political result, and elections cannot even ensure their own perpetuation—witness the Weimar Republic.

Electoral democracy is also unlikely to produce outcomes convenient to hegemonic or imperial powers. For example, if the Iraq war had depended on the freely expressed consent of 'the world community,' it would not have happened. But these uncertainties do not diminish the appeal of electoral democracy. Several other factors besides democracy's popularity explain the dangerous and illusory belief that its propagation by foreign armies might actually be feasible. Globalization suggests that human affairs are evolving toward a universal pattern. If gas stations, iPods, and computer geeks are the same worldwide, why not political institutions? This view underrates the world's complexity. The relapse into bloodshed and anarchy that has occurred so visibly in much of the world has also made the idea of spreading a new order more attractive. The Balkans seemed to show that areas of turmoil and humanitarian catastrophe required the intervention, military if need be, of strong and stable states. In the absence of effective international governance, some humanitarians are still ready to support a world order imposed by U.S. power.

But one should always be suspicious when military powers claim to be doing favors for their victims and the world by defeating and occupying weaker states. Yet another factor may be the most important: The United States has been ready with the necessary combination of megalomania and messianism, derived from its revolutionary origins. Today's United States of America is unchallengeable in its techno-military supremacy, convinced of the superiority of its social system, and, since 1989, no longer reminded—as even the greatest conquering empires always had been—that its material power has limits. Like President Woodrow Wilson (a spectacular international failure in his day), today's ideologues see a model society already at work in the United States: a combination of law, liberal freedoms, competitive private enterprise, and regular, contested elections with universal suffrage.

All that remains is to remake the world in the image of this 'free society.' This idea is dangerously whistling in the dark. Although great power action may have morally or politically desirable consequences, identifying with it is perilous because the logic and methods of state action are not those of universal rights. All established states put their own interests first. If they have the power, and the end is considered sufficiently vital, states justify the means of achieving it (though rarely in public)—particularly when they think God is on their side. Both good and evil empires have produced the barbarization of our era, to which the 'war against terror' has now contributed.

While threatening the integrity of universal values, the campaign to spread democracy will not succeed. The 20th century demonstrated that states could not simply remake the world or abbreviate historical transformations. Nor can they easily effect social change by transferring institutions across borders. Even within the ranks of territorial nation-states, the conditions for effective democratic government are rare: an existing state enjoying legitimacy, consent, and the ability to mediate conflicts between domestic groups. Without such consensus, there is no single sovereign people and therefore no legitimacy for arithmetical majorities. When this consensus – be it religious, ethnic, or both – is absent, democracy has been suspended (as is the case with democratic institutions in Northern Ireland), the state has split (as in Czechoslovakia), or society has descended into permanent civil war (as in Sri Lanka).

'Spreading democracy' aggravated ethnic conflict and produced the disintegration of states in multinational and multicommunal regions after both 1918 and 1989, a bleak prospect. Beyond its scant chance of success, the effort to spread standardized Western democracy also suffers from a fundamental paradox. In no small part, it is conceived of as a solution to the dangerous transnational problems of our day. A growing part of human life now occurs beyond the influence of voters – in transnational public and private entities that have no electorates, or at least no democratic ones.

And electoral democracy cannot function effectively outside political units such as nation-states. The powerful states are therefore trying to spread a system that even they find inadequate to meet today's challenges. Europe proves the point. A body like the European Union (EU) could develop into a powerful and effective structure precisely because it has no electorate other than a small number (albeit growing) of member governments. The EU would be nowhere without its 'democratic deficit,' and there can be no future for its parliament, for there is no 'European people,' only a collection of 'member peoples,' less than half of whom bothered to vote in the 2004 EU parliamentary elections. 'Europe' is now a functioning entity, but unlike the member states it enjoys no popular legitimacy or electoral authority.

Unsurprisingly, problems arose as soon as the EU moved beyond negotiations between governments and became the subject of democratic campaigning in the member states. The effort to spread democracy is also dangerous in a more indirect way: It conveys to those who do not enjoy this form of government the illusion that it actually governs those who do. But does it? We now know something about how the actual decisions to go to war in Iraq were taken in at least two states of unquestionable democratic bona fides: the United States and the United Kingdom. Other than creating complex problems of deceit and concealment, electoral democracy and representative assemblies had little to do with that process. Decisions were taken among small groups of people in private, not very different from the way they would have been taken in nondemocratic countries. Fortunately, media independence could not be so easily circumvented in the United Kingdom. But it is not electoral democracy that necessarily ensures effective freedom of the press, citizen rights, and an independent judiciary.

Historically, industry has always been liberating. The great emancipation of the European masses throughout the nineteenth century came from their going into cities and factories, getting away from the poverty and ignorance of life on the land. Industry gave them new hope, and it gave them the means, of course, to develop the new ideas and habits that make a democracy work. So the more American and other Western concerns are down in South Africa opposing apartheid quietly through their own operations, their own attitudes, and through allowing workers and employees of all races and tribes to mingle in the factory and the office—all these new, decent ways bring on democracy much faster than speeches from soap boxes or pulpits or lecterns or brutal attempts to give democracy through the muzzle of the cannon to the South.

Background to Exporting Western Democracy

After the Cold War ended, promoting the international spread of democracy seemed poised to replace containment as the guiding principle of U.S. foreign policy. Scholars, policymakers, and commentators embraced the idea that democratization could become America's next mission. In recent years, however, critics have argued that spreading democracy may be unwise or even harmful. This chapter addresses this debate. A permanent feature of American opinion and action in foreign policy has been the wish, the hope, that other nations might turn from the error of their ways and become democracies: "They are a great people, why can't they manage their affairs like us?" A corollary has been, let us help those governments that are democratic, make them our allies, and let us oppose the others—indeed, if necessary, take action to coerce them. A current example is the agitation about South Africa, which rages from the campus to Capitol Hill and from the board room to the living room. In these rooms, anyone not in favor of "doing something" against South Africa is deemed a traitor to the very spirit of this country, these democratic United States.

But, there remains a question on this subject that has long bothered the thoughtful. What is it exactly that we want others to copy? What is the theory of democracy that we mean to export? Not all democracies are alike. Whose constitution is the best? On what theory is it based? The demand for a theory has been especially urgent during the last 40 years because of the striking success of the opposite theory, Marxist-Leninist communism. In one region after another it has conquered what often looked like rising democracies. The rival theory was apparently more attractive, more convincing. We attribute these results to eloquent agents who had an easy time because "we" weren't there with a theory of our own. Hence such missionaries for our side might be, given the democratic idea of the self-determination of peoples, is something of a puzzle, but it is secondary to yet another, greater one: What are these missionaries to preach? Where do we find the parallel to the writings of Marx and Lenin, and what do those writings tell?

Different persons would give different answers, which is a weakness to begin with.

Some would point to the Declaration of Independence and the federal Constitution; others to Rousseau, Edmund Burke, Thomas Paine. Then there is Tocqueville's *Democracy in America* in two volumes and a wonderful little book by Walter Bagehot on the English Constitution, not to mention *The Federalist* papers and many eloquent pages from John Adams, Thomas Jefferson, and Abraham Lincoln. Taken loosely together, those writings would be regarded by many as making up the theory of democracy.

Of course, they don't all agree; they don't form a system. *The Federalist* writers are afraid of democracy; Madison repeats in *The Federalist* (nos. 10, 14, 48, 58, and 63) that full or pure democracy is a menace to freedom, and he praises the constitution being proposed to the American people for its "total exclusion of the people in their collective capacity" (no. 63), John Adams disputes Tom Paine and goes only part way with Jefferson (Cappon,1959, 1959), pp. 199, 236, 248, 279, 35 152, 456, 519, 550, 598, and passim). Burke and Rousseau sound like direct contraries.

Tocqueville calls for so many of the special conditions he found here that his conclusions are not transferable. And Bagehot does the same thing for Great Britain: you have to be Englishmen to make the English Constitution work.

All these ifs and buts make a poor prospect for unified theory, but there is worse. When we actually read these documents we find that each theorized about a few subjects among many which very properly go by different names. We have: democracy, republic, free government, representative government, constitutional monarchy. These are beside: natural rights, civil rights, equality before the law, equal opportunity. Then there are also: universal suffrage, majority rule, separation of powers, and the two-party system. Nor should we forget about another half dozen topics that are found associated in modern times with the so-called democratic process—primary elections, the referendum, proportional representation, and so on.

That array of ideas and devices cannot but be daunting to the propagandist for democracy. Which are essential? How should they combine? The very need to explain what the terms mean bars the way to easy acceptance and enthusiasm. In addition, the key words do not mean the same thing to all the theorists. To cap these troubles, nowhere in the West has there been a central authority to define an orthodoxy, even a shifting one, such as there has been on the communist side.

On that side, there is the advantage not only of unity but of broad abstraction: the class struggle, history as dialectical materialism, surplus value, society shaped by the forms of economic production, the contradictions in capitalism preparing its decline and fall, the aim and training of the revolutionist, and the dictatorship of the proletariat leading to the withering away of the state. These eight "big ideas," energized by resentment and utopian hope, make up a scheme that has the ring of high intellectuality. The scheme is readily teachable as a series of catchwords which, as experience shows, can appeal to every level of intelligence. It offers not only a promise of material advantage, but also a drama—a struggle toward a glorious end, unfolding according to necessity.

Compared with a scripture and prophecy, which amount not to theory but to ideology, the concrete plans and the varied means of the writers on democracy present a spectacle of pettifogging and confusion. Common opinion reinforces this lack of order and unity. The democratic peoples suppose that free governments did not exist before the population at large got the vote, which is not true, or that democracy is incompatible with a king and an aristocracy, though England is there to show that a monarchy with a House of Lords can be democratic. Was the United States a democracy when senators were not elected directly by the people? Were we a free government when we held millions in slavery or segregation? Finally, it takes no research to find out that the democracies of France, Italy, and Sweden, those of Brazil, Mexico, and the Philippines, and of Thailand, India, and the United States are far from giving people the same freedoms by the same means.

Take two recent illustrations. In France, the last elections brought to power in the National Assembly, and hence in the office of the prime minister, a party opposed to that of the president, whose term was to continue for another two years. This vote caused immediate and prolonged consternation. Would there be a violent clash or would government stop dead in a stalemate between the president and his prime minister backed by the Assembly? A few daring souls said that "cohabitation" (which in French has no sexual overtones) might be possible. But debate raged on. It so happened that a young musicologist from Smith College was in Paris when the dismay was at its height. Being fluent in French, he wrote a letter to *Le Monde*, which published it as remarkable. It said in effect: "Good people, don't be upset. What bothers you has happened in the United States quite often.

Democracy won't come to an end because two branches of government are in the hands of different parties" (Peter Anthony Bloom, "La Leçon des Etats-Unis," *Le Monde* (Paris), February 28, 1986). He was right. Cohabitation has begun, but it is working in ways that surprise American friends of democracy—for instance, by the use of ministerial decrees that become law or of the closure called guillotine by which debate is cut off in the Assembly. The point of the example is clear: one Western democracy is nearly stymied by a lawful result of its own system, and gets over the trouble by means that would be unthinkable—anti-democratic—in another democracy where that same trouble of divided authority seems no trouble at all. What unified theory could cover both versions of the democratic process?

The second example comes from the Philippines, where a national election was held in circumstances of violence and coercion and yielded an outcome that could therefore be questioned. A delegation from the United States Congress had to go and inquire into the events surrounding the vote before this country could assume that the democratic process had in fact been carried out, for as we saw, common opinion holds that the vote of the people is the diagnostic test of democracy—"... the right to vote is surely the Linchpin of peaceful change...," says Lloyd N. Cutler, former counsel to President Carter, and he recommends it for South Africa ("Using Morals, Not Money, on Pretoria," *New York Times*, August 3, 1986, sec. 4, p. 23). But change to peace is far from assured. Hitler's example has been imitated again and again by well-led groups aiming at one-party rule. But what if the voting itself is not free, as in parts of the Philippines and in many other countries where the doubt and confusion are never settled by inquiry? Are those democracies? Or must they be considered half-way cases in order to fit under the grand theory?

The truth is, the real subject for discussion is not "Is democratic theory for export?" but "Is there a theory of democracy?" We expect to find one not solely because a large part of the world boasts a rival theory, but also because in our admiration for science, we like to have a theory for every human activity. My conviction is that democracy has no theory. It has only a theorem, that is, a proposition which is generally accepted and which can be stated in a single sentence. Here is the theorem of democracy: For a free mankind, it is best that the people should be sovereign, and this popular sovereignty implies political and social equality.

When I say the theorem of democracy has been accepted, I am not overlooking the anti-democratic opposition. For in one sense there is none. Look over the world of the twentieth century and you find at every turn the claim that the government of this nation and that nation is a popular government—the People's Republic of China, the German Democratic Republic, the Democratic Republic of Yemen and that of Kampuchea all say so in their titles. Other nations profess the same creed and point to their constitutions. The Soviet Union has one that provides for elections and delegates at various levels.

Parties and voting and assemblies are found all up and down the five continents. The split comes over who "the people" are, what is meant by "party," and how the agents of government act for (or against) the people. Historically, the people have always been recognized in some fashion. Athens was a democracy—with slaves; the Roman emperor spoke in the name of "the Senate and the Roman people"; the Germanic tribes and the American Indians had chiefs and also general councils; kings were the "fathers" of their people—and their servants too. And the old adage *Vox populi, vox Dei*—the voice of the people is the voice of God—has always meant that rulers cannot and should not withstand the people's will.

The theorem, then, is not disputed, even when tyranny flourishes under it, for it has two parts and the tyrant can boast that the blessings of the second part, equality, are due to him. We are thus brought to the great question of the machinery of government, because it is how the wheels turn, and not a theory, that makes a government free or not free. The dictatorship of the proletariat may be the theory of communism, but in fact neither the proletariat nor its single party rules. Voting and debating is make-believe set over a tight oligarchy led by one man. There is no machinery to carry out the promise that in time the proletariat will disappear and the state will wither away, and most often, there is not even a device for ensuring the public succession from one top leader to the next.

The conclusion established so far would seem to be this: Democracy has no theory to cover the working of its many brands of machinery, whereas its antagonists use a single, well-publicized theory to cover in another sense, namely to conceal, the workings of one rather uniform machine, the police state. A further conclusion is that the demand for a theory of democracy shows the regrettable tendency to think entirely in abstractions, never bringing general statements side by side with the facts of experience, or even noticing important differences between abstractions if they happen to be linked together by custom or usage.

Democracy, for example, is thought of as synonymous with free government; "the sovereign people" is thought of as meaning all or most or some of the residents within the boundaries of a state. What kinds of freedom a government guarantees, how they are secured, and which groups and individuals actually obtain them and which do not constitute complicated questions that theorists and journalists alike prefer to ignore. They know that such details are of no use in stirring up either protests at home or virtuous indignation about others abroad. The public at large takes government itself abstractly, as a kind of single-minded entity, an engine that works only in one direction and always expresses the same attitude toward human desires. The democratic, modern style of government is the good kind, and the rest, past and present, are the bad.

For this childlike view, there is only one remedy and that is a little history. I include under this term contemporary history, for after having excluded the possibility of a theory of democracy I am concerned to offer instead a survey, or rather a sketchy panorama, of its manifestations. I do this with a practical purpose in view I think it is important to know how the so-called free world came into being, what ideas and conditions would be required for its extension, and most immediate and important, what changes are occurring in our own democracy that threaten its peculiar advantages and make its export impossible.

Let us return to our theorem. It calls for three difficult things: expressing the popular will, ensuring equality, and by means of both, distributing a variety of freedoms. These purposes imply machinery. How, for example, is the popular will ascertained? The devices we are familiar with in the Anglo-American tradition have come from two sources. One is the long, slow, haphazard growth of the English Constitution from the Parliament of Simon de Montfort in 1265 through innumerable struggles for rights won (and listed) a few at a time—Magna Carta, the Bill of Rights, and so on. Simon de Montfort anticipated "the English Constitution" by 600 years. The Parliament of 1265 included two delegates from every shire and two burgesses from every town.

The aim was that acting as Great Council to the king, they should advise him, supervise the several divisions of government afford redress, and approve taxes. The king's ministers should be responsible to it. In short, Montfort wanted in 1265 what slowly and painfully became general in Western Europe by the end of the nineteenth century. In 1265 the barons quarreled, resented middle-class participation in government, and resumed a war in which Montfort was conveniently stabbed in the back. But the people of England continued to worship him as a martyr, patriot, and saint. From this history, Montesquieu, Locke, and others variously derived the precepts and precedents that influenced the making of the United States Constitution.

The other source is antiquity—Greece and Rome—whose practices and writings on government inspired thinkers to design plans or issue warnings appropriate to their own time. The most famous scheme is that of Rousseau. His is also the most instructive, for although he is crystal clear, his interpreters divide on the tendency of his great book, *The Social Contract*. Some say it promotes freedom, others say it leads to totalitarianism. This shows how double-edged propositions can be. But let us see what Rousseau himself says. He takes democracy literally: all the people, equal in rank, come together and decide policy and choose leaders. This is the old Athenian democracy, except that there are no slaves.

Rousseau goes on to point out that only a small city-state can manage that sort of government. Knowing his ancient history, he adds that such pure democracy is too good for men as they are. He agrees with the great minds of ancient Greece—Aristotle, Plato, Xenophon, Thucydides—all were against democracy; they saw dozens of democratic cities perish from inefficiency, stupidity, and corruption. Aristotle's treatise on ancient governments influenced such eighteenth-century proponents of free government as Madison in their fear of "democracy," for Aristotle says it is the corruption of free government, just as tyranny is the corruption of monarchy (*Politics* bk. IV, chap. 2). Rousseau therefore falls back on representative government, which he calls, correctly, "elective aristocracy": the people elect those they think the best (*aristoi*) to run their affairs for them.

He also requires a lawgiver to describe the structure of the government. For "lawgiver" substitute "constitution," a set of rules for day-to-day operations. Why should anybody think that such a system must end in tyranny? One answer can be given through a quick reminder: Hitler did not seize power, he was voted in as head of a plurality party by a people living under a democratic government and with a constitution that combined the best features of all constitutions on record. If you add to the strength of Hitler's party that of the German Communists, you have a large democratic majority voting for totalitarian rule. To generalize from this example, if the people is sovereign, it can do anything it wants, including turn its constitution upside down. It can lose its freedom by choosing leaders who promise more equality, more prosperity, more national power through dictatorship. The theorem of popular sovereignty is honored in the breach. The dictator says, "I represent the will of the people. I know what it wants."

On the other hand, a new nation can ask: "Popular sovereignty, the vote for everybody, then what?" That question was precisely the one put to Rousseau by envoys from two nations, Poland and Corsica. He wrote for each of them a small book that shows how he would go about being a lawgiver, a constitution-maker. These notable supplements to the abstract outline of *The Social Contract* are conveniently forgotten by Rousseau's critics. For in prescribing for Poland and for Corsica, Rousseau makes the all-important point that the history, character, habits, religion, economic base, and education of each people must be taken into account before setting up any machinery. No rules or means apply universally. What works in England will fail in Poland; what the French prefer, the Corsicans will reject.

Political equality can be decreed, but freedom cannot—it is a most elusive good. Rousseau warns the Poles that they should go slowly in freeing their serfs, for fear that in their economic ignorance the serfs will fall into worse misery than before. This was Burke's great point about the solidity of English freedom, which is freedom under a monarchy and what we would surely call a non-representative Parliament based as it was on gradual change through history, freedom had taken root inside every Englishman. Burke criticized the French revolutionists because they did not revive the old assemblies and thereby give the French some training in the use of freedom. Instead, they wrote principles on a piece of paper and expected them to produce the right behavior overnight. On this central issue, Burke and Rousseau are at one, as a fine scholar long ago demonstrated to a non-listening world in her book *Rousseau and Burke* (Osborne, 1940).

This element of Time, of the slow training of individuals by history, carries with it a predicament and a paradox. The predicament is: How can the peoples that want to spread freedom to the world propose their institutions as models if those institutions depend on habits long ingrained in this paradox? It is easy enough to copy a piece of actual machinery, such as a computer or even a nuclear weapon. It takes only a few bright, well-trained people with the model in front of them. But to copy a government is not something that a whole population can achieve by merely deciding to do it.

One may note in passing the double error of the former colonial powers: They did not teach the ways of freedom soon enough to their colonial subjects, and they let go of their colonies too quickly when the urge to independence swept the globe. The bloodshed was immediate and extensive, and it is not over. Some of the nations that emerged tried what they thought was democracy, only to succumb to military or one-party rule—always in the name of popular sovereignty, indeed of liberation. The word is not always a mere pretense, for it is liberation to be rid of a government that cannot govern. The ancient maxim is true, *mundus vult gubernari*—the world insists on being governed.

As for the paradox, it is this: How can a people learn the ways of free government until it is free? And how can it stay free if it cannot run the type of machinery associated with self-government? On this score, the spectacle of Latin America is baffling. The several states gained their independence from Spain not long after the thirteen North American colonies gained theirs from England, during the period 1783-1823. Yet repeated efforts by able, selfless leaders have left South and Central America prey to repeated dictatorships with the usual accompaniment of wars, massacres, oppression, assassinations, and that great diagnostic fact, uncertainty about the succession of legitimate governors.

To contrast the history of the North American colonies with the history of those of the South is not to disparage Latin America, but to remind ourselves of the bases of free government. We make a great mistake in calling the American War of Independence "the American Revolution" and in bragging about the fact that it did not wind up in dictatorship like the English Revolution under Cromwell or the French under Robespierre. In 1776 the Americans rebelled against very recent rules and impositions. What they wanted was not a new type of government, but the old type they had always enjoyed. They were used to many freedoms which they claimed as the immemorial rights of Englishmen. Once they had defeated the English armies and expelled the Loyalists, they went back to their former ways, which they modestly enlarged and codified in the Bill of Rights. Needless to say, when the people of South America threw off Spanish and Portuguese rule they had no such tradition or experience to help them.

The evidence is overwhelming that it is not enough to be left alone by a royal or imperial power in order to establish some degree of freedom and to keep it safe, to say nothing of achieving egalitarian democracy. One should remember the travails of Spain itself throughout the nineteenth century and down to a few years ago. One should think of France, eager for freedom in 1789 but hardly settled in it during its five republics, two empires, one partial dictatorship, and twelve constitutions. For 200 years in Central Europe, various peoples, unhappily intermingled by centuries of war and oppression, have been longing to form nations and nations to form free states. Even under the iron heel of local communism and Russian hegemony, a working system seems beyond reach. A recent headline read: "Ethnic Mini-states Paralyze Yugoslavia" (*Washington Post* June 28, 1986). The lesson here is that *the people* must first define itself through a common language and common traditions before it can hope to be *the sovereign people*.

Nor are grass-roots aspirations alone enough to ensure either nationhood or liberal rule. We should recall the forgotten example of Russia. At the turn of the nineteenth century there had developed there a widespread, home-grown movement toward constitutional government. In 1905 several well-organized parties ranging from conservative and liberal to socialist and revolutionary had obtained from the tsar a representative two-chamber assembly based on nearly universal suffrage. Important civil rights and religious toleration were granted and able leaders arose from the middle class and professional groups, but the parties and leaders were unable to keep united behind their gains and the whole house of cards soon collapsed. Politics were, so to speak, immature and the popular will confused. A symbol of that confusion was the crowds cheering for the Archduke Constantine to replace the tsar: "Constantine and Constitution" was the shout, and it turned out that many thought that Constitution was Constantine's wife.

That first experience was not forgotten. Ten years later, in March 1917, a second democratic revolution occurred, backed at first by everybody—not just do-or-die liberals and revolutionaries, but business and professional men, trade unionists and conservative landholders, urban workers and army officers. The force behind the call for reform was the desire to win the war, and the institutions set up to carry out the one and carry on the other were perfectly adequate. Again, those in charge were unable to make the new institutions work, and in eight months they perished under the onslaught of a new autocracy led by Lenin and Trotsky. In less than ten years, then, two intelligent attempts to modernize government in Russia had failed—and Russia was a country where Western ideas had long since penetrated, a country whose educated class was at home in all the democratic capitals of Europe.

Our second large conclusion must therefore be that a democracy cannot be fashioned out of whatever people happen to be around in a given region; it cannot be promoted from outside by strangers; and it may still be impossible when attempted from inside by determined natives. Just as life on the earth depended on a particular coming together of unrelated factors, so a cluster of disparate elements and conditions is needed for a democracy to be born viable. Among these conditions one can name tradition, literacy, and a certain kind of training in give-and-take, as well as the sobering effect of national disaster—France in 1870 and Germany in 1945. The most adaptable of peoples, the Japanese, took a century to approximate Western democracy, aided no doubt by the harsh tutelage which followed a grievous defeat. And another people might have taken these same experiences the other way, as spurs to resist change.

The absence of theory and the rare occurrence at one time and place of the right pieces to assemble might seem enough to rule out the export of democracy from nation to nation, but there is today a third and last obstacle: the present character of free governments in the West. This difficulty may be made clear by comparing our times with the heyday of enthusiasm for democratic freedom, 1918-20. The First World War had been fought against monarchies and empires, and this country joined in to "make the world safe for democracy." There is nothing foolish in that motto of Woodrow Wilson's. Victory seemed to give the Allied powers a chance to replace two conglomerate empires with a galaxy of new, true, and free nations. It is worth noting that tsarist Russia and the Communist Soviet Union joined the Western powers in the last two world wars without preventing those powers from proclaiming that they were fighting to put down autocracy and advance the cause of freedom. Theories, theories! Russia itself seemed to have jumped the gun in March 1917.

What was not foreseen was the backlash of the war. Emotionally, it was a revulsion against four years of carnage. In practical effect, it was nothing less than a social revolution. The war itself was revolutionary, having moved the masses out of their routines-the men into the trenches, the women into the factories. What happened under Lenin in Russia, and for a time among her neighbors, advertised this social upheaval. The masses were now sovereign in their outlook and behavior. Henceforth, whatever was done must be done for their good and in their name. Their needs and wants, their habits and tastes, marked the high tide of democracy as Tocqueville had foreseen it in this country.

The message was clear to all, because it had been preached with growing intensity for 100 years. Universal suffrage; the end of poverty; identical rights for everybody; social, economic, even sexual emancipation; popular culture, not elite esthetics—these demands went with a distrust and hatred of all the old orders, old leaders, and old modes of life that had brought on the four years of homicidal horror and destruction. The new modes were to be anti-capitalist (obviously); anti-Victorian in morals, and anti-parliamentarian as well, for many thought representative government a corrupt and contemptible fraud. Democracy needed better machinery. In that mood it is no wonder that fascism and the corporate state triumphed so rapidly. The theory of the corporate state, or socialism in the guise of state capitalism, was expounded in France and Germany and promulgated in Italy. It had intellectual adherents for a time; Winston Churchill praised Mussolini, and David Lloyd George, Hitler. The defeat of the Axis powers silenced such advocates, which shows again how dependent on current events theorists are. If England and France hung on to their constitutional freedoms amid this turmoil, it was due largely to historical momentum, the same force that threw Russia back into its old groove.

After all this, it would be a mistake to think that what is now called the free world is just the continuation of the liberal regimes which existed before 1914. The social revolution has changed them all into welfare states, and this transformation, which is one expression of the socialist ideal, has so altered the machinery of free government that it no longer resembles the model one could previously define by a few plain devices, such as voting, the party system, and majority rule. Although the changes of the last 60 years in democratic nations have been similar, they have been uneven. In different countries the notions of freedom and equality have taken varying and sometimes contradictory meanings.

It is essential to raise some probing questions here. Does a national health service increase freedom or reduce it? Does workers' compensation give equal treatment to workers and employers when it disregards contributory negligence in causing accidents? Are the rules for zoning and landmark preservation a protection of property rights or an infringement of them? More generally, can the enormous increase in the bureaucracy needed to enforce endless regulations and the high taxes levied for all the new services be called an extension of freedom or a limitation? Where it is clearly a limitation, the argument advanced is that it is imposed for the sake of equality, thus fulfilling the prediction of the earliest critics of democracy—that it begins by talking the language of liberty but ends in promoting an equality that destroys one freedom after another.

One can readily understand how the modern constraints to ensure rights came into being. The old inequalities were so flagrant, so irrational, and so undeserved, the exclusions and prejudices were so heartless and often so contrary to the laws even then on the books, which only concerted action by the government could bring the conditions of life for the masses into conformity with the democratic theorem—the popular will absolute implies equality also absolute. But the steady drive toward social and economic parity for all has brought about a great shift in the source of day-to-day authority over individuals. The guarantor of rights and freedoms is no longer political; the government we live under is administrative and judiciary. Hence the diminished interest in political life and political rights: the poor turnout at most elections, the increase in single-issue partisanship, the rare occurrence of clear majorities, and the widespread feeling that individual action is futile. To exercise his or her freedom, the free citizen must work through channels long and intricate and rarely political.

To see this situation in perspective, open your Tocqueville and see what he saw as the essence of the American democracy. For him, the federal government is of small importance compared to the government of each state—and so it was in 1835 for every American citizen. "The government" meant the legislature at the state capitol. What is more, in all the small things that affect individual life, from roads and police to schools and taxes, Tocqueville tells us that it is the township or county that is paramount. He gives New England as proof: the town meeting determines the will of the people and the selectmen carry it out. That is democracy at work. Everybody has a voice in decisions, everybody has a chance to serve in office, everybody understands the common needs, as well as the degree to which anybody's opinion or proposal is worth following (Alexis de Tocqueville, *Democracy in America*, vol. I, pt. I, ch. 5). The democracy is that of Athens in its best days, the one Rousseau said was too perfect for human use.

Today, the government machine is more like the circuitry of a mainframe computer in that it is too complex for anybody but students of the science. And this elaboration of devices for equality can only be endless. The lure of further rights is ever-present, because among men and women in society "equal" is a figurative term, not a mathematical one. For example, the justice of rewarding talent with higher pay has been gravely debated; the word meritocracy has been invented to suggest that merit violates democratic equality, because merit is not earned, it is as it were unmerited. Other attempts are being made, under the name of comparable worth, to legislate the equality of very diverse occupations. Equality of opportunity has come to seem too indefinite and uncertain.

Please note that I am describing, not judging. The point here is not the contents or wisdom of these new rights conferred in batches on the minorities—ethnic and sexual, on the employed and the unemployed, the disabled, the pregnant, the nonsmokers, the criminal, the moribund, and the insane, to say nothing of the fanciers of old buildings, the champions of certain animals and plants, and that great silent minority, the consumers. What is in question is the effect of ever-extended rights on the conception or definition of free government. One such effect is a conflict of claims, a division in the body politic. Many complain that others have become not equal but superequal, that reverse discrimination has set in. The rights of women and those of the unborn are clearly opposite. Perhaps the smoker and the nonsmoker form the emblematic pair whose freedoms are incompatible.

The upshot is that the idea of the citizen, a person with the same few clear rights as everybody else, no longer holds. In his place is a person with a set of special characteristics matched by a set of privileges. These group privileges must be kept in balance by continual addition if overall equality is to survive. State constitutions are continually being amended. In 1984-85, the last year for which figures are available, 158 of the 338 proposed changed in state constitutions were approved. Many of these proposals dealt with rights and of these, 77.7 percent were approved (Council of State Governments, *The Book of the States:*

1986-87, Lexington, KY, 1986, p. 4). This progression has a visible side effect: it tends to nullify majority rule, for in seeing to it that nobody loses through any decision, it makes majority and minority equal.

Finally, progressive equality and bureaucratic delay encourage the thing known as "participatory democracy," which is in fact direct minority rule, a kind of reverse democracy for coercing authority by protests, demonstrations, sit-ins, and job actions in order to obtain the rapid satisfaction of new demands. For example, when budget cuts forced the Library of Congress to reduce its hours of service, readers staged protests by various forms of obstruction. Arrests were made, and so were concessions. Again, acting on behalf of eleven monkeys, a group of simophiles camped outside the National Institutes of Health and commanded attention. Such sequences have come to be called civil disobedience, but they are not always civil and they bypass the traditional procedures guaranteed by the Bill of Rights—peaceful assembly and petition. It is felt, no doubt justly, that the old devices presuppose a different society, less hurried, better integrated, and used to articulate communication.

Regardless of one's like or dislike for the great complication the different society, less hurried, at the original ideal of government by the people and for the people, has undergone, one must admit yet again that devising a theory for its actual working is impossible. To say, "Here it is, come and observe, and then copy it" would be a cruel joke. For one thing, the Western world still believes, rightly, that it is free. But though at one in the resolve to establish equality, its institutions remain wide apart in their allotment of freedoms. For example, an American citizen would find the extent of regulation in Switzerland or Sweden oppressive. He would call Switzerland's indirect elections at every level a backward, undemocratic system of representation. A Swiss (or an Australian) would retort, "You haven't advanced as far as the initiative and referendum for important national issues. You don't know what freedom is." The latest "initiative" in Switzerland proposes to abolish the Swiss army.

So radical a change will doubtless elicit a large turnout at the polls, but usually no more than a quarter of the electorate votes on the initiatives, of which there is usually a large backlog. In France, that same American would be shocked at the practices by which the police regularly gather and use information about every citizen and would not be pacified by the reply that it is an old custom quite harmless to freedom. Elsewhere, the drag on democracy would seem to be the inability to act within a reasonable time, the result of government by coalition. In Holland, for example, because of the system of "pillarization"—the forming of groups according to religious, occupational, and ideological preference—there are over twenty parties competing at the polls and there is no majority.

"Pillarization" was made official in 1917 to satisfy the demands of the Catholic, Protestant, and "Humanist" factions that divided the Dutch professions, trade unions, sexes, and ideological groups. Each permutation of these combining allegiances was recognized as a pillar of the state and given a place on the ballot. In the last ten years, a demand has grown for more comprehensive parties, but it has not yet made headway. It is precluded by proportional representation, which many regard as essential to democracy. As for Germany and Italy, the same need for coalition works in the usual way to give extremists leverage against the wishes of the actual but disunified majority.

Which of these complexities would one recommend to a new nation eager for free government? If a detached observer turned to the American scene, he would note still other obstacles to the straight-forward democratic process: gerrymandering, the filibuster, the distorting effect of opinion polls, the lobbying system, the maze of regulations governing registration for voting and nominating, the perversities of the primaries, and worst of all, the enormous expense of getting elected, which entails a scramble for money and the desperate shifts for abating its influence, including financial disclosure, codes of ethics, and the like. Nobody wants to play according to the rules.

In addition to the deliberate evasion or twisting of the rules, their administration is inevitably slow and poor. This evil is only partly the fault of the bureaucrats who are so readily blamed. The art of administration has not been brought up to date; no one has thought about it since Frederick the Great and Napoleon, or, it often seems, since Charlemagne. Although courses and certificates are offered on every conceivable activity of the modern world, administration is ignored. There are courses in management, but they take it for granted that psychologizing and manipulating people is the sole avenue to efficiency.

Add the use of television to make quick bids for popularity through inane, fictional dialogue, and the employment of public relations gurus to guide the choice of ideas to propose to the electorate, and you can gauge the decay of political campaigning. A symbol of the loss is the four-yearly spectacle called a debate between presidential candidates—no debate but an amateurish quiz program. As one listens to any current campaign or "debate," one cannot help comparing its quality and methods with those of Lincoln and Douglas in 1858, or even of later presidential aspirants, such as Woodrow Wilson, Theodore and Franklin Roosevelt, or John F. Kennedy. One difference is in the span of attention required. Its dwindling is suitably met by the use of "30-second spots" on the air.

A last feature of modern democracy which should baffle would-be imitators is the contempt in which politicians are held. Here is a system that requires their existence, endows them with power, and throws a searchlight on all their acts, and yet the same people who choose them perpetually deride and denounce them. The educated no less than the populace resent the politician's prominence but would not trade places with him. Writers multiply more or less witty epigrams about the breed and defamatory little essays against them. See, for example: two sections in *A Casual Commentary* by Rose Macaulay (London: Methuen & Co., Ltd., 1925)—"Problems for the Citizen" and "General Elections."

In the second, the author suggests a nationwide refusal to vote, which would result in "a ridiculous little parliament that could be ignored," to everybody's advantage. The title "honorable," used to address them, is obviously a bitter irony. How to explain all this to a visitor from Mars? For politicians not only represent us, they represent the scheme by which our changeable will is expressed. They are, as a group, the hardest working professionals; they must continually learn new masses of facts, make judgments, give help, and continue to please. It is this obligation, of course, that makes them look unprincipled. To please and do another's will is prostitution, but it remains the nub of the representative system.

With these many complex deeds and chaotic demands, American democracy would have little to show the world with pride if it were not for another aspect of our life that Tocqueville observed and admired, that is, our habit of setting up free, spontaneous associations for every conceivable purpose *(Democracy in America,* vol. II, pt. II, ch. 5). To this day, anybody with a typewriter and a copying machine can start a league, a club, a think tank, a library, a museum, a hospital, a college, or a center for this or that, and can proceed to raise money, publish a newsletter, and carry on propaganda—all tax exempt, without government permission or interference, and free of the slightest ridicule from the surrounding society.

Here is where the habits of American democracy survive in full force. Robert's Rules of Order are sacred scripture and the treasurer's report is scanned like a love letter. Committees work with high seriousness, volunteers abound, and the democratic process reaches new heights of refinement. It is not uncommon, for example, that after a strenuous debate in committee, a vote of seven to five will prompt a chairman to say, "This business needs further thought; we shouldn't go ahead divided as we are." This admirable tradition enables us to accomplish by and for ourselves many things that in other democracies require government action. But this very habit of self-help, contrasting with the huge helpless bulk of government, has lately bred the conviction that popular sovereignty, like equality, should be unlimited. More and more often it is taken for granted that every organization, from businesses and churches to magazines and universities, should become a little democracy, with everyone voting, regardless of his position or knowledge. The former governing bodies—board of directors or elected vestry— should no longer act for their constituency because their decisions "affect everybody." In some instances, indeed, the geographical neighbors of an institution have claimed a voice, on the irrefutable ground that they too are affected by what it does.

It is plausible to regard this tendency as a result of the feeling that government at the top is unresponsive and in some ways unrepresentative, even though it is busy enacting privileges and protections. The bureaucracy then tries to homogenize the fates of citizens; they, in turn, appeal to the courts, which establish and often widen the rule; and thus a hopefully contentious atmosphere keeps everyone's attention on his or her rights. These are the occasion of a continual free-for-all. The latest of these to arouse angry debate is "language rights," aimed at making the United States officially multilingual. It is not said how many languages other than English would be included under these rights; at the moment Spanish is the one contender. One can find the arguments on each side in Gerola Bikales's "Comment," *International Journal of the Sociology of Language* 60 (1986), 7785.

There is undoubted freedom of a kind in a free-for-all. In how many countries, for example, would it be possible for a visiting head of state to make half a dozen speeches in New York attacking the President for his foreign policy? Where else would avowed partisans of subversion be allowed to teach in state universities? Such things are commonplace with us, but, again, they betoken group rights. Dissenters nowadays are tolerated only when their views are already group views. On our campuses, where academic freedom is claimed by the faculty, it is not extended to unpopular lecturers from outside. Their invitations are cancelled under pressure and their talks disrupted. The notion of a "free market for ideas," the belief that truth comes out of unrestricted debate, are vindicated only when a vocal group favors the freedom.

The disruption of others' speech, coupled with the claim to free expression for oneself, seems to be triggered by something besides unpopular views, namely holding office. Members of the cabinet or of the diplomatic corps have been assailed at colleges (and at a writers' conference) even before they spoke, and university officials have apologized for issuing the invitations. Faculty members doing "government research" or aiding intelligence agencies are suspect. These symptoms of disaffection may not be grave, but they indicate something less than support for the American form of government.

That, unfortunately, is an old story in this country. Tocqueville observed in 1835 that "he knew of no nation in which there is so little independence of mind and real freedom of discussion" (*Democracy in America* vol. I, pt. II, ch. 7). He attributed this lack to the weight of majority sentiment. Now the majority is that of the group to which one belongs by profession, status, or region. But if in those early days of democracy free discussion thrived better elsewhere, it was not solely because free speech was a legal right, it was also because of property rights. Their sanctity was something all the early proponents of constitutional government insisted on. They knew that liberties must have a material base—independence of mind is wonderfully spurred by an independent income. And this underpinning has been progressively weakened, by industrial civilization as much as by public law. Even in public opinion, property has become an unsavory word.

These various developments of democratic life help to account for the generalized feeling of oppression that pervades the free world. It manifests itself in common talk, in novels and plays, in the medical concern with stress, in the rise of cults, and in the recourse to drugs. Tocqueville again has something to say on the subject: "If social conditions, circumstances, and laws did not confine the American mind so closely to the search for comfort, it might be that when the Americans came to deal with immaterial things, they would act with more maturity and prudence and would keep themselves more readily in hand. But they feel themselves to be imprisoned within bounds that they are seemingly not allowed to escape, so that once they have broken through these barriers their minds do not know where to settle down and they often rush heedlessly far beyond the limits of common sense." (vol. II, pt. II, chap. 12). Such feelings of oppression are now so pervasive that optimism and the love of life are felt to be almost indecent. Consider in this light the universal demand for liberation, or emancipation, which has come not from the former colonies, but from long-united parts of great nations. The Scots, the Welsh, the Basques, the Bretons want to be free, just like the smallest islands of the Pacific or Caribbean, and indeed of our own waters.

Martha's Vineyard was clamoring to be free of Massachusetts. It sounded like a joke, but it expressed the widespread illusion that if only we could be "by ourselves" all our frustrations would end. It is an individual desire before it becomes a group demand, a demand generally called nationalism. But that is the wrong word. It is separatism, the very reverse of wanting to form or belong to a larger group. Hence the call for decentralization and what has been termed in this country the New Federalism, each a type of separation from the great machine built on the plan of popular sovereignty and absolute equality. Students of government in the United States report that it is in the counties that flexible adaptation to modern circumstances is most visible and innovative. Howard L. Griffin in his address to the American Studies Association of Texas, Huntsville, TX, November 15-17, 1984, explained this fact in "Stasis and American County Governments—Myth or Reality?"

Being at the end of this rapid survey, I must repeat the caution I urged before: do not take description as disparagement. We do live under a free government, and it has enormous advantages over any that is not free or only part free. We could all name these advantages and show their rational and emotional value, but that would not help our present inquiry, which is to find out what foreign nations could use to model themselves on our polity, could adopt from our complicated practices. The answer, I think, is: Nothing. The parts of the machine are not detachable; the organism is in fact indescribable, and what keeps it going, the "habits of the heart," as Tocqueville called them, are unique and undefinable. In short, we cannot by any conceivable means "show them how to do it."

This must be our third and last conclusion. What is more, if Rousseau were approached today by some liberal-minded South African and asked for advice of the kind he gave to Poland and Corsica, he would be at a loss where to begin, for he would not be facing one nation trying to modify its institutions, but several peoples, with diverse traditions, each trying to keep or gain its freedom by power. In the democratic theorem, the sovereignty of the people implies the practical unity of that people. How to create it when it does not exist is a different task from that of developing free institutions and is probably incompatible with it.

The nagging question here is: has the West any responsibility to export and defend democracy abroad? No. First, democracy has no theory to export, because it is not an ideology but a wayward historical development. Second, the historical development of democracy has taken many forms and used many devices to reach the elusive goal called human freedom. Third, the forms of democracy in existence are today in a state of flux. The strong current toward greater equality and the strong desire for greater freedom are more than ever in conflict. Freedom calls for a government that governs least; equality for a government that governs most. No wonder the institutions of the "free world" are under strain and its citizens under stress. The theorem of democracy still holds, but all of its terms have changed in nature, especially the phrase "the people," which has been changed beyond recognition by the industrial revolution of the nineteenth century and the social revolution of the twentieth.

Cold War Origins of Western Crusade for Democratization

While both sides accepted the status quo in Europe and embraced mutual deterrence through MAD (mutually assured destruction), the Cold War continued to rage in the so-called Third World or developing nations. From 1946 to 1960, thirty-seven new nations emerged from under a history of colonial domination to gain independent status. Both the United States and the Soviet Union, backed by their respective allies, competed intensively for influence over the new nations of Africa, Asia, Latin America, and the Middle East. Strategists in both camps believed that ultimate victory or defeat in the Cold War depended on the outcome of Third World conflicts. Moreover, many of these areas harbored vital natural resources, such as oil in the Middle East, upon which the developed world had become dependent. With American and allied automobiles, industry, and consumerism dependent on ready access to vast supplies of crude oil, maintaining access to foreign energy sources emerged as a key element of U.S. foreign policy.

Both the United States and the Soviet Union abhorred neutralism, that is, they demanded that their allies and Third World nations side with them against their Cold War rival. Both powers equated neutralism with appeasement and sought to punish not just states that sided against them but those that attempted to remain equivocal. Both the United States and the Soviet Union worked tirelessly in Asia, Africa, Latin America, and the Middle East to convince Third World leaders that their ideology was on the right side of history and held out the best hope for those nations to grapple with their pressing social problems, including poverty, disease, and rampant population growth. The Soviets had less money and a weaker economy than their Western rivals, but they did have the advantage of arguing that communist ideology offered liberation from the legacy of colonialism.

Adopting a much harsher line toward the West than Khrushchev and China's leader, Mao Zedong, called on Third World revolutionaries to launch "wars of national liberation" against the capitalist world. The message had resonance since the overwhelming majority of Third World states had been under the control of foreign powers, including Belgium, Britain, France, Germany, Holland, and the United States, for much of the previous century. Washington sought desperately to counteract the Soviet message and to contain revolutionary movements in the Third World. U.S. leaders went to great lengths to stave off defeat in even the most obscure and strategically insignificant corners of the globe out of fear of a bandwagon or domino effect. They insisted that a communist victory anywhere would encourage other revolutionaries and thus precipitate the much-feared red avalanche.

While the United States was most sensitive to revolutionary movements in neighboring Latin America, Cold War intervention was a global phenomenon. For years Washington coveted as a strategic partner South Africa, at the time a racist white minority regime that attempted to isolate and contain black radical movements in southern Africa. In North Africa and the Middle East, Washington backed Egypt and Israel against more radical regimes, some of which, such as Syria, became close Soviet allies. The United States and the Soviet Union supported different sides in the Middle East Arab-Israeli conflict. The United States backed the Zionist state, a policy supported by most American Jews—the largest population in the world in any one country—but also by a majority of overall public opinion. While Washington became Israel's chief diplomatic benefactor and weapons supplier, the Soviet Union embraced the cause of Arab nationalism and Palestinian statehood. When wars erupted in 1956, 1967, and 1973, however, Washington and Moscow ultimately found the common language to work together to prevent the conflicts from escalating into longer wars.

While the Soviets and Chinese appealed to the Third World on the basis of Lenin's theory of imperialism, Washington offered its democratic ideology as well as its advanced economy to woo Third World nations. Through its supervision of the World Bank and the International Monetary Fund, the United States offered aid and loans on the condition that the recipients join the capitalist camp in the Cold War struggle. The United States confronted serious obstacles, however, in its efforts to win over the Third World. First of all, most of the Third World consisted of populations of people of color. The leaders and peoples of those nations condemned America's history of slavery, racism, and support for imperialism based on a racial hierarchy. Many scholars believe, in fact, that the Cold War played a significant role in the slow emergence of federal government support for the civil rights movement, which culminated in the United States in the mid-1960s. U.S. leaders recognized that they could not hope to appeal successfully to the Third World while sanctioning segregation, denial of voting rights, and other forms of racial discrimination in the United States itself.

Theorizing Globalization and Democratization as Rewesternization

Globalization is a complex and controversial process. It has changed the world in many ways and has brought several countries together. However, as well as bringing countries together in some ways, it has also driven them apart. One of the most controversial changes it has made is to the political culture of many countries around the world. Many scholars such as David Held would agree that democracy is commonly being regarded as the best form of government. However, is globalization solely responsible for the spread of democracy around the world?

The concept of democracy is derived from the Ancient Greek term *dēmokratía* which means "rule of the people" and it defines "a form of government in which the supreme power is vested in the people and exercised directly by them or by their elected agents under a free electoral system." (Dictionary.com Unabridged. Random House n.d.). This form of government, however, has become increasingly popular since the demise of communism in the late 1980's. Hence it is widely regarded that *"Democracy is a cornerstone of human dignity and the good society. A public should shape its own destiny, even if some might doubt the wisdom of certain of democratic decisions taken. A society that is not striving after democracy tends to be a less worthy and also more dangerous place."* (Scholte, 2005).

Parallelly, globalization has also become an increasingly popular process that countries are opening themselves too. The concept was created in the late 1800's by American entrepreneur Charles Russell, but was only popularized in the 1960's by economists and social scientists. Pro-globalists would argue that it is inevitable for countries to open themselves up to globalization. There are too many benefits and the ones that do not, become isolated from the rest of the world. Hence, this essay will examine if globalization has led these countries to opt for a democratic form of government and if so, what the reasons were behind it.

Many scholars such as Jens Bartelson would agree with the idea that globalization poses a threat to the democratic state instead of aiding its expansion. It is believed that it undermines the essential requirements of state autonomy, patriotism and national identity (Bartelson, 2004). For this reason, one could argue that political globalization could be a contradiction in terms. One of the anti-globalist theories is that globalization is causing the decline of the nation state, as governments no longer have control over their economy, their trade and their borders. Nation states may have in the past been in complete control of their markets, exchange rates and capital. Now, trans-national companies are becoming increasingly imperative to the economy, and the state is becoming obsolete. This supports the argument that globalization is reducing the power of democracy and the state, resulting in hollow democracy.

Sceptics believe that while globalization promotes opportunity for growth and increase in wealth, it has also increased the socio-economic disparity between people, making nations less democratic and progressively more ruled by the wealthy multi nationals. This means that "governments now try and compete for foreign capital and design their policies to please global investors and firms, who may not act in the best interest of, nor be held accountable to, the voters. It follows that the level of democracy declines." (Quan & Reuveny, 2003). Also, scholars such as Peter Drucker argue that globalization cripples even more those who are less fortunate, as previously stated. Companies which are unable to compete with multinationals on an international scale lose from more economic openness. The results of this loss cause a weakening in the country's democracy (Drucker, 1994).

The unfortunate losers in the globalization battle thus, tend to seek support and unity with their identities, usually based on religion or ethnicity. This encourages the prosperous economic winners to maintain their edge over the poorer and reduce their competition. These actions intensify social inequality and undermine the progress democracy has made (Robertson 1992). This inequality, however, is not only carried out on a national scale. Even in the international community, globalization has increased the cleavage between the developed countries from the north and the developing countries from the south. In international organizations such as the United Nations it is commonly witnessed that the elite wealthy countries always have the final say in conflicts or important issues that are discussed, which ends up swaying the domestic politics of less developed countries to their favor (Amin, 1996).

Another argument made by many such as O'Donnell is that in order for a stable and functioning democracy to work, the concept of citizenship and participation must be active and embedded in the population. Globalization has transformed the common citizen into an individual who is more willing to pursue its own economic interest than to be concerned with the content of public policy (O'Donnell, 1993). As observed, there are many reasons as to how globalization has weakened democracy around the world. However, like any controversial issue, it is important to evaluate the two sides of the argument to fully comprehend the implications of the statement. For this reason, there are several claims of notable scholars that defend the idea that globalization has spread democracy around the world. According to Schumpeter's *Capitalism, Socialism and Democracy* globalization has helped promote economic development which has augmented the number of educated and well trained citizens, which has resulted, contrastingly to previous statements, in a decrease in economic inequality. This illustrates the freedom and development of the people in allowing them to prosper from the benefits of globalization.

As previously stated, globalization has increased the power of multi-nationals. However, differently to what has been stated, international businesses demand an increase in democracy. In order for businesses to grow, peace and stability must be entrenched in all potential investment countries. Subsequently, as democratic countries scarcely ever fight with each other, there is an increase in the demand for a democratic form of government. As economic links among states expand, authoritarian countries experience an increase in pressure from trans-national companies for political liberalization. These authoritarian states, as a result of globalization have fewer incentives to cling to power or proceed with their radical policies. Globalization encourages authoritarian states to decentralize power as they hand over their control to make progress for the market, which is fundamentally democratic. This concept of allowing the economy to fluctuate is known as laissez-faire, a French expression meaning "let it be" which allows industries to be free from state involvement in restrictions such as taxes and state monopolies.

Many other advantages of globalization also help promote democracy. The reduction in information and travelling costs mean that people have access to a lot more information not only from their government but from all over the world. This means democracies can now promote their values and ideals to autocratic countries a lot more freely, as autocracies have diminishing control over information. (Hanen, 1990) Other advantages of globalization reducing borders is that it strengthens the distribution of democratic values over borders. The more democracies border non-democratic countries, the more the chances that country has of becoming democratic.

In addition, with the increase in the demand for human rights and humanitarian interventions in countries which abuse power, democracy is progressively becoming the only alternative to autocratic regimes.

As the preponderance of states withholds democratic values, it is expected that any other state that is non-democratic is in violation of human rights as they are not allowing their citizens to voice their opinion and have a say in the way their government is run. Hence, interventions have contributed to the democratization of numerous countries such as Iraq and several other countries in Sub-Saharan Africa. Currently, international organizations such as the IMF and the World Bank have reformed numerous of these authoritarian countries so that they become potential investment opportunities for multi-nationals, and this is only due to the result of the expansion of globalization to such nations (Kura, 2005).

This, however, is one of the main causes of rising military conflict and tensions amongst nations in the international community. Many sceptics and especially countries with alternative values believe that the process of globalization has pressured them into becoming liberal democracies and believing in western capitalist values. Since the beginning of the cold war, there has always been a great tension between the western democracies and the rest of the world. Now, the few countries that do not uphold western values feel threatened and ever more forced into opening their economies and becoming a democratic system.

Globalization encourages democratic institutions which promote democracy. As the global market relies on capitalist democratic values, it is inevitable that organizations that reinforce these values are rewarded meaning. This implies that can expand into countries with other forms of government and promote these ideals. Hence, the increase involvement of INGO's and other businesses furthers the transparency and liability of institutions that reduce state intervention, all which of facilitate democracy according to Dalpino who opines that:

> *Western policymakers and nongovernmental groups trying to promote greater political liberalization have placed their faith in the indirect effects of globalization. An authoritarian government agrees to a global regime to gain benefits of one sort but is forced to accept the political consequences that follow.* (Dalpino, 2001)

In conclusion, the question of globalization and the spread of democracy is a complex one. On one hand, it may be considered a threat to democracy as it is believed that it undermines the essential requirements of state autonomy, of patriotism and of national identity. Many argue that globalization is the sole reason for the decline of the nation state, as governments do not have control over their economy, their trade and their borders anymore. Now, transnational companies are becoming increasingly imperative to the economy, and the state is becoming obsolete. Even though globalization has many advantages and one of them is the opportunity for economic growth both at an individual and a national level. This means that governments now try and compete for foreign capital and design their policies to please global investors and firms. The result of which is that such governments do not necessarily act in the best interest of its citizens and thus disregard their primary purpose (Quan & Reuveny, 2003).

Many people, however, cannot benefit from the advantages of globalization. Small companies which are unable to compete with multinationals on an international scale lose from more economic openness. The results of this loss cause a weakening in the country's democracy. Hence, globalization has transformed the common citizen into an individual who is much more willing to pursue its own economic interest than to be concerned with the content of public policy. On the other hand, however, globalization has expanded greatly the values of the democratic state. According to Schumpeter globalization has helped promote economic development which has increased the number of educated and well trained citizens, which has resulted, in a decrease in economic inequality.

Also, international businesses demand an increase in democracy. In order for businesses to prosper, peace and stability must be established in all potential investment countries. As economic links among states expand, authoritarian countries experience an increase in pressure from transnational companies for political liberalization. Globalization encourages authoritarian states to decentralize power as they hand over their control to make progress for the market, which is essentially democratic. Another proof that globalization has expanded democracy is through the reduction in information and travelling costs.

People have access to a lot more information not only from their government but from around the globe. This means democracies can promote their values and ideals to autocratic countries, as autocracies have less and less control over information (Hanen, 1990). It is because of these and other reasons like globalization encouraging democratic institutions and INGO's which promote democracy, that democracy had expanded so drastically over the past decades. Hence, if one were to analyze carefully how globalization had reduced democracy and how it has expanded it, one could safely affirm that even though it has somewhat decreased the power of the nation state, on the whole, the process has in fact spread democracy around the world.

Globalization and Legal Rewesernization of the South

It would not be surprising if, in the context of an international conference, a group of jurists from different nations identified a set of common juridical references based on different legal systems. This occurrence would be attributed to the process of globalization. However, it might also not be considered curious if a historic study about law in the nineteenth century were to conclude that legal systems from various corners of the world shared a set of common legal principles. It is common for jurists from a significant variety of countries to encounter the same legal and hermeneutic models as well as the same conceptions of fundamental rights, accountability, governance, and democracy.

In the past, as in the present, these models were imposed on different contexts and realities always with the justification that they assure a future state that is better than the current one. From this perspective, it is possible to affirm that the global acceptance of jurists with these legal methods is based on concepts such as "overcoming deficiencies," "progress" or "development" and, in this sense, justified by the moral dichotomy of good and bad. From a philosophical point of view this concept of a morally universal law is related to the model of humanism and rationalism developed in the West. In my view, this kind of approach presupposes the existence of a set of values belonging to everyone in the world, without distinction, as a sort of universal essence of human beings. These supposed universal characteristics not only require that everyone should be treated equally, but also that legal procedures destined for the protection of human values have to be implemented in the same way. In my opinion, this approach should be reassessed.

Although it claims to be neutral and uniform, an exclusive definition of humanity leads to many contradictions. One of them is the risk of attributing moral superiority to Western legal institutions. This risk is particularly insidious because the adoption of Western normative standards is justified through the universalizability of human values. This is a result of one of the projects of rationalizing the world, known as the Enlightenment. The argumentative "strategy" is simple: on the one hand, there are civilized spaces imbued with the supposed virtues of intellectual rationalization, and on the other, there are presumed to be pockets of injustice, governed by irrational and backward norms. As a result, institutions, values, and ways of life that were defined as rational acquire superiority.

Since the universalized institutions and standards closely correspond to the historico-social traditions of Europe and the United States – their laws, legal orders, and economy – a legal culture of a few countries is presented as globally applicable. Therefore, the attempt to solve conflicts by imposing universal procedures originating in north-western societies is destined to fail. In this respect, it is emphasized that the origin is not a problem in itself, but it becomes a problem because of the contradictory structure of discourse that combines morality, humanism, and universalization. By claiming for itself universality, this discourse does not recognize other rationalities, on the contrary, it treats them with condescension as irrational. As I have stated above, the result is an imposition from a position of superiority, by means of the election of only one world-view as rational.

Asymmetries and domination are, therefore, part of the fabric of a humanist discourse. This contradictory trope creates images of a civilized North in relation to the observance of rights, making its practices and institutions exempt from questioning, and, at the same time, providing the criteria against which the rest of the world is judged. I would like to stress that these double standards become evident in situations in which countries of the North openly violate human rights. I am thinking, for example, of the connivance of official supranational agencies and courts with detention camps for irregular immigrants, with security policies against terrorism, or with the legal prescription of the death penalty. Furthermore, on a micro-social level, one can think of the many denunciations of human rights violations in Latin America presented to the Inter-American Commission on Human Rights and Court by law clinics at law schools in the USA – particularly considering that the USA, together with Canada, have not ratified the Pact of San José, Costa Rica.

Starting with the research of Edward Said (1978/2003) on Orientalism, post-colonial studies have developed a critique of these claims of universalization. Said maintains that the West's knowledge of the Orient serves a self-referential logic. Influenced by Foucault's notion of discourse, Said presents Orientalism as an imaginative European invention aimed at the reaffirmation of the very idea of the West. The Orient is artificially constructed as the "other" and "inferior." In opposition to this Oriental "other", Western values constitute the identity and superiority of the West.

With the rise of other post-colonial approaches the "other" projected as inferior or backwards includes not only the Orient, but also the rest of the non-western world. The distinction between the West and the rest of the world is discursively constructed in an asymmetric way by the imaginary of Northern countries, to establish their identity and fabricate their superiority. Since, however, this discourse is imposed as a universal morality inherent in nature. This process leads to monopolization on the part of the Western semantic of concepts such as human progress and modernity. This discursive strategy of domination has been termed the 'Coloniality of Knowledge' in Latin American post-colonialism. I would argue that this kind of coloniality legitimates politico-military interventions and the imposition of models on other regions – even if this has meant support for dictators in many parts of the world or the global diffusion of techniques of torture.

By demonstrating that the Western legacy does not correspond to an objective reality, but rather to a discourse that is constitutive of identity by opposition to the other, post-colonial studies identify strategies of exclusion, colonization, and hierarchization of global processes as central to the universalizing projects of Western modernity. In this way, dominant social forces are not established exclusively through the use of violence. Even if this dimension is not ignored, domination is only established when the dominated conceive and accept the vision of the world of the dominator as the "natural order of things", as Chimni (2006) indicates. I believe that applying this notion to the realm of a post-colonial sociology of law would enable a reinterpretation of the social function of legal discourses from the perspective of the asymmetric relations of power between global regions.

As a synonym for humanity, development, and modernity, Western legal culture has become an instrument for Northern domination in the South. In this process Chimni (2006) identifies the role of legal language as ideological and legitimizing: Northern legal discourses are presented as rational and fair, producing rules that should be accepted by the South. Because of its supposed quality and neutrality, Western legal discourse elevates itself to a superior position in the scale of civilization, and Western Societies act as protagonists in the South. What is involved here is a process of obscuring colonial relations by means of legal discourse and legal tools.

Given this, the universalization of legal rationality can be re-read. This rationality was presented by mainstream European thought in the nineteenth century as a superior discourse, supposedly resulting from the accumulation of knowledge about the world, and scientific methods which according to logical schemes of deduction and induction were capable of promoting a generalization of rules based on cases. According to Anghie (1999), by affirming itself as the sole condition for modern law, legal rationalization separated the world between civilized regions (those that have this knowledge) and uncivilized ones (with "irrational and primitive" legal forms). This distinction justifies the global imposition of Northern legal models, and the colonization of the discordant manifestations of law in the rest of the world.

In relation to current issues, we can consider for example legal frameworks presented in the North as universal, owing to their alleged neutrality, and ethical or moral quality. Governance, accountability, democracy and so forth are concepts that when mobilized construct a field of comparison in which the socio-legal development of the North is considered the only one to be valid. This claim of superiority becomes a criterion for judging and excluding alternative legal rationalities in the rest of the world. In this sense, Chimni (2006) states that in the global South institutional designs, guided by the degree of concordance with ideas of citizenship or governance of the "true" democracies, reproduce the same logic as used by the "civilizing missions" of the past, and thus authorize recolonizations or rewesternization.

In short, the universal legal discourse reproduces the following paradigm: given that it adopts Western standards as synonyms for "humanity," "development," or "modernity", the legal reality of the conceptually maladjusted countries of the South is reconstructed in opposition. The absence of these Western characteristics is understood as backwardness, and, therefore, those standards from the North, which supposedly the South lacks, should be imported. Hence, hierarchical positions of global power are maintained. According to Hall (1996), this reproduces, by means of law, the same logical structures as colonial relationships: the notion of "universalism," monopolized by the semantics of the countries of the North, not only oppresses empiric and cognitive manifestations of the South (incompleteness, irrationality, deviation, but also demands their conformity (modernization).

While Western formal or material legal rationality is based on a claim of universality, Chatterjee (1998) demonstrates that the semantic schemes of "other societies" are supported by the recognition of difference, or on their ethnic, cultural, religious, and social particularities – even as resistance to the expansion of the enlightenment project. Thus, without autochthone equivalents, the imposition of the model of European or U.S. law has led to a split in colonized spaces between legal discourse, which follows the Western archetype, and social dynamics, which require statutes that respond to its specificities. From this perspective, the commonplace diagnosis about the separation between law and society in the global South acquires another meaning. On the one hand, it explains how the discourse of reform is considered to be routine by legal protagonists in these regions: the reality always appears to frustrate the expectations generated by institutional designs based on the U.S.A or European model. On the other hand, it reveals the empirical and theoretical obstacles to projects of democracy based on the universalization of a model of law and of a particular type of society.

This does not involve a defense of cultural relativism or of multiculturalism. These constructions are not alternatives, but, on the contrary, they are part of the universalist discourse to the degree to which the "other" is built by techniques of "exoticization" and subalternization. Likewise, universalist discourse, cultural relativism, and multiculturalism produce cultural hierarchies that exclude the "other" from decision-making processes, transforming them into exotic, mystical or primitive characters who should be frozen and preserved. The universal project of legal enlightenment is, in reality, full of tension. It involves apparently neutral semantics, which serve to conceal positions of power and block the emergence of different semantics. From the perspective of colonial history, it is clear that this violence was and still is essential to the expansion of capitalism.

I am not rejecting the possibility of the world law and society thesis. However, this thesis should be established by taking into account alternative legal regimes and different political societies.

Western democracy does not deserve the semi-sacred status accorded to it. In Europe, democratically elected politicians such as Jörg Haider, Jean-Marie Le Pen, Silvio Berlusconi, Umberto Bossi, Gianfranco Fini and Pim Fortuyn are a reminder of democracy's defects: an anti-racist dictatorship is preferable to a racist democracy. Democracy is expanding globally, but not because of its moral superiority. Military intervention is now the standard origin of democratic political systems. Any universal ideology will tend to crusades and messianic conquest, and democracies feel entitled to 'bring freedom' to other countries.

Democracy has brought societies which are monotonous and uniform, at least to some of the people who live in them. But not only that. Democracy has failed to bring utopia. That is, it has failed to bring into existence any proposed ideal society, or any other proposal of a 'utopian' type. Democracy itself can be labelled a 'utopia', and the present liberal-democratic societies are historically unique - nothing like them existed before the 19th century. So, in that sense, democracy has brought at least a new democratic society, which is itself an ideal society for some people. But nothing else!

No dramatically new type of society has emerged among the democracies, differing from the standard model of these societies. And most liberal-democrats would in fact be hostile to the label 'utopia' being applied to these liberal-democratic societies.

The liberal tradition is resolutely hostile to utopias: anti-utopianism seems a defining characteristic of liberal ideology. That hostility has shaped the present liberal-democratic societies. Liberal anti-utopianism and democratic anti-totalitarianism are in practice the same thing. Some liberals explicitly equate the two, and see totalitarianism as the result of utopian ideals. They believe that the 20th-century totalitarian regimes derive from the European utopian tradition. The early-modern ideal city, the ideal city-states of the type described in Thomas Moore's original book *Utopia*, were for them the source of all later evil. Many postmodernists share this distaste for utopia, and the belief that there is a direct line from Thomas Moore to *Auschwitz*. In other words, there are liberal-democrats who believe that the political system should be so structured, as to save society from utopian experiments. To them, democracy is (at least partly) a mechanism to prevent utopia. I think they are right about the nature of democracy: but it is democracy, not utopia, which must disappear.

Western Bastardization of Democratization

The thesis that democracy can grow in virtually any soil is inherently appealing and even enlightened. In fact, what could be more idealistic than the notion that no culture is inimical to democracy? It may be true as well. Plenty of countries once condemned to perpetual authoritarian rule have managed to reinvent themselves as thriving democracies. The nations of Latin America during Wilson's time were regarded as a cesspool of authoritarian vices; nowadays, with the obvious exception of Cuba, they are ruled entirely by democratic governments. Spain and Portugal, paradigmatic examples of corporatism and dictatorship through the mid- 1970s, are today highly successful pluralist democracies. Germany and Japan, two other miracles of postwar democratization, were once regarded as infertile ground for democracy due to the conformist culture of their people and the authoritarian orientation of their political leaders.

What appears to have turned former authoritarian enclaves into democratic models is the capacity to nurture internal conditions favorable to the maintenance of democracy. These generally include a civic culture able to accommodate compromise as well as dissent and pluralism, significant social and economic development, a strong sense of national identity, stable and competent political institutions, and a free and vibrant civil society. Whether these are "preconditions" or "by-products" of democracy and how precisely they facilitate democracy remains a source of debate among social scientists. But two things about the rise of these conditions are clear, which American presidents tend to overlook.

First, attaining the conditions that favor the installation and maintenance of democracy is a long-term process not immune to backsliding. It cannot be abbreviated, expedited, or circumvented by introducing political practices such as free elections and a democratic constitution. As Wilson learned in Latin America, "electoralism" and "constitutionalism" do not guarantee democracy; indeed, they do not even ensure its survival. The attempt to impose democratic practices throughout Mexico, Central America, and the Caribbean in the years between 1913 and 1921 failed to yield stable democratic governance. In the wake of the American intervention of 1914, the Mexican political class turned not only authoritarian and nationalistic but also intensely anti-American. Democracy would not arrive in Mexico until 2000, following decades of economic and political modernization. In Central America and the Caribbean, Wilson's military occupations and attempts at creating democracy paved the way for a new generation of brutal tyrannies, including those of Fulgencio Batista in Cuba, Rafael Trujillo in the Dominican Republic, and Anastasio Somoza in Nicaragua.

The reasons for the failure of Wilson's policy in Latin America include some of the same ones that prevented democracy from taking root in the aftermath of Iberian colonialism. Most republics that were created during the 1820s and 1830s adopted democratic institutions of their own free will and most, interestingly, took the American Constitution and presidential political system as their model. But few of these democracies were able to overcome their undemocratic colonial legacies, especially an illiberal ruling class, a powerful and reactionary Catholic Church, widespread poverty, and underdeveloped state institutions. Post-independence, this hindered a consensus on national identity, the development of coherent political institutions and autonomous civil societies, and respect for the rule of law. Reverting to authoritarianism seemed almost natural after democratic politics proved chaotic and unable to solve pressing social issues. Small wonder that in the end Wilson came to accept authoritarianism in a Mexico led by revolutionists "because he had become convinced that agrarian and other socioeconomic reforms were more pressing than electoralism" (Drake, 1991,p.16).

141

Second, although the United States can assist in encouraging the conditions that favor democracy, it can neither create them nor sufficiently develop them to determine whether democracy succeeds or fails in the long term. As noted by the Harvard political scientist Samuel Huntington(1984) "There is little that the United States can do to alter the basic cultural tradition and social structure of another society or to promote compromise among groups of that society that have been killing each other" (p.218). Instead, the conditions that favor democracy depend for their emergence largely upon the political skills of a given society. This is the lesson we can absorb from the experience of Germany and Japan, two countries where democracy's success is often linked to an effective American occupation. "Because we and our allies were steadfast, Germany and Japan are democratic nations that no longer threaten the world," remarked Bush in a speech, "Freedom in Iraq and the Middle East," delivered on November 6, 2003, on the occasion of the twentieth anniversary of the National Endowment for Democracy.

However, much of the historiography on the democratization of postwar Germany and Japan cautions about giving too much credit to America for having engineered a democratic miracle (Schwartz, 1991; Dower, 1999; Bellin, 2004). Prior to the Second World War, Germany and Japan were economic powerhouses with a strong sense of national identity facilitated by ethnic homogeneity and well-developed state bureaucracies. Indeed, it was economic might and ultranationalism that made these countries such formidable military powers. Both countries were also eager to return to the generally democratic life they had during the interwar period. Although flawed and unstable, Japan's Taisho democracy and Germany's Weimar Republic provided templates for the re-creation of democracy.

Paradoxically, Iraq, where a demonstration effect is expected to serve as a catalyst for spreading democracy across the Middle East, presents one of the most challenging environments for democracy. There is a dearth of democratic consciousness within Iraqi political society. While political pluralism is on the rise, it is hard to gauge the intentions of nascent parties and social movements. Some of

142

the country's most powerful political organizations, such as those headed by powerful Shiite clerics, including Muqtada al-Sadr, the young cleric who incited the Fallujah uprising in April 2004, and the all-powerful Grand Ayatollah Ali al-Sistani, Iraq's most respected religious leader, participated in the country's first democratic elections. But as the Iraqi people begin the process of crafting a new constitution it is unclear how committed to the democratic process these groups actually are. Many of them are calling for the merging of religious and secular authority so typical of other Middle Eastern societies, notably Iran (Wong, 2005).

Moreover, under Saddam, the state bureaucracy in Iraq did not function as a coherent, merit-based system (as was largely true of prewar Germany and Japan) but rather as something more typical of Latin America during Wilson's time: a hotbed of clientelism, corruption, and loyalty toward the dictator (Makiya, 1989). Equally worrisome are Iraq's economic prospects. In recent decades, Iraq has experienced a staggering reversal of development, best suggested by the collapse of per capita income. In 1979, when Saddam Hussein came to power, Iraq's per capita GNP stood at $12,000ßtwenty-first in the world, ahead of Spain and Hong Kong. Today it stands at less than $3,000, behind the Philippines and Ecuador (Barro, 2003, p.28).

According to democratization experts, for democracy to endure in Iraq, per capita income will need to almost double to $5,500 (Przeworski *et al*, 2000, p. 94). This is a tall order, to be sure; one that the Bush administration hoped will be made possible by Iraq's oil riches. But this assumption is contradicted by cross-national data on the connection between oil and democracy. In Indonesia, Nigeria, Mexico, Venezuela, and much of the Middle East, an oil-dependent economy has become the seedbed for authoritarianism, corruption, and civil war. Indeed, the collective experience of these nations has given rise to the so-called resource curse, with oil becoming a hindrance to rather than a facilitator of democracy.

The picture of civil society, the social actor believed to grease the wheels of democracy by inculcating such public values as trust and tolerance and by providing a sturdy defense against state abuses, is also bleak, to say the least. Islamist groups, the most prominent face of civil society in Iraq and across the Middle East, do not commonly frame their objectives in terms of democratic values. Many of them have in recent years moved to fill the void left behind by a failing government by offering a wide range of social services from education and transportation to healthcare. But this has come at the expense of the general "Islamization" and radicalization of society resulting from the rigid and often intolerant character of religious organizations now performing functions previously in the hands of state authorities (Berman, 2003).

Lastly, there is Iraq's ethnic and religious diversity, with Shia in the south, Sunnis in the center, and Kurds in the north. This volatile mix discourages a strong sense of national identity, making it difficult for democratization to rest on widespread societal solidarity. It also increases the possibility that democracy will become a source of conflict in its own right. In the last three decades, few multiethnic states have been able to orchestrate a successful transition to democracy: witness the case of the Soviet Union and its successor states (most notably those in Central Asia and the Caucasus). More tragically, there is the case of Yugoslavia, where "ethnic cleansing" was an early fruit of majority rule. Ironically, contributing to the collapse of these states as they undertook to democratize was the existence of federalist structures, which the Bush administration seemingly did not regard as a prescription for dealing with Iraq's ethnic divisions.

Perils of Imposing Western Democracy

The belief that the United States is uniquely endowed and therefore especially burdened with the task of spreading democracy is problematic on many fronts. Efforts by American presidents to articulate this mission have often had unintended consequences. Early references to the war in Iraq as a democratizing "crusade" were dropped from Bush's speeches once reports from the Middle East indicated how offensive the term was to local audiences. More problematic are the political dynamics unleashed by the imposition of democracy. Democratic imperialism entails the fundamental paradox of making the transition to democracy more complicated than it otherwise would be. The liberalization of a people from dictatorship by an external force entails the abrupt, usually violent, end of the old regime. This mode of regime change is effective in purging authoritarian forces deeply ensconced within the bureaucratic structures of the state. But it sets an inauspicious stage for the transition to democracy by creating a void in political authority, not to speak of the considerable chaos that can ensue.

Iraq tellingly suggests how an occupation can itself become an obstacle to democratization. The "systematic looting and destruction of practically every public building in Baghdad" created by the American invasion made restoring basic services such as electricity more difficult to accomplish while imbuing the emerging political culture with a great deal of incivility (Rieff, p.44). More serious was the vacuum in political authority created with the sudden passing of the old regime. A month into the military occupation, U.S. administrator Paul Bremer announced the disbanding of the Iraqi Republican Army, some 400,000 strong, and the lustration of 50,000 members of the Baath Party. The aim was laudable: to cleanse Iraq of Saddam's political influence once and for all. Unintentionally, Bremer's actions created a formidable resistance to American authority and exacerbated the fault lines of domestic political conflict. As reported by one Iraqi observer, "May 15 was the day the United States made 450,000 enemies in Iraq" (*Ibid.,* p. 72). This resistance is, if anything, stronger than ever, and in an effort to stamp out the violence spawned by terrorist groups, Iraq's new leaders have curtailed civil and political freedoms.

Another flaw in America's self-anointed role as a democratic crusader is that it entails creating democracy through undemocratic means. Imposing democracy requires one country to intrude itself in the political affairs of another country, thereby robbing democracy of its indigenous legitimacy. Arguably the most intrusive step in the imposition of democracy is the creation of an interim or provisional government. They are generally designed to meet short-term interests, such as securing political order, rather than the more complex task of developing democratic institutions. Less intrusive but equally problematic is the staging of post occupation elections, a key benchmark of democratic imperialism. In an attempt to ensure the desired outcome, the invading power will likely seek to influence (if not manipulate) the elections by deciding what groups can participate and which cannot.

Wilson's experience in Latin America vividly illustrates how external intervention in the construction of democracy is hardly an exercise in democracy. His administration wrote electoral laws and constitutions, and went so far as to encourage or discourage particular candidates or parties, seeking those most likely to govern effectively (and to serve U.S. interests). Unsurprisingly, forced and manipulated elections often provoked internal disputes. Complicating matters, many of the institutions relied upon to guarantee the survival of democracy evinced scant respect for democracy and its values. The task of consolidating democratic political life was often given to the military, ushering in a long and tragic history of military intervention in politics.

The case of the Dominican Republic is especially instructive. The United States ruled the country between 1916 and 1924, and oversaw the organization of the judiciary, the Treasury, and the Ministry of Agriculture, and the creation of a provisional government in 1922. Before leaving, the Americans also created a national constabulary (national guard) in the hope of improving the capacity of civilian leaders to sustain constitutional rule. This was meant to "depoliticize the armed forces, serving to bolster stable, constitutional government" (Hartlyn, p. 58). This strategy backfired spectacularly. Soon after the Americans left, the Dominican Republic plunged into a civil war that ended in 1930 when Trujillo assumed control by virtue of his command of the National Guard. Trujillo abolished the liberal reforms instituted by the Americans, harshly repressed the opposition, and terrorized the country's neighbors, not least by massacring some 12,000 Haitians along the Haitian- Dominican border in 1937. "Wilson's dreams of a constitutional order had become a nightmare," concludes one scholar of Wilson's Dominican policy (Smith, *Op.Cit.*, p. 73).

Similar dynamics to those of the Latin American experience are already visible in Iraq. There is the obvious lack of legitimacy of the interim governments the Americans have installed in the country. The Iraqi Governing Council, dismantled in June 2003, was widely

146

criticized for its lack of autonomy, for consisting primarily of Iraqi exiles, and for failing to incorporate the whole spectrum of Iraqi political factions. The same fate befell the "sovereign" government inaugurated on June 28, 2004, led by its American-approved head, Iyad Alawi, the former president of the Governing Council. Charges that these governments were essentially a cover for Washington were underscored by the restrictions on national autonomy incorporated into the declaration of sovereignty likely to perpetuate American control of Iraq for years. As of this writing, Iraq continued to be ruled by edicts enacted by the Bremer administration covering a wide range of subjects from crime to the economy to foreign affairs, including shielding every U.S. soldier, coalition employee, and private contractor from Iraqi law.

In Iraq, as in Latin America, the United States is employing intrusive political engineering with uncertain consequences for the development of democracy. Iraq's first free democratic elections, remarkable in many respects, failed to become a symbol of national unity and reconciliation. To the contrary, the Sunni parties boycotted the elections on the grounds that they lacked legitimacy since the voting was taking place under the American occupation. Yet to be worked out are a new democratic constitution and the relationship between the new Iraqi government and the thousands of Americans expected to remain in the country. How the United States manages these sensitive tasks will play a critical role in determining whether the new government is perceived to be legitimate and working toward Iraqi, rather than American, interests.

Finally, America's commitment to spreading democracy is often at odds with the reality of protecting the "national interest," as defined by strategic economic and political goals. Reconciling these often contradictory objectives leaves U.S. foreign policy vulnerable to the criticism of being inconsistent, even hypocritical. It was this clash between professed ideals and the pursuit of the national interest that ended Wilson's efforts to impose democracy in Latin America. His administration found it very difficult to insist on a uniform standard of democracy since Wilson was unprepared to defend the policy across the region. It was applied uniformly and coercively to the nations of Central America, the Caribbean, and Mexico, but ran afoul in South America, where Wilson was less willing to deny diplomatic recognition to authoritarian governments, much less to intervene militarily against an autocratic regime. In Peru in 1913, and again in 1919, the Wilson administration denied recognition to a provisional government because it had been established by force. However, Wilson later reversed course and granted recognition anyway.

The Bush administration was similarly caught between its desire to spread democracy and the pursuit of such "national interests" as fighting terrorism, giving American policy in the Middle East an egregious "split personality" (Carothers, 2003). Despite his ringing calls for democracy, President Bush actively cultivated warm relations with numerous regional tyrants. The evident hypocrisy of this approach was vividly demonstrated during his June 2003 visit to the Middle East. Rather than pressing the leaders of Bahrain, Egypt, Jordan, and Saudi Arabia to implement democratic reforms, the president spent almost all of his time talking about the fight against terrorism and extremist groups. This only reinforced "the widespread perception that the United States uses democracy as a whip to punish its enemies, like Iraq, while doing business as usual with its autocratic allies" (Gerges, 2003).

Hard Lessons of Democratic Imperialism

Who needs Western democracy? In Afghanistan as in Iraq today and every day since more than a decade, heavily armed troops from the "mature democracies" strut about waving their high-tech weapons—and justify their invasion and military occupation of Afghanistan with the claim they are "bringing democracy". In their home countries this is already judged surplus and useless. In their home countries democracy is worthless: why force it down the throat of Afghans at the point of a gun? To Afghanistan they bring a typically derisory version of so-called "democracy". This is rule by a group of organized criminals practicing total and permanent corruption—but is simply a more intense version of the corporate kleptocracy which operates in the ex-democracies, and has now

148

stripped off its mask and moved to take total power. To Iraqis, Western democracy has birthed the bloodletting quest for the Islamic State of Syria and Iraq.

The inescapable realities of Iraq are gradually forcing a second look at democratic imperialism. Speculation about the current target in the Middle East for coercive democratization (Syria or Iran?), which was intense following the invasion of Iraq, is continuing.

Neoconservatives are contending with a resurgent "realpolitik" critique of American policy in Iraq (Tierney, 2004). The *National Review*, a bible of conservative thought, has already dismissed the Wilsonian ideal of implanting democracy in Iraq and has recommended instead settling for an orderly society with a nondictatorial regime (Tierney, *Ibid.*). This rising skepticism is welcome, although one hopes it does not signify deemphasizing democracy in American foreign policy. Despite the many faulty principles that over the years have mocked American efforts, the United States remains the main force for democratic change around the world. The real issue is what type of democratic promotion is best suited to advancing democracy abroad.

America's own experience with democratic promotion suggests that this mission is most effective when its coercive, heavy-handed approaches are checked and its energies focused instead on facilitating the conditions that enable nations to embrace democracy of their own free will: promoting human rights, alleviating poverty, and building effective governing institutions. These were the policies that helped the people of Latin America and the former Communist bloc embrace democracy. The Republican president who subsequently sought to repair relations with Latin America following Wilson's aggressive attempts to democratize the region understood this point. While traveling throughout South America in 1928, President Herbert Hoover promised to promote democracy by example rather than by force. In remarks that must have come as a great relief to Latin American audiences weary of American aggression, Hoover remarked: "True democracy is not and cannot be imperialistic" (Smith, 1996, p.64). Really?

Let us look at the U.S. adventures of imposing democracy elsewhere. The collapse of the Soviet model helped trigger the third wave of democratization. There are at least five strategies the domestic politics of democratization in former European colonies is influenced by Western, especially American, factors: 1) modelling, 2) demonstration effects, 3) foreign support or intervention, 4) bandwagoning with hegemonic powers or challengers to hegemons, 5) militarization of domestic politics which undermines local democratic forces and processes. Countries undergoing transitions to Western democracy are often consciously modelling themselves after existing democracies. The political and economic success of Western nations, as the claim goes, makes their political system seem desirable and feasible to nations with different systems, particularly if these nations are undergoing recurrent political crises.

Conscious modelling after the West and EC nations in particular is most obvious since the democratic transitions in Spain and Portugal as these nations made both political and economic changes that paved their way for the entry into the EC they both desired. When the Soviet bloc collapsed many eastern European nations clearly desired to join the EC and NATO and consciously emulated the West in both economic and political transitions away from socialism. But modelling can work in the other direction too. European and Latin American transitions to fascism were clearly influenced by the perception that first Italy and later Germany offered new roads to the modern world. Many states in the 1920s and 30s consciously emulated Italian fascist political institutions. Even more clearly the Soviet Union and its form of socialism provided an alternative model to liberal democracy in the second reverse wave against democracy.

This explanation demonstrates that the current Western crusade for democratization of former European colonies is not permanent and has its nauseating and contested cases. Historical hindsight is helpful in driving home the point. In fact, the operation of the global economy precludes the exercise of real national sovereignty and the implementation of truly democratic decisions by the people, of the people, and for the people, especially in Third World countries. The reasons for this impossibility of liberal representative democracy are many, and we can here recall only a few, which are internal and external to the countries concerned.

Even the best of newly democratically elected parliaments can be no more than an ineffective talk shop if it's powers are limited by a constitution and/or a judiciary, as well as parts of the executive branch that are hold overs from a previous undemocratic regime. That is the case today in Chile for instance. General Pinochet deliberately had the Constitution written so that it would preclude the exercise of democracy. The judiciary is also a holdover from his dictatorship and continues to rule or threaten to rule all sorts of democratic initiatives to be unconstitutional or otherwise illegal. General Pinochet himself continued as Commander in Chief of the Army and publicly declared the Army independent of and not subject to the control of the democratically elected president, not to mention the parliament. Just before leaving the presidential office moreover, General Pinochet also introduced changes into the administration of the economy in general and the Central Bank in particular, which intentionally and now effectively preclude both parliamentary and presidential influence over a whole series of vital economic decisions. However, this was only some icing on the cake; for the new democratic government in Chile, just as elsewhere, is in any case obliged to continue pursuing the selfsame economic policies, which were initiated by the undemocratic military predecessors.

Indeed, these specifically Chilean arrangements are only particular examples of widespread general limitations to the exercise of democracy by, of, and for the people. The most obvious general limitation is that imposed by the generals themselves. All around the Third World from the Philippines through South and West Asia, throughout Africa, and in Latin America armed military power continues to stand behind the new democratic throne. Democratically elected governments in Pakistan and Thailand were recently again overthrown by their armies. President Aquino in the Philippines and both Presidents Alfonsin and Menem in Argentina have suffered various military coup attempts. Civilian presidents, not to mention the legislatures, in El Salvador and Guatemala are powerless in the face of the effective power of their military forces. In Brazil and elsewhere in Latin America as well as throughout Africa, the options of any civilian government are ever conditioned and limited by the ever present threat of governing under a military sword of Damocles. That sword may fall again elsewhere as it did in Thailand and Pakistan. These military forces and their commanding officers were often trained by, and are still under manifold influence of, the Western powers.

However even if they were not, these militaries would still be an arm of anything but that of democratic economic elites in their respective countries. They did and continue to pursue economic policies, which are in their own and their foreign partners' interests. These policies are certainly not designed or implemented in the interests of the majority of the people or in accordance with the desires they express through their democratic votes. Certainly not the democratically elected parliaments and hardly even any democratically elected presidents or their ministers are in a position to pursue any alternative economic policies.

However, the greatest structural limitation to the exercise of democratic policy by, of, and for the people is their participation and place in a world economy, over which they have and can have no control whatsoever. To put it the other way around, effective democracy is limited indeed if it extends only to the formulation and implementation of relatively unimportant domestic political policy; and it is barred from effective intervention in the most important economic policy decisions, which are made outside the range of democracy by, of, and for the people. What is worse, the economic policy of others elsewhere not only conditions the economic policy of the government at home; but that foreign economic policy may also intervene directly in the political process and the very nature of the government at home.

We may briefly review only two related examples of American economic policy decisions, which had far reaching worldwide economic and political consequences. The October 1979 decision by the Chairman of the US Federal Reserve, Paul Volker, to raise the rate of interest and thereby also to increase the value of the dollar was the single most important cause of the debt crisis and therewith the depression and "lost decade" of the 1980s in much of the Third World. The same decision also promoted the recession, which began in 1979 and helped elect Ronald Reagan to the presidency. By law, the American electorate and Congress, and even the American President, had and have no right to intervene in such a decision by the Federal Reserve. Law and political "sovereignty," as well as of course all economic reality, prevent any democratic or other influence by, of, or for the people in any part of the Third World on any such decision which is vitally determinant of the economic welfare and political options for its people.

The Reaganomic response to the 1979-82 recession at the American presidency and Congress then set the stage for the major events in the world of the 1980s and into the 1990s. Contrary to the ideology of "getting the government off our backs" and eliminating the US deficit and debt, Reaganomic Military Keynesianism increased the budget deficit, promoted the trade deficit, tippled the foreign US debt to $ 3 trillion, and already in 1986 converted the United States into the world's greatest foreign debtor. However, the pump priming demand created through heightened military expenditures and domestic and foreign borrowing for the same by the United States maintained afloat not only its own economy in the 1980s, but also that of the entire West and of the East Asian NICs to boot.

The costs were borne unwittingly and unwillingly by the Soviet Union, Eastern Europe, the Middle East, Africa, and Latin America, among others. The world recession since 1979 and American economic policy already occasioned the decline in the Soviet Union's sources of foreign exchange through the export of oil and gold. Then, President Reagan's military spending for "star wars" and in support of "regional" armed insurgencies against the governments of Afghanistan, Ethiopia, Mozambique, Angola, Nicaragua and others outcompeted the Soviet Union into bankruptcy and currency inflation. Perestroika and its failure as well as the end of the Cold War were the economic and political results.

The global examples are multiple. This statement from the influential Indian-American pundit Fareed Zakaria about Hungarian Prime Minister Viktor Orban's controversial speech in July, 2014 is revealing:

"But even I never imagined that a national leader – from Europe no less – would use the term (illiberal democracy) as a badge of honor." According to Zakaria, Hungary has enacted and implemented a version of what can best be described as "Putinism," whose crucial elements are nationalism, religion, social conservatism, state capitalism and government domination of the media. He points to other examples of political systems embracing core elements of Putinism. Turkey's recently elected President Recep Tayyip Erdogan has adopted Putin's authoritarian and anti-Western brand of politics.

Zakaria and other mainstream commentators in the West argue that Putin, Orban and Erdogan have created strikingly similar systems – albeit by different methods – built around their personal leadership and open contempt for separation of powers, pluralism and transparency. These leaders manipulate the legacy of national heroes and seek to reclaim past imperial glory to imbue their autocratic regimes with democratic mysticism, and wield cultural relativism as a weapon against constitutional freedoms. This new style of political system is seen most clearly in the revival of czarism in Russia, xenophobia in Hungary and fundamentalist Muslim traditions in Turkey. The defenders of liberal democratic exceptionalism note that Putin, Orban and Erdogan are in no hurry to relinquish power. For them, ideology, politics and the formalities of democracy are only means to an end. They believe they know intuitively what their people need. They resurrect dreams of former greatness and glory and construct ideologies based on national exceptionalism, patriotism and xenophobia.

Liberal advocates of "justice" have rendered their verdict. But are they right? Is this a common model emerging in these three countries? Or do they merely overlap at certain points, including a rejection of liberalism? Viktor Orban, who has consistently spoken about the demise of the liberal model for fifteen years, earned the wrath of Western – primarily American – media with his lecture at Hungary's University of Culture criticizing the tenets of liberal democracy. He said that the new Hungarian state was based on an illiberal foundation. He argued that Hungary's liberal systems failed to protect collective property and plunged the country into debt, turning Hungarian families into debt slaves.

The tectonic shifts underway in the global economy have shown that liberal systems are struggling to remain competitive and that their promise of prosperity for all was an illusion. But, according to Orban, a search is underway for a form of collective organization that can make nations and societies competitive internationally. Political science experts around the world are less interested in Western, liberal or even democratic systems than systems that make countries prosperous – Singapore, China, India, Russia, and Turkey. Orban's liberal detractors intentionally distort his words, claiming that Hungary is abandoning the system of European democratic values.

Most publications offer only a selective reading of his speech and the simplistic suggestion that Budapest is modeling itself on Moscow. The New York Times even urged the EU to reduce Hungary's infrastructure funding and suspend its voting rights. Of course, Mr. Orban has parted company with the liberal, or more accurately neoliberal, economic system, not democracy. All he did was reaffirm a growing international trend and question the salutary nature of the market. He wants to create a state that protects its citizens, nationalize utilities and raise taxes on banks, the retail sector and media outlets. Orban is not alone in his market-bashing. The West will have to come to terms with leaders placing their national interests ahead of the interests of global capital.

The EU faces not only a grave economic crisis, but also a crisis in values. This is why the valid critique and alternatives offered by Orban and others have caused such a vexed reaction in the West. They are particularly frightened by the Hungarian government's "anti-liberalism" – which it decided not to translate into English in the version of the speech it released – though, in fact, Orban criticized market fundamentalism. They are even more alarmed by any praise of the Russian model.

It was no coincidence that they tried to present Orban as a Putin supporter (while disregarding the other countries that fit the mold) because he advocates a foreign policy based on pragmatic interests rather than liberal values. Viktor Orban has signed a major bilateral deal with Vladimir Putin, supporting the building of the

South Stream pipeline and condemning the EU sanctions on Moscow because it is in Hungary's best interests to do so.

Even staunch supporters of liberal democracy acknowledge that history is on the move again, heightening the competition between political systems. The Western system is noticeably losing ground to others that are forging ahead. This would be unfortunate, though not terrible for the West, were it not for the fact that Hungary is not the only example of the growing "illiberal" trend. In Central Europe, there are politicians like Slovakia's Robert Fico and former president of the Czech Republic Vaclav Klaus, who are equally critical, if not more cautious in their wording. Add to this group Putin-hater Jaroslav Kaczynski who, like Orban, is critical of EU liberalism and gearing up for a comeback in Poland, and it becomes clear that liberal democracy faces a serious challenge.

Chapter IV

Toward Liberation from Western Democracy's Cognitive Imperialism

Overview

During the European Renaissance and the Enlightenment, coloniality emerged as a new structure of power to colonize the Americas and built on the ideas of Western civilization and modernity as the endpoints of historical time. Europe then became the center of the world. Hence, coloniality became the darker side of Western modernity. It has become a complex matrix of power that had been created and controlled by Western men and institutions from the Renaissance, when it was driven by Christian theology, through the late twentieth century and the dictates of neoliberal globalization. This cycle of coloniality is coming to an end. Two main forces have been challenging Western leadership since the early twenty-first century. One of these is dewesternization, an irreversible shift to the East in struggles over knowledge, economics, and politics. The second force is decoloniality. This decoloniality requires delinking from the colonial matrix of power underlying Western modernity to imagine and build global futures in which human beings and the natural world are no longer exploited in the relentless quest for wealth accumulation.

Introduction

Democracy is a form of government in which people are sovereign and supposed to have the final say in politics, but there has been intensive debate for centuries about what democracy is, what it ought to be, and whose democracy it should be. Today, political scientists and politicians have long been accustomed to the narrow, yet pragmatic, definition of Western democracy in accordance with the notion of "procedural democracy" or "electoral democracy," which states that democracy is simply a method or mechanism for choosing political leadership. Legislative bodies and executive heads at each level of government are subject to full electoral competitions in which citizens have unrestricted and equal rights in political participation. There are no arbitrary laws on civil organizations that ban the formation of political parties. There exists no censorship that restricts people's freedom of speech and publication. For the notion of the elitist view of liberal, procedural, representative, democratic system (Schumpeter, 1943; repr., 1976, p.260. Taking a more pluralist view of democracy, Dahl stresses the importance of a democratic system that is responsive to the preferences of its people and provides institutional guarantees of political equality among its citizens to formulate and to voice their preferences (Dahl, 1971, p, 3).

Yet, a broader and more comprehensive notion of democracy, suggested by David Held, argues that democracy must be considered not only in political affairs but also in social and economic life. Real democracy should incorporate the concept of democratic autonomy, for without a high degree of accountability and responsibility by both the state and a civil society, there will be no equal opportunity for participation and for discovering citizens' preferences in a polity. For those proponents of equal opportunity for political participation, the inherent nature of a capitalist system regarding resources, wealth, and status has created social and economic inequality among citizens, and the social, economic, and political liberties of the have-nots are systematically deprived and disrupted because they have less resources and time to invest in voicing their preference (Bowles and Gintis,1986, pp. 177–81, 183–87, 203–13).

As an idealist, I believe that once a polity achieves the state of procedural or liberal representative democracy, it should engage in reordering civil society and political practices to achieve the real principle of popular sovereignty. Further political development that goes beyond the procedural, representative, democratic system of government should aim at searching for social and economic equality with the intervention of the political hand and social justice to ensure adequate resources for citizens' political participation.

Therefore, it is too early to assume that the universalization of Western liberal representative democratic system of governance is the final form of human government and to predict that "the end of history" will soon arrive. A real liberating democratic system of government has to deal with equity not only in political rights but also in social and economic issues.

The Bandung Liberation Idea: Decoloniality/Delinking

The study of regime transformation has faced the difficulty of defining what democracy is and what it ought to be. To many scholars, the highest human achievement in political development is equated with the establishment of a liberal representative system of governance through open competitive elections. Nonetheless, such a concept has been challenged constantly by the more progressive ideas of participatory democracy and democratic autonomy. In addition, while scholars conduct their research they inevitably fall into the trap of Western-centered ethnocentrism and omit the impact of cultural differences and contexts faced by those non-Western human communities in the course of political development. Finally, previous research on democratization has offered only partial explanation of the phenomenon of regime transformation, solely examining either transition or consolidation stages or simply building a single-dimensional analytical framework and discarding other explanatory factors as insignificant.

Let us start by underlining two "particularities" of the "wounds" inflicted upon the colonies by Western imperialism. The first was brought about in the Bandung Conference, in 1955. In a nutshell, what Sukarno was proposing was "neither capitalism, nor communism but decolonization." Not a third way à la Giddens or Beck, but something else, away from the two sides of the coin of the European enlightenment (Wright, 1956). Notice also that representatives of 29 countries attended the conference. Sukarno made clear that the "belt" of countries present at the conference were a third part of the world and were people of color and of non-Christian persuasion. That is, he was pointing at racism in its religious and secular manifestations. Secondly, the "wound" is both colonial and imperial, and they interact through history in very interesting ways. The humiliation China suffered after the Opium War is better described as "imperial wound", similarly to the Ottoman Sultanate, for example, while the humiliation that Indigenous people suffered since the sixteenth century, and Africans from the slave trade to the European partition of the continent in 1884, is better described as "colonial wound", that to distinguish coloniality without colonialism (China, Ottoman Sultanate) and coloniality with colonialism (Africa, South America and the Caribbean, Native Americans and Africans in the US). Let me elaborate on this by referring to the historical trajectory of the concept and the needs to which it responded.

Historically, the project known as modernity/coloniality/decoloniality and sometimes for short modernity/(de)coloniality, originated in South America. Two years later Enrique Dussel (2007), Argentine philosopher of liberation, residing in Mexico, introduced the concept of transmodernity. Transmodernity which means both, that modernity was a historical process in which Europe was marching all alone, but was a process in which Europe made itself through its imperial/colonial expansion. That is the analytic of transmodernity. The prospective is that the world of the future shall be transmodern and not postmodern, for postmodern is an expression that only recognizes Europe as a protagonist of history, while transmodenrity points towards a future in which the entire world will participate.

We are already at the beginning of that process. The shakiness of the European Union, the crisis in the US today (after Enron, Iraq and Wall Street), indicates that the European Union and the US are losing their credibility and their leadership carries the future on their own shoulders. Now, all that will involve economic and political decisions, but much of the struggle for the control of the colonial matrix of power will cross by the colonial difference (colonial wound) and the imperial difference (imperial wound). This important dimension of feeling, sensing, memories, and wounds cannot be superseded by economic calculus and political strategies. Dependency theory in Latin America was as much theoretical as it was existential. Dependency was not only an economic analytic but also the feeling and the realization that being dependent was being somewhat inferior or at least living in inferior conditions.

Quijano (1992) was involved, in the 70s, in the debates on dependency theory, while Dussel was engaged, at the same time (late sixties and early seventies), with the beginning of theology and philosophy of liberation. Historically, the concept of coloniality came into being in the early nineties as a consequence of the collapse of the Soviet Union. However, it would not have been possible without the previous work of Peruvian intellectual José Carlos Mariátegui (1971), contemporary of Gramsci, in the 20s. It was Mariátegui who connected the colonial history in Latin America with capitalism. Thus, the underlying logic that connects both is "coloniality." That was Quijano's touch of genius, to see that colonialism and capitalism are based on the logic of coloniality and that the logic of coloniality is also what explains racism: basically the idea is that you cannot exploit and expropriate an equal. You have to make people inferior in order to be able to manage them and take away their labor and their land.

That is why racism emerged in the modern/colonial world, that is, in the sixteen hundreds. I am telling this story to help in dispensing with the idea that European genealogy of thoughts is the only point of reference. It is one; it is a genealogy of thought that from the right to the left belongs to European and Euro-US imperial history. We are getting used to the idea that the intellectual loci of enunciations are multiplying, and the world is becoming polycentric not only in economy and politics, but also in epistemology and hermeneutics. What is important to underline here is that genealogies of thoughts are ingrained in "structures of feelings" (as Raymond Williams had it), and structure of feelings are imbedded in the legacies of colonial and imperial wounds (something Williams did not take into account).

The colonial wound had been inflicted through history in the complicity between an economy of growth (e.g., capitalism) that sacrificed everything to its success and racism. The Atlantic commercial circuits connected the globe and the process known today in its latest version (the neo-liberal one), globalization, began. A new type of economy emerged. The historical foundation of the colonial matrix of power brought together a type of economy that was non-existing until then: an economy of inversion of the surplus and of dispensability of human life to increase economic gains (e.g. massive commodification as well as enslavement of Africans to work in the Caribbean plantations), a new form of political organization in which the metropolitan centers managed their colonies; which at their turn prompted the invention of international law to protect it.

Last but not least, racism was needed both for political and economic reasons. Racism, as we know it today, goes hand in hand with capitalism and with the modern state, both in its monarchic, Renaissance version, as well as in its nation-state, Enlightenment version: racism is the invention of those who controlled and managed discourses and knowledge and are able to make certain people feel that they are less human. Racism allows for the justification of indigenous genocide and African slavery: lesser humans, as they were considered, their lives were and are still dispensable. Lesser humans are people who are both epistemically and ontologically deficient. They are not quite rational, and therefore they are inferior or, they are inferior and, therefore, they are not quite rational.

From the trade of women and human organs, to the commercialization of migrants to the poisoning of land and rivers where people lived for millennia, to extract gold for the global market, one will see that the economy of growth comes first and live (the planet and us), second. coloniality, the colonial matrix of power, and the colonial and imperial wounds are important aspects of it. The colonial matrix of power is a complex structure that we describe as five interrelated domains: the domains of knowledge and subjectivity, of the economy, of authority (e.g., politics), of gender and sexuality and of the "natural" world (e.g., that in which our bodies are part of and what constitute our constant "becoming" as "human being" organized in communities (Caliphates, Empires, Monarchies, Churches, Mosques, Nation-States, Inter-communities relations, etc.).

This is why the spheres of feeling and sensibilities (what the Greeks called *aesthesis)* was colonized by modern philosophy and

162

turned into aesthetics: a theory to control "taste". There is no such thing as the colonial matrix of power before the sixteenth century. One cannot find it in Ancient China, in Ancient India and Persia, in Ancient African Kingdoms, in Ancient Greece, in Rome, in the Islamic Caliphate or in the Andean Incanate (the Incas were not an empire in the same way that Romans were not an Incanate. The colonial matrix of power is precisely what allowed the West to build itself as overcoming all existing civilizations in the name of modernity.

In other words, what came to be known as capitalism (e.g., Weber and Lenin) is for mankind a new type of economy that emerged in the sixteenth century as with the Atlantic commercial circuits. But it came together with the process of building new knowledges and forming new subjects: the modern and modern/colonial subjects. For humanity, the economy is only one domain of the colonial matrix of power, albeit since the 1970s, it became the privileged domain. What for liberal and Marxists is "capitalism" for us, the subjected people, is "economic coloniality", meaning that there are other forms of economy that are not tied up with coloniality. In the some five hundred years of economic coloniality, the economy was part of society until WWII but since then, society became part of the economy. Neo-liberalism was the last moment of that trajectory.

Economic coloniality began to be formed with the massive appropriation of land in the New World and the massive exploitation of labor, Indians first and enslaved Africans secondly. There thus arose the triangular trade in which enslaved Africans were bought, sold and transported to the Americas; the commodities (gold, silver, sugar, cotton, tobacco) from America transported to Europe and generating a global market; weapons transported from Europe to Africa to trade for enslaved people. The surpluses of such an economic exchange were re-invested instead of being stored, as it was the case in all other co-existing economies. This new type of economy introduced also the dispensability of human life: because of that subjectivity it was possible to believe in a hierarchy within the human species. And those who were inferior (that is the economic need and justification of racism), their lives were dispensable in pro of economic growth and benefit of the superior beings. Once again, if we review the Opium War we will realize that the profit the British made was their first concern, not the millions of Chinese who ruined their lives because of the drogue, as well as people in England and the US becoming "consumers" who contributed to the wealth of the British Empire.

It is here that the concept of *transmodernity*, introduced by Dussel comes into the picture. And why is this concept important? Once again, postmodernity was a concept that emerged in Europe to account for the transformations that European intellectuals were "feeling." Postmodernity and transmodernity are inscribed in different structures of feelings of the actors elaborating and promoting them. Transmodernity carries the memories of the colonial wound, and is open to dialogue with the imperial wound, since it is a concept that emerged from racialized and marginalized sensibilities: being of European descent in South America and the Caribbean is not being European. The feeling was that the concept of "modernity" was no longer capable of accounting for the experience of men and women of European descent, and even less of the majority of non-Europeans on the planet.

Post-modernity responded to feelings and sensibilities of the time in Europe, to the closing of the universal time of historical macro-narratives (e.g., Hegel). However, postmodernists couldn't escape to the Eurocentered linear concept of time. That is why for European intellectuals postmodernity naturally follows modernity; there is a change, but it is a change within the same. That is a very alien experience for 80% of the people of the world for whom modernity was always one side of the story; the other was coloniality.

For ex-Third World intellectuals modernity was, and will continue to be in different forms, transmodern; that is modernity/coloniality is transmodern. And it was, is and will be transmodern for the emerging economies that are living behind the Third World (like East and South East Asia). Transmodernity opened up the views to the work of coloniality, while conflictive modernities shut it down. What unites and divides modernity and coloniality is not only military, economic, and political, but it touches and forms subjectivities: thus, racism and imperial and colonial wounds. It is within modernity/coloniality where the colonial and imperial wounds dwell and where transmodernity is becoming the orientation to global futures.

In sum, dependency theory, philosophy of liberation and theology of liberation, the New World Group in the Caribbean (parallel to dependency theory in the continent), were the responses from the Atlantic to the process of decolonization in Asia and Africa. All that was before the idea of postmodernity emerged and postcoloniality was conceived. The postcolonial needed the postmodern (Lyotard: *The Postmodern Condition*, 1978). So the postcolonial is an idea of the 80s, while the decolonial goes back to Bandung.

The Bandung Conference and the meeting of the Non-Aligned countries (Belgrade, 1961) were not alien to Latin American and Caribbean intellectuals and intellectuals/activists, who were at the same time scholars. Frantz Fanon's *The Wretched of the Earth* was translated into Spanish and published in Mexico in 1962. Now *The Wretched* was read by Sartre as a fundamental decolonial statement. Homi Bhabha appropriated it for the postcolonial, but Lewis Gordon and many other Caribbean intellectuals (Paget Henry, Nelson Maldonado-Torres) are taking Fanon back to his decolonial vain. French Caribbean thinkers and literature did not need the postcolonial in order to be Caribbean thinkers and intellectuals. On the contrary, the postcolonial needs Caribbean thinkers and writers, as well as Africans, to be postcolonial scholars. Since the decolonial is the way of thinking that unveils the colonial matrix of power, the difference with the postcolonial is obvious. Catholicism and Protestantism are two positions within Christianity. It is same with the decolonial and the postcolonial. One should avoid any attempt to find equivalences, that is, whether the post– or the deco– correspond to Catholicism or Protestantism. Within the same frame there are different roads.

Preamble of Liberation Epistemology

Epistemology is crucial to decolonial thinking because ontology is always an epistemic construct. For us it is necessary but not sufficient to "study" the economic and political aspects of "capitalism." Capitalism is possible because its architects and supporters were able to build a structure of knowledge, epistemology that justifies the building of capitalism in spite of all the disasters that many of us know capitalism brings with it. However, the knowledge we have about the deadly consequences of capitalism is always superseded by the control of knowledge of actors and institutions that created it, transformed it, maintain it and now are "saving it." And the control of knowledge means also formation (e.g., education) and transformation like the media) of subjectivities.

The development of epistemology is essentially coextensive with the bourgeois epoch — the epoch of production for exchange, of commodity production. As capitalism develops, all facets of human existence become commodified, transformed into objects to be bought and sold, alienated from the individual human producer and coming to appear as if they were natural "inhuman" objects, as "forces of nature". This mode of production divides people into two classes—the buyers/users of human labor power and the producers/sellers of labor power. Those who live outside of this trade in human energy are "outside the economy" and "don't count" – women engaged in unpaid domestic work, members of self-sufficient or subsistence communities as well as the aged, disabled, etc.

Those oppressed under this social system, particularly those whose labor is exploited in the production of social wealth, struggle for recognition and freedom, and identify themselves in whatever way they can, by means of the forms of organization and consciousness possible within bourgeois social relations. Workers form themselves into cartels to bargain more effectively for the price of their labor power, and those doubly exploited by the under-valuing of their labor or whose labor is directly consumed in unpaid labor, likewise struggle to increase the value of their labor and to

166

participate on an equal footing with others in the labor market. However, in general, this struggle of "the excluded" is manifested only at a time when their labor begins to have value, to be exchanged, or at least the conditions for such commerce are coming into existence.

It is in this sense that we say that "trade unionism is bourgeois consciousness". Trade union consciousness has no place before, after or outside of the labor market. Trade unionism does not in essence call into question the right of the capitalist to use labor slavishly and the need of the worker to sell labor power cheaply. While anti-capitalist, socialist consciousness may develop within organizations of workers, such consciousness which aspires to a higher form of society in which wage-labor is abolished is nothing to do with trade unionism whose very foundation is wage-labor. Socialist consciousness grows up in the same conditions and on the same basis as trade union consciousness, namely modern conditions of production and the self-activity of organized workers — but it is something quite distinct from the forms of bourgeois consciousness with which workers fight to improve their lot within capitalism.

It is in this same sense that I shall refer to "liberation epistemology" as a form and part of "bourgeois philosophy". By "liberation epistemology" I refer to the philosophical production of the women's movement, in particular beginning with Simone de Beauvoir in the 1950s and later Betty Friedan, Kate Millett, Shulasmith Firestone, Dale Spender, and many, many others and such contemporary writers as Linda Nicholson and Drucilla Cornell, and many, many others, but also Black Liberation writers such as C. L. R. James and Frantz Fanon (2004) and US Blacks such as Stokeley Carmichael, Hughie Newton, Malcolm X, and others. Michel Foucault in particular, but also many other post-modern writers continue the same tendencies which find political application in combating a wide range of forms of the discounting of human labor.

There is no implication that one or another liberation struggle is "secondary" to the struggle of workers or the socialist movement or that I am in some way labeling such tendencies as bourgeois while reserving the tag of "proletarian" for other philosophical currents.

In fact, I think that to talk of a "proletarian epistemology" would be essentially meaningless. While the philosophy of Karl Marx is something else again and the subject of a separate consideration, the various Communist Parties have shown little evidence of the creative and mass development of epistemology which can in any way be compared to the Women's Movement and the Civil Rights movement and nothing of the kind is under consideration here.

By "Bourgeois Epistemology" I mean the whole organic development of epistemology from the Copernican Revolution till today. In it I include the Royalist Hobbes, the cleric Berkeley (though perversely), as well as the socialist-humanist Feuerbach and, with important qualifications, Marx, in so far as he was concerned with that subject. I use the word "bourgeois" in the sense that we say that "trade unionism is bourgeois ideology", even though it is clearly the ideology of proletarians, because it reflects the historic tasks of the bourgeois epoch. Bourgeois epistemology will only complete its development when the market is well and truly buried. It is nonsense to think that we can invent "proletarian epistemology" in the same sense that Trotsky reserved the conception of "proletarian culture" as something which could come into being only in some far, distant future:

> "[Marxism] was formed entirely on the basis of bourgeois culture, both scientific and political, though it declared a fight to the finish upon that culture. Under the pressure of capitalistic contradictions, the universalising[sic] thought of the bourgeois democracy, of its boldest, most honest, and most far-sighted representatives, rises to the heights of a marvellous[sic] renunciation, armed with all the critical weapons of bourgeois science. Such is the origin of Marxism. ..."

And that,

> "One cannot turn the concept of culture into the small change of individual daily living and determine the success of a class culture by the proletarian passports of individual inventors or poets. Culture is the organic sum of knowledge and capacity

168

which characterizes the entire society, or at least its ruling class. It embraces and penetrates all fields of human work and unifies them into a system. ...

... We have the literary works of talented and gifted proletarians, but that is not proletarian literature. . ." (*What Is Proletarian Culture, and Is It Possible?*, Trotsky 1923).

Furthermore, on the social and political level, the completion of the tasks of the bourgeois epoch is by no means exclusively the role of the bourgeoisie. As Trotsky put it in *The Permanent Revolution*:

> ... the victory of the democratic revolution is conceivable only through the dictatorship of the proletariat which bases itself upon the alliance with the peasantry and solves first of all the tasks of the democratic revolution. ...

The dictatorship of the proletariat which has risen to power as the leader of the democratic revolution is inevitably and very quickly confronted with tasks, the fulfilment of which is bound up with deep inroads into the rights of bourgeois property. The democratic revolution grows over directly into the socialist revolution and thereby becomes a *permanent revolution* (Trotsky, 1924).

Nevertheless, it is of considerable theoretical importance to be able to understand those tasks which are essentially those of capitalism (right of free speech, right of association, universal suffrage, separation of Church and State, equality before the law, freedom from racial vilification, national self-determination, etc.), and (so far as is possible) those forms of human activity and relationship which are essentially characteristic of a completely new and qualitatively different form of human society (such as the Russian Revolution). In this context, the anti-capitalist politics of many feminist, civil rights or anti-colonial currents by no means contradict the placing of the epistemological import of such movements as part of the 400-year long development of "bourgeois" epistemology.

Does such a characterization somehow mean that as a socialist one is necessarily opposed to or "not interested in" women's liberation, anti-racism or national liberation? Emphatically "No!" And if for reasons of not wanting to be misunderstood by trade unionists and feminists, I were to compromise this understanding, we are reduced to bourgeois radicalism, in which class characterization is used simply as a label to mark out friends and enemies. After this preamble which may encourage the reader to at least suspend judgment, let us now look at the development of liberation epistemology.

Rise of Liberation Epistemology: Decoloniality

There is no unanimity amongst scholars regarding the impact of Western Colonialism and Imperialism on Asia and Africa. On the one hand, some scholars hold that it greatly contributed to the civilizing of the backward people and contributed to the improvement of their living standards. They argue that the various colonial powers set up schools and colleges, constructed roads and railways, built canals and bridges; provided law and order, improved sanitation and health, promoted trade and commerce and thus contributed to the welfare of the native people.

On the other hand, writers like John Conard and Holison are highly critical of the role of western imperialism in Asia and Africa. They associate imperialism with exploitation, misery, poverty, cruelty, conversion, degradation and racial segregation. Holison says that imperialism was 'rapacious and immoral'. John Conard says "In many cases the motives for empire building have been selfish and the people in the colonies have frequently been exploited for the benefit of the mother-country." Both the above views contain only partial truth. In fact, the western colonization and imperialism was a mixed blessing. Its effect can be conveniently studied under the following heads.

1. Political Impact:

In the political sphere, Imperialism proved to be a blessing in disguise for some countries. For example it provided political unity to India which had been torn by dissensions and strife before the arrival of the western powers. Thus the British provided political unity to India which she had not achieved at any stage in her past history. This was rendered possible by the development of railways, modern means of transport and communication, press, introduction of English language which served as lingua franca, and a uniform system of administration throughout the country. This unity paved the way for the growth of political consciousness amongst people and ultimately motivated them to overthrow the colonial and imperialist yoke.

Secondly, western colonialism and imperialism was responsible for the introduction of western ideas like nationalism, democracy, constitutionalism etc. in Asia and Africa. The various imperialist powers tried to implant their ideas and institutions in their colonies and thus unconsciously let loose liberal forces in the countries of Asia and Africa. Thirdly, the colonial powers introduced efficient system of administration in the country. It is true that the administrative machinery was evolved primarily to promote the interest of the imperialist powers and paid little attention to the wellbeing and welfare of the natives.

Further, the natives were not given adequate representation in the civil services and generally excluded from higher positions. Despite these shortcomings, the system of administration, provided by the imperialist powers, exposed the colonial people to the system of western administration. Fourthly, the imperialist rule also led to the rise of slavery. The slaves began to be sold and purchased as part of personal belongings. The practice commenced when Portuguese in the 15th century raided the African villages and enslaved the people.

These persons were then transported to America. In fact there existed a regular market of slaves in Lisbon. Even the English engaged themselves in the slave trade. This slave trade resulted in the uprooting of millions of Africans from their homes. What is still worse is that they were made to work under the most inhuman conditions and were treated with great cruelty. Finally, colonialism and imperialism led to bitter rivalry among the European powers and they fought various wars for the possession of the^ colonies.

For example France and Germany clashed over Morocco in Africa. In India also the French were involved in a long drawn-out struggle with the British.

2. Economic Impact.

In the economic sphere western imperialism also had a mixed impact. On the positive side it led to development of industries in Asia and Africa. The various imperialist powers set up industries in their colonies to make profits and thus paved the way for the industrialization of the colonies. The colonial powers established long lines of railways, built banking houses etc. in the colonies to fully exploit their resources. They also set up certain industries in these colonies to make quick profits and fully exploited the resources available there. All this proved to be a boon for the colonies and led to their industrialization. On the negative side, the imperialist powers exploited the colonies by importing raw materials at the cheapest possible rates and exported the finished products at very high rates. They also tried to cripple local industries, trade and commerce by enacting necessary industrial and taxation laws. This policy of systematic exploitation resulted in the draining of wealth and greatly contributed to poverty, starvation and backwardness of the colonies.

3. Social and Cultural Impact:

In the social and cultural spheres, colonial and imperialist rule produced serious consequences. In the first place it adversely affected the religions of the local people because the local people were encouraged by the Western Missionaries to embrace Christianity by offering them certain material benefits. As a result soon Christianity became a thriving religion in many Asian and African countries. Secondly, Christian Missionaries played an important role in providing certain social services to the local people in the form of hospitals, dispensaries, schools, colleges etc. and thus greatly contributed to the enlightening of the people of Asia and Africa. Thirdly, colonial and imperialist rule led to racial segregation. European rulers treated their culture as superior to the Asian and African cultures and tried to impose the same on them.

Further, they believed that white races are superior to the black races and tried to keep aloof. They often enacted discriminatory laws against the local people. For example, in India the Indians could not travel in the railway compartment in which the Europeans were travelling. This policy of racial segregation greatly undermined the moral tone of the local population. Fourthly, the imperialist rule undermined the moral principles. They foreshook all norms of morality to keep their hold on the colonial people. They tried to divide the local people and made them fight among themselves to retain power. The policy of 'divide and rule' followed by the British in India best exemplifies this policy of the imperialist powers. It is well known that this policy of 'divide and rule' ultimately led to the partition of India.

Finally, the policy of colonialism and imperialism caused untold misery and suffering to the people. The various imperialist powers were involved in a number of wars with the local people as well as amongst themselves which resulted in loss of millions of lives. Thus colonialism and imperialism resulted in untold misery to humanity. In the light of the above legacies we can say that colonialism and imperialism left a deep impact on Asia and Africa in the political, economic as well as social field. The enduring impact of colonial imperialism compelled the world to embark on decolonization.

Decoloniality has a different genealogy of thoughts. It goes back to Indonesia, to the Bandung Conference, when Sukarno gathered the leaders of 29 Asian and African countries. China was one of the 29th. At that point China was part of the Third World. Religion and racism were two of the major issues in Bandung. The goal: neither communism nor capitalism, but decolonization. So, decolonization was born at the same time as the idea of Third World countries, neither capitalist (First World) nor communist (Second World). It is in that genealogy of thoughts that we can understand Frantz Fanon, dependency theory, Ali Shariati in Iran, and, more recently, thinkers as Ashis Nandy and Vandana Shiva in India, the concept of "coloniality" and therefore "decoloniality." For decolonial thinkers, whether in India, Africa or the Caribbean, the point of reference of coloniality is the sixteenth not the eighteenth century. The eighteenth century is the "second stage" of modernity and Western formation and expansion.

Decolonial thinkers may have taken a step forward in relation to postcolonial ones because we have been always taking a step backward. That is, while the postcolonial has the Enlightenment as its point of reference, the decolonial has the Renaissance. The 500 years of world history are the years in which Western Civilization emerged, asserted itself through the first three centuries and expanded globally since 1750, approximately. The colonial history of India that provided the impulse for postcolonialism (including the subaltern studies project), endured Western interferences since the second half of the eighteenth century. For that reason, post-colonialism is grounded in both the colonial history of India and in post-structuralist (Foucault, Lacan, Derrida) and Marxist (Gramsci) thinkers. While decoloniality is historically grounded in the history of the Americas, since 1500, and theoretically in the Bandung Conference (1955). But, both moments are connected in the history of global coloniality although they are disconnected if you look at them either from the perspective of particular empires (Spanish, English or French) or of national/colonial history (Indonesia or Bolivia for example).

One of our tasks is precisely to show the underlying network, the colonial matrix of power that connects all those moments and places and make them dependents of Western imperial expansion. But coming back to the language of decoloniality, the Bandung Conference made visible a common concern of many countries in Africa and in Asia in the fifties; Aimée Césaire's *Discourse on Colonialism* was written in Paris, and published in 1955 and Frantz Fanon (born and raised in Martinique) lived in France before moving to Algeria where he wrote his decolonial political treatise, *The Wretched of the Earth,* in 1961. Here you have geopolitics of knowing and knowledge at work. Even if Césaire and Fanon were in Paris, their conceptualization of colonialism and their decolonial thinking did not come from the history, experience and memories of Europe but of the colonies. Let's go back to the Bandung Conference.

Sukarno of course was not in Paris, but in Indonesia, sensing, feeling to the bones the experience of colonialism. In one of the transcriptions of his opening address at the Bandung Conference (remember that China was part of the Third World at that time and was one of the 29 countries at the Bandung Conference), Sukarno is quoted as saying:

> All of us, I am certain, are united by more important things than those, which superficially divide us. We are united, for instance, by a common detestation of colonialism in whatever form it appears. We are united by a common detestation of racialism. And we are united by a common determination to preserve and stabilize peace in the world.

We are often told 'Colonialism is dead.' Let us not be deceived or even soothed by that. 1 say to you, colonialism is not yet dead. How can we say it is dead, so long as vast areas of Asia and Africa are unfree. China, we should remember, was one of the third world countries (the division into three worlds was invented in France at that very time) at the conference. Let's remember in passing that Mao Zedong considered Russia a First World country. And that is understandable: Russia was Second World seen from France, Western Europe and the United States. From Mao's China things look different. That is why in our theory we pay a lot of attention to the enunciation and to the geopolitics of knowledge.

Liberating Knowledge

Knowledge is always situated. Liberating knowledge from Western cognitive imperialism must therefore relate to being non-Western, be connected to the philosophy and principles of the non-Westerners, take for granted the validity and legitimacy of non-Westerners, i. e., the importance of their languages and cultures, and, lastly, be concerned with the struggle for autonomy over the cultural well- being of the non-Westerners. Here, it has to be acknowledged that there is a distinction between colonialism and coloniality. Coloniality doesn't need colonialism as the Opium War demonstrated. Coloniality is the underlying logic (e.g., the colonial matrix of power upon which Western empires founded themselves, justified their imperial expansion and their intervention all over the world. Coloniality, in short, is the very foundation of Western civilization.

Another reason why the concept of "coloniality" did not call scholarly and intellectual attention (in China as in other places) is because it originated in South America and not in Europe. People, and progressives at that, are still taking for granted that concepts theoretically relevant have to come from Western Europe (France, Germany and England, and some from Italy) and the US but not from any place else on earth. In many other places people are afraid of their own thinking and need the legitimization of Western institutions and publishing houses. But that is changing, as is changing the sphere of political economy and theory. A few decades ago the rest of the world was praying to the IMF and the World Bank. Now many are learning to say, thanks, but no, we have our own way of doing things. Well, coloniality is a concept that emerged from this spirit and attitude in the Third World, at the moment in which it was becoming ex-Third World: the concept was introduced in Peru, by sociologist Anibal Quijano, in 1990.

Philosophically, "coloniality" next to "biopolitics" are two key concepts of contemporary intellectual and political debates. "Biopolitics" originated in Europe at the beginning of the twentieth century but it was Michel Foucault (1997) who gave the theoretical foundation of the concept in the second half of the same century. Through "biopolitics" and then "biopower" Foucault confronted and explained specific issues of the past and present of European history. Basically, how since the second half of the seventeenth century emerged in Europe and increased in the following centuries, a form of control of the population that consisted in the control of the bodies. "Biopolitics" and "biopowers" are the concepts through which the control of the population was a need of the emerging nation/states. Since nation/states at that time were only European phenomena, an outcome of its own history, bio-politics and bio-power were not crucial concerns in the non-European world. The concern was "coloniality" where Europe expanded and with the

176

imperial expansion racism in the way we understand it today was born. From the colonies, racism is one of the key elements of coloniality.

Coloniality/racism is a decolonial concept while biopolitics/biopower is a postmodern concept. However, since biopolitics and biopower were based in the history of France mainly, and the core of Europe, with the core of Europe (England, France and German) leading countries of European imperial expansion, the nation-state became also a form affirming local histories and gaining independence from Europe (e.g., China in the process that led to the 1912 Revolution led by Sun Yat-sen, or the subsequent struggle for decolonization since the end of WWII). The modern nation-state is also a European invention responding to European needs (like the separation of Church and State), and then expanded all over the world. The modern nation-state was built by an emerging ethno-class (the white European bourgeoisie), displacing the monarchy and the church and becoming a potent tool of political coloniality.

These are precisely the historical experiences and the conditions that brought about the concept of "coloniality." No one in Europe was thinking "coloniality", they did not see it; they did not feel it. They can understand "colonialism" but "coloniality" is another matter. It is more difficult to see, they only see modernity and invent concepts like alternative, peripheral, subaltern etc. modernities, assuming that there is only one real one. By multiplying modernities eurocentered scholars and intellectuals continue to hide coloniality.

In Latin America — where the concept of coloniality emerged—the history is five hundred years old, and it is only related to the history of Europe because Europeans were the conquerors, colonizers, slave traders and slaveholders. After all of that "importation" you do not want again to "import" biopolitics and biopower to deal with the problems that Europe created. Biopolitics and biopower are important regional critical concepts that cannot be converted into a single story as if Europe has the goodwill to create the problems and the solutions while the rest of the world will watch the unfolding, like watching a tennis match as unlookers. "Coloniality" is one of the concepts that introduced a different story, literally, and released repressed sensibilities rationalization, memories and above all, needs. "Coloniality" is in the genealogy of Frantz Fanon's crucial concepts such as "sociogenesis" and the "damnés" but not on the same channel with biopolitics, biopower and multitude. That is why the geopolitics of knowledge is a necessary companion to coloniality and why the universality of knowledge is taken for granted in all European (and Euro-Anglo-American) debates on bio-politics and bio-power.

The type of management and control that is described by the concept of coloniality (short hand for colonial matrix of power) goes back to the seventeenth century (where Foucault locates the form of control he describes as bio politics). The processes that we describe as coloniality go back to the fifteenth century and the formation of the Atlantic commercial circuits. That is, when the Atlantic was incorporated into the global economy, when Western globalism started and with it the foundation of Western civilization began to unfold. What emerged there and we describe as coloniality or colonial matrix of power, was a global structure of management and control that lasted until today.

In other words, coloniality is what allowed Europe to be Europe and to manage not only its own population, but also the population of the planet. The Opium War was the moment in which China felt the effect and the consequences of coloniality: it took a while to recover, and now China is disputing the control of the colonial matrix of power that, for five hundred years, was in the hands of Western imperial countries and the alliances between them. There is a conversation today among Western progressive intellectuals making sense of China and East Asia who are talking about "contested modernities." That makes more sense than "alternative modernities." But still, they hide coloniality. What we have been witnessing in the past few decades is an increasing struggle for the control of the colonial matrix of power in the name of modernity and modernization. Coloniality is embedded among "contested modernities.

One can therefore begin to understand how biopolitics/biopower (unveiled and analyzed by European intellectuals) is only one aspect of the complex colonial matrix of power (unveiled and analyzed by Third World intellectuals). Crucial here is then the point of origination of both concepts and the geopolitics of knowing and understanding. I am not saying that one shall be displaced by the other. I am saying that both shall and will co-exist but that they are irreducible to each other. We have to start thinking in terms of geopolitics of knowledge and leave behind the modern set of mind according to which only one story is possible and desirable and you have to eliminate everyone who does not bend, think or feel like the single story tells you to do, feel or think.

Biopolitics/biopower are regional not universal concepts. And if they are global, they are also partial for in the colonies and ex-colonies there are other concerns and needs that are not accounted for with those concepts. Crucial for European sensibilities, these concepts are not in the skin of billions of people of the non-European world, except of the few who are followers and promoters of what is going on in Europe. The concepts could only account partially for some European strategy of control but they are far from helping to understand the complexity of the colonial world. Hence, "coloniality" is global, but not universal. In time, it is restricted to the world order that began in the sixteenth century with the formation of the Atlantic commercial circuits. It doesn't make sense for us to talk about coloniality in the Roman Empire, in ancient Chinese Dynasties or among the Incas before the conquest: coloniality goes hand in hand with capitalism and none of the civilizations before 1500 were based on a capitalist economy, as history attests abundantly.

Coloniality introduced the perspective of people at the receiving end of biopolitics and biopower, it accounts for the wide spectrum of colonial worlds. The difference is that the colonial matrix of power that originated in the history of the colonies subsumes the history of Europe and of the colonies, from the perspective of the colonies. In that regard, it brings to the foreground the other stories that European narratives hide when the story of the world is told from the perspective of Europe. As you see, decolonial thinking focuses on the enunciation, not so much on what is said but on who is saying it, when, why, and what for. The analytic of coloniality is always already a decolonial statement. Decoloniality, however, is not limited to the analytic but it is also a prospective concept, as one talks about progress and development.

Now, this is the crucial point. Europe built itself over the control of knowledge, which allowed for the organization of itself, politically, economically, intellectually, artistically, religiously. And "biopolitics/biopower" is part of that control, even if the concepts are critical of state regulations. "Coloniality/colonial matrix of power" first of all unveils that imperial history built itself in the name of salvation (by conversion to Christianity, by the civilizing mission, by development and modernization). Secondly, it shows that the underlying matrix of European imperial power and of Western Civilization lies in its rhetoric of modernity (which is the rhetoric of salvation) and its constitutive part, the logic of coloniality. Thus the strong thesis I am advocating here is that coloniality is constitutive of modernity and it is the underlying structure of Euro-America imperial expansion and domination. That is why "contested modernities" implies a "struggle for the control of the colonial matrix of power."

From here we can derive two conclusions: one is that biopolitics/biopower is a small part of the colonial matrix of power (and to talk about colonial biopower is really a fancy word game without theoretical and historical foundation), and that now, in the twenty-first century the main conflicts are around the control of the colonial matrix of such power. The West (European Union and the US) can no longer control. The economic strength of China is that it has the means to dispute the control of the colonial matrix, and so do the BRICs countries. Sure, they are all capitalist countries, EU, US and the BRICs. But there is an enormous difference. All BRIC countries (population, languages, religions, skin color, writing system) has been racialized and therefore made inferior to Europe from the perspective of Europe. No longer! So, we can explain the history of the formation of the modern/colonial world since 1500 by explaining the formation, transformation and lately dispute for the control of the colonial matrix ("contested modernities" for Western progressive intellectuals- (See for instance the much discussed book by Martin Jacques, *When China Rules de World, When*

China Rules the World: The End of the Western World and the Birth of a New Global Order, 2012).

To understand modernity from the perspective of decoloniality one must first accept that the idea of modernity was built on the celebration of newness. The very idea of newness was ingrained in the idea of modernity since Europeans baptized the New World; the lands and people that appear in their consciousness at the end of the fifteenth century. So that post-modernity captured in and by the European mind was, they felt, the sign of a new era. For people in the non-European world the "feeling" was different. They were entangled with European history but were not living that experience. South America (as well as in Asia and Africa —let us leave the US aside for the moment), knew that "modernity" was something alien to their own history. Their history was/is that of modernity/coloniality—the history of the formation of the Atlantic commercial circuits; of the historical foundation of capitalism; of racism as it is known today; of the beginning of the Western project of economic expansion, of converting and civilizing the planet. Someone from the non-Western world cannot understand modernity in the way Giddens and Beck do. They live in different skins, have different memories, non-Western memories are not that of imperial England or the memories of Germany's genocide in Africa (the Herero) and in Europe (six million Jews and another nine or ten million of non-Jews).

For non-Westerners modernity is incomprehensible without coloniality. Not for Giddens and Beck. Dussel pointed out that, historically, that in the sixteenth century, with the European Renaissance, and then the Enlightenment, the history of Europe is entangled with the non-European world that Europeans want to have under their wing. So that modernity is indeed trans-modernity in the sense that the entire world participated in the making of Europe and then Euro-America from fifteen hundred on. And the future will be also trans-modern but no longer having Europe and US at its center.

The trans-modern future will be (is already underway) built on the principles of pluri-versality. The world is already witnessing this mutation. The BRICs countries are decentering the world order, although maintaining the economy of exploitation, expropriation and expropriation that Weber and Lenin named capitalism. However, BRICs countries are neither liberal nor neo-liberal. That is why Confucianism is gaining ground in China. Dewesternization seems to be the common ground of BRICs countries leading the way. And of course, Confucianism is one way of dealing with dewesternization, not the only one, even less the model for all processes of dewesternization.

However, what the project of modernity/(de) coloniality promotes is not a polycentric capitalist world. This view is part of our analytic. What should be promoted is decoloniality, a march toward a polycentered and non-capitalist world, a world in which economic coloniality has been barren. This would be a world order in which the myths of modernity will not be needed because the horizon of life will be to live in harmony, in plenitude and to compete for progress and to modernize as if modernity would provide in the future what has not been provided in the past, since the idea of modernity was put in circulation.

Dewesternization is an important step toward non-imperial futures. Instead of contested modernities let us talk about the struggle for the control of the colonial matrix of power. Dewesternization, in its several trajectories, is a case in point. The colonial matrix of power was built, maintained and transformed by the West (Christianity, Liberalism, Neo-liberalism and even Marxism, its oppositional force within the same rule of the game) at the same time that the West became the West because of the colonial matrix. Today, the economy of accumulation is global, so then is economic coloniality.

However, what is changing is that economic coloniality is no longer responding to one set of political rules and principles. China is a clear case in point. If China's leaders' decisions in 1979 would have been to follow the rules of the game and be dependent on the US, China would not be at its current economic level. At the same time, economic growth contributed to regain the confidence that was lost with the Opium War. That is to say that next to economic growth there is the process of healing the imperial wound. What is disputed are Western designs and of the will of self-appointment to rule the world. Disputing the control of the colonial matrix is the challenge that BRICs countries are presenting to Western imperial legacies (Western Europe and the US).

But not only BRICs countries are engaged in processes of dewesternization. Also there are other countries in the Middle East, in Africa and in South America and the Caribbean. That means, that under dewesternization, economic coloniality will continue its march and its life, at least for a while in and by the US, the European Union, China, India or Brazil. But new venues will be opening up by the process of dewesternization as people enduring the legacies of coloniality (whether colonized like India, South America or African countries or not colonized like China and Japan) began to regain the confidence that the myth of modernity took away from them. One of the consequences of dewesternization at the international level is what is currently being witnessed in the European Union and the US: their internal collapse also, as they can no longer enact coloniality beyond Europe and the US while maintaining a comfortable middle class in their own countries.

There is another reason, and for us the most significant, of why dewesternization is relevant. Since the collapse of the Soviet Union and the end of the Cold War, there is clear evidence, not in process of transition but in a revolutionary process in which the entire world is participating. That revolutionary process makes of "left and right" an obsolete conceptualization of the world. Left and right are valid in the limited and regional world of post-enlightenment Europe and its aftermath, the Soviet Union, Mao's China, Castro's Cuba. Today, dewesternization and decoloniality have exploded the narrow and limited European conceptions of politics and the political (friends and foes). The Bush's "either you are with us or you are with the terrorists" is dead and buried.

First of all, the famous French Revolution was a revolution of an emerging ethno-class, the European bourgeoisie, which was growing economically and finally asserted themselves in front of the political and economic states of the monarchy supported by the church. It was an ethno-class revolution — a part it involved whites, Christians, French and Europeans. Before that, something similar happened in England with the Levelers, mid seventeenth century, and then with the Glorious Revolution toward the end of the century, where John Locke emerged as its leading ideologue. It was, furthermore, a revolution that on the bases of mercantile capitalism (one form of economic coloniality, others are free trade, industrial revolution, technological revolutions) and the enrichment of Europe with gold, silver, sugar, cotton, tobacco, slave trade of the colonial period, solidified the bourgeoisie and created the condition of the industrial revolution.

It was in other words a capitalist revolution built upon the European three centuries of colonial wealth. Today, the celebration of the French Revolution goes hand in hand with the critique of capitalism. Absurd! Indeed! But the point is that if the French Revolution (and before that the British's Glorious Revolution) was an ethno-class one, the world is now witnessing a racial revolution. Simply said, while the white and Christian bourgeoisie grounded in their economic growth overthrew the white and Christian aristocracy, now the non-European bourgeoisie of color and non-Christians are if not overthrowing yet stopping the global hegemony that the white Western bourgeoisie set up (i.e., the colonial matrix of power) and controlled during the past two centuries (nineteenth and twentieth.

The racial revolution that dewesternization is enacting maintains capitalism. And that is true. But at the same time the French Revolution and the American Revolution were revolutions that consolidated capitalism. We tend to forget it but remember the nice words "democracy, freedom, equality, etc." So in a parallel way we should pay attention that while dewesternization maintains capitalism that the Glorious, the American and the French revolution consolidated (by consolidating a new ethno-class controlling knowledge, the economy, politics, gender and sexual relations, and affirming themselves through patriarchy and racism), dewesternization opens up the doors to a racial revolution parallel to a class revolution that took place through the eighteenth century.

Beyond dewesternization, and coexisting with it, are the variegated decolonial processes that are enacting racial and patriarchal revolution and working toward a world without capitalism and therefore without coloniality. This is the moment in which the legacies of Bandung become relevant again: what it was proposed was to delink from European enlightenment legacies and to regain the racial and religious dignity that Western imperial civilization took away from most of the planet. But decoloniality, contrary to dewesternization, confronts head on economic coloniality: there cannot be peace, non-poverty, flourishing of life in the planet, while the principles that sustain the economy of growth (economic coloniality) are not changed to an economy of administration of scarcity. And this is no longer capitalism vs. socialism. It is something totally different based on decolonial visions of the alternative futures.

Decoloniality, then, is the third global force re-orienting the present toward global futures. We see its manifestations in South America in the growing forces of indigenous and peasant epistemic and political participation, in the so called "social movements", chiefly in the potent organization claiming for the rights to life acting to stop the depredation of open pit mining in all the Andes Mountains, from Colombia and Ecuador to Chile and Argentina going through Peru. "Juicio Etico Popular to the Transnational Corporations" is a telling example of these processes (http://www.youtube.co...ia campesina.org/en/). "La via campesina" is another example (http://viacampesina.org/en/).

Lately, the uprising in Tunisia and Egypt, the "indignados" of Spain and Greece, the students in Chile and in Colombia against the corporate transformation of the university, even the "Occupy" in the US, and of course the growing global intellectual awareness that if decolonization was a specific moment during the Cold War, decoloniality transcended it. And decoloniality transcended decolonization in the same way that coloniality transcended colonization. Colonization refers to specific historical moments and countries in the past 500 years while coloniality refers to the logic of domination behind the salvation rhetoric of modernity. Imperial modernity doesn't need colonies to install coloniality (as China knows it very well since 1842), but it needs coloniality. In parallel fashion, decoloniality means to delink from the colonial matrix of power. Decoloniality is thus an epistemic, ethical and political project. *The world cannot be changed if the people who run the world do not change. And people do not change submitting to public policies and obligations.* Here is where Karl Marx had good intention but it was difficult for him to see coloniality and decoloniality at the other end of the spectrum. Instead, he projected the European experience (the proletarian class) toward global futures.

Postcoloniality, Decoloniality and Delinking

Much confusion has raged concerning the differences between post-colonial and decolonial phenomena. There are clear differences between both. The so called postcolonial is the particular local histories in which postcolonial and decolonial intellectuals inhabit. Willy-nilly, coloniality is an unavoidable experience for 80% of the world, that is, the non-Euro-US world. However, there are in these regions and countries Native Americans and enslaved Africans, and in Europe Romans, Romanians, Gypsies, and Jews who couldn't escape coloniality. Hence, the postcolonial makes no sense since the colonial matrix of power is still right there and calling the vital economic and cultural shots. The basic difference between decoloniality and postcoloniality is that the latter depends and piggy backed on the concept of postmodernity while the former is an unfolding of the Bandung Conference, in 1955. That is why the past in the present toward the future, is crucial for decolonial thinking and that is why without an epistemic revolution there cannot be political or economic revolutions: politics and economy are tied up and grounded together in Western political theory and political economy.

What has changed is that re-westernization and dewesternization as an option coexisting with the decolonial option have come into the scene. China is responding well to that in the process of political dewesternization, which means to manage capitalist economy beyond the rules of the IMF. If you read the IMF boss, Christine Lagarde's speech delivered on March 18, 2012 as you read a literary text, you will see several interesting indicators: although she is a French officer at the IMF, she speaks as if her position at the IMF allows her to be impartial and above developed and emerging economies. Second, she cannot avoid honoring China's economic growth, and she cannot avoid being "ma/paternalistic." She knows that the time when Western officers of international institutions give advice to emerging economy has passed. However, she couldn't restrain from offering some advice. And third, she delivered a congratulatory push to suggest changes in China's fiscal policies. Finally, she quoted Confucius. The fourth point showed that re-westernization continues but now can no longer stand on a bully pulpit. It has to be condescending but presented as respectful recognition of China's achievements.

The fact that the gap between these third world countries and the first world countries is not narrowing but widening invokes "contested modernities" or "the struggle for the control of the colonial matrix of power." But From the beginning: there is no way to avoid coloniality once you enter the road market economy and under the belief that "modernity" is something you have to catch up with. The belief that modernity is something you have to catch up with was the most successful fiction of the European imaginary. And we are still struggling with it, in the name of modernization. However, from decolonial perspectives, modernity is not something you have to catch up with. The second more pressing question is that of development and growth. Once again, what does modernity have to do with growth and development? We need to delink, as Amin said it in the 80s, but not from capitalist economy but from the colonial matrix of power of which economic coloniality is one sphere.

First of all, we have to delink from the idea that economic growth is the road to happiness for all. It is for a minority, that minority that is growing bigger in wealth while the majority is growing bigger in poverty. So, economic growth is a lie, a lie that keeps the logic of coloniality hidden under the rhetoric of modernity. I am not talking here about a socialist distribution of wealth but of a radical change of horizon in which growth, development = wealth is not the guiding light of governments (which shall not necessarily be States), financial institutions (which shall not be necessarily banks), industries (which do not necessarily need to be corporations), institutions for nurturing and education (which shall not necessarily be corporate universities that support research for national security and for transnational corporations). If the horizon of life is to live in plenitude and to enjoy the life of the planet, well, it is necessary to delink from the fantasies and illusions of modernity.

To be frank, we are now in a world order significantly different to the one Samir Amin was looking at when he made that observation. As a matter of fact, that observation was also made in the 1950s by Argentinian economist Raul Presbisch (Executive Secretary of the United Nations Economic Commission for Latin America and the Caribbean (ECLAC), 1950 – 1963). Presbisch observed that the plan of development and modernization for Latin America and the Caribbean that United Nations asked him to report, was impossible in the current state of international economic relations for, as we know, developed countries are such because they live from the resources and the surplus extracted from underdeveloped countries. Dependency theory emerged precisely to think how to get out of the trap, that is, of the entanglement of modernity/coloniality. The Caribbean New World Group has a very interesting economic history as a "plantation economy." This plantation economy is common to other parts of the world, like in South East Asia as Syed Hussein Alatas demonstrated in *The Myth of the Lazy Native. A Study of the image of the Malays, Filipinos and Javanese from the 16th to the 20th Century and its function in the ideology of Colonial Capitalism* (1977).

It was a frustrating experience for people and honest politicians and intellectuals to see how the gap between developed and underdeveloped countries continue to grow. What have developed are not the economies but the gaps, and millions of people know that development is not convenient for them but they do not have a say and if they protest, they are considered delinquent or terrorists that prevent progress and development. In many parts of the world, "Foreign Debt" was the killer since the end of the 60s. Now it is the killer in Europe, as Greece, Italy, Spain and Portugal know very well. Now we are seeing it in Europe! The situation has changed, and Greece, Italy and Spain are (next to former-Eastern European countries), in conditions similar to Third World countries before the collapse of the Soviet Union.

But let me say this before continuing: dewesternization refers to "emergent" economies that discovered the way to maintain capitalist economy and at the same time to struggle for the control of all other domains of the colonial matrix of power, chiefly political decisions in the international arena and the dispute for the control of knowledge. Dewesternization thus calls into question the foundation of western knowledge and brings out how to modernize without reproducing coloniality so that not only the middle class enjoys standards of living but the entire planet; not sameness by inclusion but equal, separate, discrete and equivalent in power and authority without forgetting the colonial wound inflicted by racial difference. Humanity in difference then means to delink to think according to Western epistemological prescriptions.

China is no doubt a paramount example of economic take off disobeying the IMF and the World Bank. Now, that doesn't solve the problems within each country and even less the question of coloniality. The good thing about dewesternization is to avoid one and only global imperialism; perhaps it was what Hardt and Negri (2000) were thinking about when they wrote *Empire*. They wrote the book in the nineties when still many believed in the end of history and in the infinite economic growth, the illusion of the techno-bubble and the "irrational exuberance". But dewesternization doesn't solve the problem of coloniality — as far as capitalism is preserved, economic coloniality is preserved too.

So, what has changed, what is going on? China was a Third World country during the Cold War, as was India and Brazil. And Russia (or Soviet Union) was the Second World. Now four of those countries constitute BRICs that is power emerged, rather than emerging, economies. What happened? What happened is that the leaders of these countries understood that it is impossible to narrow the gap if the country follows the instructions of the IMF, the World Bank and the political dictates of the Washington Consensus. I will not say that China and Russia or Brazil are First World Countries now. I will say that that division doesn't hold any more. We are in a polycentric and capitalist world order and there are more than two contenders in the arena. I call that "dewesternization." Dependency theorists were saying that in the seventies, you cannot "develop" if you follow the instructions of the IMF on how to develop.

You have to figure out yourself, that is, to become economically independent in decision-making and interconnected in the negotiations. That, once again are dewesternizing projects that BRICs countries are leading. China understood that before Brazil and India. Russia needed a decade to figure out how to build a strong economic and political state (?) after the disaster induced by neo-liberalism that made 10 Russian multi-billionaires in a couple of years. Vladimir Putin is controversial internationally and contested inside Russia. But imagine what may have happened to Russia if the country was in the hands of Yeltzin's friends? A no-win situation, indeed! Now Russia is one of the BRICS states and these countries are learning what a capitalist economy is and instead of following Western instructions they are rather thanking the West for letting them know what capitalist economy is and to manage it in their own way. That is precisely what dewesternization is. Amin was not seeing deweseternization as an unfolding of history. He was too much programmed by Marxist teleology and the Right vs. Left conflict and because of that, Amin was unable to understand the role of the Muslim Brothers in Egypt, in North Africa and in the Muslim World. This misunderstanding plays out clearly in the last chapter of his book on delinking.

Politico-economic dewesternization is viewed here as mainly secular as it is among BRICS countries. But a second aspect of dewesternization is politico-religious, and Islam is one of the strong forces moving in that direction. Malaysia, Indonesia and Iran are three such countries. Dewesternization is making the world poly-centered, a world order with a common economy and many centers of decision. If capitalist is "the common", that is, the common ground of world economy the other domains of the colonial matrix are being disputed: the control of authority, the control and management of knowledge and subjectivity, of gender and sexuality, and racism is contested at a global level: "Eastern" people were considered "Yellow" and inferior to "White." No longer!

Coloniality is not "maintained by the networks weaved by capital" but, on the contrary, that it is the persistence of "the networks weaved by coloniality that maintains capital(ism)." Here one can now see the difference between Marxist and decolonial thinking. "Capitalism" is something that Max Weber and Vladimir Lenin did not agree upon. Weber liked it, Lenin did not. But they both agree that there is something we can call capitalism. For us what is crucial is the colonial matrix, and "economic coloniality" is one sphere of the colonial matrix, the sphere that (neo) liberals and Marxists have fetishized.

So, the persistence of the colonial matrix of power has maintained economic coloniality and, in the past decades, economic coloniality has become the sphere of the colonial matrix that governs the other spheres. But it was not always like that. In the history of the American colonialism mutated into internal colonialism from 1776 to 1830 approximately, the US (called "American") Revolution (1776), the Haitian Revolution of 1804 and several independences in Spanish America, 1809 – 1830, all showed in different and complex ways that the first cycle of colonialism ended, but not coloniality. In fact, the logic of management and control behind the rhetoric of modernity. Coloniality mutated into four different forms: a) internal colonialism in the US and in the Spanish American new republics. Internal colonialism means that the colonial matrix of power was now in the hands of Creoles (e.g., people of European descent born in the New World, basically Anglos in the North and Latin (Spanish and Portuguese in the South) and b) imperialism without colonies. China and Japan were brought into the colonial matrix without being colonized like India or French Indochina.

That happened in South America and the Caribbean where the British and French, displaced Spain and Portugal, and "supervised" the local elites that were collaborators of the new stage of imperial/ colonial expansion and capital accumulation; c) the Creoles Anglo elite in the US who also transformed British colonialism into US internal colonialism took a different path: the road to imperialism, a project that was achieved after WWII; and, d) the most unexpected decolonizing act that took place in Haiti in 1804 –

unthinkable revolution made by the bottom of the New World population, enslaved Africans and their descendants. That people of European descent lead the US revolution and the Spanish America independence is understandable. They belonged to the ruling class. But Creoles were played down by the metropolitan elites occupying all the key monastic, economic and political sites. The dream that the enslaved will take freedom in their hands was indeed unthinkable, and that so-called unthinkability cost Haiti the troubles it has endured until today.

So, the second stage in Asia and Africa, that is, decolonization from 1947 to 1970 is nothing else but the continuation and mutation of what happened in the Americas at the end of the eighteenth and the beginning of the nineteenth century: local elites sending the imperial colonizer home and doing themselves what the colonizers were doing. Imperialism/colonialism ended in Africa and Asia, but not coloniality. To understand that what happened in America and the Caribbean at the end of eighteenth and beginning of nineteenth century equivalent to what happened in Asia and Africa in the second half of the twentieth century (well India independence in 1947), you have to bet out a lineal concept of history and understand how the modern/colonial world system came into being, was transformed, maintained and engendered decolonial struggles.

Now after WWII the increasing role of the US as global leader was the sign of another important mutation of the malleability of the colonial matrix of power. The Cold War was an interesting interregnum for the Russian Revolution that took place between the first wave of the decolonization in the Americas and the second wave in Asia and Africa, is interesting because it is not decolonization but a different form of imperial expansion: the expansion of communism instead of the civilizing mission. In other words, at the time it happened, the Russian Revolution was not so much a decolonial revolution but extension of Europe in the borders of Europe, a second class empire as Madina Tlostanova (Uzbek-Cherkess scholar and intellectual living in Moscow) would have it.

Just think of it. How shall we understand the Russian Revolution in the context of the first wave of decolonization in the Americas and the second wave in Africa and Asia? The Russian Empire was not a colony of Europe. So that the Russian Revolution doesn't follow the same logic as the decolonial trajectory in the Americas. It follows, rather, the logic of the French Revolution: the French Revolution was the revolution of a new class, the bourgeoisie. The Russian Revolution was a revolution in the name of the proletarian class. The Cold War was indeed not a clash between the colonies and the metropolis but a clash between two post-Enlightenment ideologies — liberalism and capitalism vs. communist economy, that is, between laissez faire capitalist and state regulated communism.

As for the world order today, I see it in relation to the previous historical scheme to what, of course, it is necessary to add the trajectory followed by China since the Opium War. As I see it, the overthrowing of the Qing Dynasty in 1911, was quite different from all the revolts that took place up to that time in the modern/colonial world (that is, in the world system whose historical foundation we, the modernity/coloniality project, date in the sixteenth century). It is different in the sense that a) the revolts in the colonies of Americas were all against European Christian imperial monarchies; b) the Russian Revolution was a revolution against the Czardom in the name of the proletarian class and c) the Chinese revolution of 1911 was a nationalist revolution, that is, the idea of the nation-state that was put in place in Europe after the French Revolution was the frame of the Chinese Guomindangs overthrowing the Qings.

A nationalist revolution is very different from one based on a social class. A nationalist revolution appeals to the past of what is being formed as a nation, and that is what Sun Yat-Sen made clear in his "Three Principles of Livelihood" (1927). In this regard, the nationalist revolution in China has this in common with all the struggles for decolonization in Asia and Africa since 1945: all decolonization struggles since the nineteenth century were made in the name of nationalism, which Fanon theorized in his classical *The Wretched of the Earth* (1961). Mao Zedong's efforts attempted to turn the nationalist revolution into the internationalization of communism.

However, contrary to the Russian Revolution, Mao never left behind the millenarian history of China while the Russian Revolution made a drastic cut with the past and came empty handed: Russians were not Europeans and the Soviets, who enacted European theories of emancipation, did not have a history to back up their revolution. The history of the formation since the fifteenth century was cut and denied by the Soviets. Today's Russia, with Vladimir Putin, turned the legacies of the Soviets into a State controlled capitalism but devoid of historical foundations while China has the legacies of Confucius and Mencius to refurbish national and moral values to confront the aggression of Western neo-liberalism and to detach themselves from Mao's legacies. In a nutshell, coloniality (short hand for colonial matrix of power) was formed, transformed and controlled by Western imperial countries from 1500 to 2000. Today, dewesternization maintains the colonial matrix, but disputes its control, while decoloniality aims at transcending it. Hence, decoloniality means to undo and to overcome coloniality. In other words, decoloniality is epistemological focusing on decolonizing knowledge rather than territory. It is therefore the analytical task of unveiling the logic of coloniality and the prospective task of contributing to a world in which many worlds will coexist That is the most important difference with the way decolonization was conceived during the Cold War.

The current notion of "progress" is basically related to the "mission civilizatrice" that gained currency in the nineteenth century. However, it can be traced back to the Renaissance. When the US took over from Britain, after WWII, the "progress" was translated into "development." It is known that Harry Truman in his presidential address of 1949 introduced the word "underdeveloped countries." That was the justification to start the project of "modernization and development." Latin America was the first showcase.

Africa was in full decolonizing struggle and the US was supporting decolonization to displace Europe in world leadership and to confront the Soviet Union. The ideas of "modernization and development" collapsed in 1968 (the uprising in Beijing, Paris, Prague, Mexico) and since then US started a new project, known now as "neoliberalism". The first showcase where neoliberalism experimented was Chile, with Augusto Pinochet, after the fall of Salvador Allende. Then came Videla in Argentina, Gonzalo Sanchez de Losada in Bolivia, Menem in Argentina in the 90s. In the middle of all of that, the financial crisis in East Asia and in Russia exploded. A new "development" now was the Neoliberal Doctrine and the Washington Consensus.

This is a mutation of the colonial matrix in the last attempt of maintaining the project of Westernization (self-defined as globalization and modernity). By the beginning of the twenty-first century it was obvious, although in Latin America this discussion began before; that "progress" and "development" are a dream that cannot be sustained. We analyze (in the project modernity/coloniality) "progress" and "development" as the rhetoric of modernity, which is a rhetoric of salvation in the words of the G7, the World Bank, The European Union and the US. But, the rhetoric of modernity hides the logic of coloniality: to develop you need to expropriate land, exploit labor, poisoning the fields with transgenic and fumigation to allow the soya beans to grow clean and colorful, while people die of leukemia and cancer; the gaps between rich and poor is growing; *Forbes Magazine* celebrates that in the past decades the number of multi-billionaires increased, many of those are outside Western Europe and the US, where the wealthy were before.

In the meantime, the economic system is collapsing; the political system is engendering all kinds of manifestations, which are an awakening of the civil society and the formation of the global political society. The world is in flames, and the world is in flames because it has been built on the chimera of progress and development instead of collaboration and communal peaceful organization of societies. Communal is not communism, which is a Western idea derived from the enlightenment, thus it is not the universal common, but the non-modern communal (neither communism nor the liberal common good or common wealth). The communal is by definition pluriversal, for it doesn't accept the idea of a "new abstract universal" that will be good for everyone because it is good for one folk. The communal is the decolonial door opening up to the pluriversal, beyond capitalism and communism.

The idea of "progress and development" is what capitalism and communism had in common. They are all part of Western Civilization and what we are witnessing now is the collapse of these ideals. China and many countries in East Asia have followed this path, have appropriated and are following their own path on what Western Civilization achieved, economically and politically (liberalism and communism), and it is confronting the same problems that the West confronted. But since in Asia, Africa, South America and the Caribbean, Central Asia and the Caucasus are the living seeds of non-modern ways of life (notice that I say non-modern and not pre-modern) that have always co-existed with modernity, the hope is that the decolonial will take over in all those places. In South America and the Caribbean there is, since the sixties a growing and powerful discourse on decolonization. And so it subsists in Africa and in Asia. Briefly, "progress and development" are no longer a desirable horizon of life because they are part of the rhetoric of modernity that carries with it coloniality, that is, expropriation, exploitation, pollutions and death.

Neo-liberalism has already become the dominant "structure of feeling" in most parts of the world! But, it is now in bankruptcy all over the place, in the financial crisis, the end-road to find solutions, the proliferations of unhappy people expressing it all over, organized communities in South America stopping the corporations from destroying the environment and poisoning the lands and the water with transgenic and cyanide in open pit mining. And secondly, let us not confuse neo-liberalism with market economy and the fetichization of commodities. Certainly, neo-liberalism contributed to that, but neo-liberalism wants a weakened state and a free invisible hand. China, Singapore, Japan are on the contrary, strong states regulating the economy. That is not neo-liberalism and that chasm is one aspect of dewesternization.

The questions of delinking shall not, on the other hand, be limited to the State and continue to hope that States will do what people want States to do. What we are seeing in the sphere of the States is dewesternization. And that is a form of delinking, delinking from Western scripts and from transnational institutions, like IMF and the World Bank, still controlled by the West but already under heavy scrutiny from the rest of the world ((http://www.wpfdc.org/index.php?opti on=com_content&view=article& amp;id=862: we-need-a-new-world-order -at-the-world-bank&catid=41:ec o nomics&Itemid=92&lang =en).

What is surprising in this respect is that the politicization of the civil society (the civil society was not politicized, it was civil). There is widespread agreement on the failure of the neoliberal doctrine and the Washington Consensus. So, then, neo-liberalism is no longer the dominant "structure of feeling." The "structure of feeling" is a growing rage from the politicization of the civil society. Rage and disenchantment is the consensus. They are of course, dewesternizers. They are neither decolonial nor even Marxists. So, what connects the world is capitalism, but not neo-liberalism. The politicized civil society is not denying capitalism; it is denying neo-liberalism. Delinking is first of all an epistemic question: without thinking otherwise is difficult to imagine global futures beyond Western structures of thoughts and structures of feelings (that is, epistemology, ontology and aiesthesis — sensing).

Now, in the same way that we cannot confuse economy with capitalism, we cannot confuse capitalism with neo-liberalism. China is capitalist, but I will not say for a second that it is neo-liberal. That is why Chinese Confucianism is being re-articulated. If you do not re-articulate Confucianism, or something that is in your history, you run the risk of entering into neo-liberalism or being convinced that you have to start with Machiavelli, Locke, Rousseau, etc. Chinese leaders and intellectuals need Confucius rather than Milton Friedman, which was the economist behind Reagan-Thatcher duo promoting neo-liberal ideals. Dewesternization is already a way of delinking, not from capitalism but from neo-liberal global design. And dewesternization is the politics of China, of Singapore, of Russia, of Brazil, and, in part at least India. This politico-economic delinking is one aspect of dewesternization.

On the other hand, Dewesternization or Islamization are being, had been, predicated in the sphere of the politico-religious. And this is another form of delinking that could take the form of dewesternization (like in Malaysia and Indonesia) or decoloniality (politico-religious project run by the political society independently from the State). This is also a way of delinking and clearly not following the globalization of Western values. That is Islamism taking charge of the economy. Sure, Indonesia and Chinese capitalism are no better that German or US capitalism, but certainly are not the same. It should be noted that polycentered capitalism is not better than monocentered capitalism. There is an important difference and we should pay attention to it. "Delinking" is a process, a huge and global process that is happening now at different levels and will continue during the twenty-first century, at the same time that forces preventing delinking will continue to operate: that force is the constant updating of re-westernization as the West "resist" losing the privileges that they enjoyed for such a long time. Re-westernization means to keep total control of the colonial matrix of power. Delinking are processes difficult to see because CNN and CCTV are hiding it with music and colors and the triumphal smile of their program anchors.

One should therefore not expect "delinking" to be something that happens at once, by decree or revolution, There are thousands of cases around the world (perfectly silenced by main stream television in the East and the West, Al Jazeera being always the exception), like what is going on now in Argentina: they call it a "pueblada" the getting together of the people (the pueblo) of the town to stop mega-mining and kick out the transnational corporations. Delinking is something that the political society and members of the political society, have to build constantly at different levels. We need a vision of the future, delinking is the first step, but we cannot have a blue print and force everyone to fit the model. We know what happens when that case is presented. "Pueblada" is a manifestation of the political society that carries its own leadership. And they are doing it, as exemplified by the Zapatistas in Mexico. That is another clear case of the growing political society.

What is at stake is no longer improving working conditions and providing jobs: that is the concern of the IMF and the States. The IMF and the capitalist States want people who live to work, while delinking means that we want a society where people work to live. What is at stake is life, not jobs to the benefit of those who take away and provide jobs. When open pit mining forms lakes of water with cyanide used to extract the metal from the stone, and the people are dying of cancer and leukemia, the problem is not to have a job but to have a life: the life of nature is the life of our bodies. That is the growing global political society.

Certainly, banks are big, corporations are transnational. The state works with the corporations and the bank and the media with all of them. It seems like a structure that will never collapse. But think that such a structure keeps happy probably one billion of seven billion of people in the planet. And the awareness that our lives are at risk because of the organized and legal delinquency ruling in the name of development, is growing. There is much more going on than the mainstream media knows or do not want to know. Depending whether you watch the news or read US or German information, or Chinese or Singaporean, you will hear a lot about rewesternization and dewesternization but not about decoloniality. This is being covered by what is now called "self-managed journalism." Rewesternization as used here is a process predominant in neocolonial societies that are hell-bent on saving capitalism, maintaining its leadership, promoting science and technology geared toward corporate knowledge for capitalist development and creating consumer subjects living to work to consume. This process is at variance with epistemological delinking.

Delinking means to delink from the magic of the media that keep us glued to what the States and the Corporations do, as if that was the entire world; and from the myth of the expert that takes away the capacity of people to think and have their own opinion about what the expert hides. It means to delink from education, it means learning to unlearn what have been taught to us in order to relearn. The reason is that the expert is a one-dimensional-man who at the same time is ignorant about the larger picture of his or her expertise. The global political society a fourth crucial actor, next to the politicization of the civil society, the traditional third actor that now is getting up on its feet due to the degree of aberration we find in the States and the Corporations. This map for delinking is based on the analytic of the colonial matrix of power and, therefore, is decolonial thinking in action.

Is capitalism the best way to go? First, if your goal is development then the best way to do it so far and fast is capitalism. The fundamental question is, shall development be the only vision and goal of human conviviality? The second point, when Chatterjee (1997) talks about "our modernity" and underlines that our modernity has to be built on one hundred years of British colonization and one hundred years before 1857 based on commerce in India, he is talking about the conditions that lead to "contesting modernities" and dewesternization. It is not clear whether decolonial projects will likely keep "modernity" as a goal, since in our view there is no modernity without coloniality.

So, while one may agree with Chatterjee in his emphasis on delinking from "Western modernity" one should not think that modernity can be pursued without coloniality. Therefore, Chatterjee's claim as formulated looks like a program for dewesternization. The third point is the position sustained by Wang Hui. In fact, it seems to me that he is very well describing China's effective dewesternization. The open question is whether there is a difference between the politic of the State and that of the New Left.

When one describes China's state politics as dewesternization one already engages in a decolonial analysis; that is, one is making the distinction between decolonial perspectives that are of my discourse, and dewesternization that is a concept through which East Asians make sense of their own practices and goals. Singaporean Kishore Mahbubani, Dean of the School of Public Policy Lee Kuan Yew elaborated the concept as precisely the politics of accepting development and capitalism but taking your destiny in your own hands. That is precisely what China and Singapore are doing. It seems to me then that Wang Hui's position coincides with that of Mahbubani. And that is showing the changing winds of the world order based on the three major trajectories, namely, rewesternization, dewesternization and decoloniality. This makes obsolete the distinction between Left and Right that emerged from the European enlightenment. Hence, Mahbubani and Hui's ideas coincide in the need to dewesternize, although they may differ in the way to do it; they coincide in the goals, while they may differ in the methods.

China is different to most of the ex-Third World countries for many reasons. One of them is its long, lasting and rich history which carries with it ways of thinking and doing. The ways that China embraced capitalism and market economy compatible with a strong State cannot be understood as reproducing Western capitalism and Western communism through Mao Zedong. There was and is something else that is neither Western (neo) liberalism nor Western communism outside of the West. Let us avoid falling into the easy interpretation and explain it by Confucianism. There is a specific way Chinese of today make sense of their past, their memories, their own ways of thinking, living and doing. It is the same way one can explain that deep experience Western civilization built grounded in Greece and Rome. Similarly, in Africa and the indigenous nations around the world, there is not a name that explains the persistence of their way of thinking and being.

Similar observations can be made through the Islamic world, from the Middle East through South East Asia: there is something there that is their own and which the Koran is obviously a crucial moment, but it is safe to think that is not all: there was already something built in communal formations that made the Koran needed and possible. So, in that sense, China is different from many Third World countries, but is very similar to many civilizations in the world that were disavowed and humiliated by the narratives of Western modernities that are coming to terms with a period of history that now is being overcome. Dewesternization and decoloniality are two of those wide ranging trajectories. And, interestingly enough, both dewesternization and decoloniality are projects that have much to do with overcoming the Western imperial humiliation, whether one carries the traces of the colonial or the imperial wounds.

Another question that could be asked: is it possible to think decolonially in China and to carry on decolonial projects in different walks of life? Certainly it is because decolonial thinking renders it irrelevant whether a people was colonized or not. For instance, China did not escape coloniality, and dewesternization and decoloniality are two different responses to coloniality. Dewesternization doesn't delink from capitalist economy, but delinks in all other spheres of the colonial matrix: who decides about what? This doesn't mean also that the one billion plus Chinese will endorse dewesternization: it means that dewesternization is a project and a Chinese response to coloniality whether or not 100% of Chinese will know or accept it. That is an important issue for everybody expecting that when a project is not Western, it shall "represent" all the people. A Western Democratic Party system doesn't mean that all the citizens of France, Germany or the US would agree with the politics of one party.

It means also that not all Europeans and US citizens would agree with the project of rewesternization led by the US and supported by the EU. It means that rewesternization is a Western project, whether it "represents" all citizens or not. So, then, since dewesternization and decoloniality are responses to delinking from the colonial matrix of power, decolonial projects could very well unfold in China. Not necessarily from the government, it is too much to expect at this point. But it should come, if it comes, from the political society. There is no need of public manifestation here. It is a question of beginning to think and act otherwise. Decoloniality is basically an epistemic project with political, economic and ethical implications.

Now let's go back to the situation described through Partha Chatterjee and Wang Hui. Let me say first that I am sympathetic with their views. From what I said before, you can see that I do not fully endorse them. What is important are the issues they are raising, even if you do not agree with the way they frame the issues they are raising. The dilemma "modernity of anti-modernity" is a complex issue but, basically, it is an example of the entanglement and the fact that the imperial force of modernity forces responses that cannot be detached from modernity.

Let us be very clear here. Delinking doesn't mean that you reject modernity and go to the mountain. It doesn't mean either that you oppose modernity following its logic. That is, that you contest the content but not the logic, that you contest the content but do not change the terms of the conversation. So, what Hui and Chatterjee are pointing out is happening in India, in China, in Latin America, in the Caribbean, in Central Asia, in the Middle East, and in Africa. Briefly, it is happening all over the world that had to respond to the ideals of modernity that Western actors and institutions encroached upon them. Some rejected, some embraced it and some embraced modernity but defended their own nationalist interests. None of this is delinking. All of these are examples of imperial/colonial entanglements. "Delinking" are projects whose very beginnings and foundations are the theorization of the very idea of "delinking." Delinking is what the decolonial option is proposing. It means that there is no way out if the terms of the conversations are not changed. Delinking is proceeding in two directions, sometimes complementary and sometimes confrontational: dewesternization and decoloniality.

Many people may consider delinking as mere shop talk and ask: how can we delink if we are in the colonial matrix of power? Advocacy—if you really want a minority student to do well, you need faculty who can produce decolonial knowledge; show the student's options how to delink, that is, going to the university to be a doctor or lawyer is one option, but there are other options in education; decoloniality is not a field of study, but it permeates all the disciplines where one can make students aware of options; the ultimate decision is not epistemic or political but it is ethical because what the student chooses, whichever option he chooses, he is responsible for his option. Ethics is about responsibility in whatever one chooses to do, all one's acts.

One has to be aware of the decisions one makes and the consequences. A decolonial education, therefore, is making students aware that they are living among options. That is, you cannot force a student to take an option, but you can say that you have to be aware and responsible for that option. We are conditioned by modernity not to question our actions—we don't question the messages of accumulation. What is hidden is how we arrived at this state of accumulation. You start with your own personal ethics. Create a space whereby we question each other's frameworks of what is right and wrong—begin to dialogue. If the ethics is controlled by hegemony, how is a student to see options? The colonial education limits this, but a decolonial education has to provide how communication functions, how we have been conditioned to accumulate, talking to them about their own life and what they know to show how they have been conditioned; a decolonial education needs questions; it is not about information but it is about being able to understand the world in which they are living unconsciously. We don't have to live unconsciously. The teacher opted to bring this to the classroom and now students have to think about options, but they are not always rational choices.

Rational argumentation for why you chose an irrational option locates your ethical decision. In other words, advocating for others and making ethical choices may seem irrational but that is a good sign that you are delinking from the age old systems of control that dehumanize our global society AND that system that is now dressed in a modern garb. What is justice and how does decoloniality bring forth justice? Mignolo first suggests that there be a shift in the meaning of justice to "economic justice." Considerations of economic justice compel us to think about what it means to live within the law. Civilians are living within the law, but the state and corporations are not. What kind of justice can we talk about when the people in the army and with the money are living beyond the law? So what is a decolonial sense of justice? If the rhetoric of modernity is the defense and rationalization of the use of the matrix, and justice, human rights and democracy are being used to preserve acting beyond the law, then justice will be in the delinking —to thoughtfully engage the global society to practice inclusivity, but I think it is fundamentally to show options.

Alternatives to Western Democracy

The prevailing system of competitive Western democracy is proving itself unjust and unsustainable in an age of increasing global interdependence. Yet this system is not repairable because its problems lie in its deepest internal assumptions. The corrupting influence of money, the exclusion of diverse perspectives, the inability to solve complex issues, the short-term planning horizons, the lack of cross-boundary coordination, the rise of incivility and mean-spiritedness, the aggravation of social divisions, the cultivation of public cynicism and disaffection, and the generally corrosive effect on the human spirit—these are the culmination of this system, the sour fruit inherent in its seeds.

"How long will humanity persist in its waywardness?" asks Bahá'u'lláh, "How long will injustice continue? How long is chaos and confusion to reign amongst men? How long will discord agitate the face of society? The winds of despair are, alas, blowing from every direction, and the strife that divideth and afflicteth the human race is daily increasing." (Bahá'u'lláh, 2005, Op.Cit., p. 216). Competitive democracy has now become a costly anachronism. How long will the populations who bear these costs continue to live in a state of denial? It is time to move on. History is just beginning.

Alternatives to Western democracy fall into four main categories: the systematic modification of democracy to remove its ethical defects; the simple overthrow of democratic governments; a non-democratic political systems, and innovation in the system of states outside the Westphalian model, with redistribution of territory and populations. But first it is useful to reconsider what they would replace: the relevant characteristics of the existing democracies. The older Western definitions of democracy referred to historical origins, or simply to 'the rule of the people.' They were followed by the polyarchy definitions, and later by rights-and-procedures checklists. None of these give a complete picture of modern democracy. A new definition would have to start at the global level, the level of world order, not the capitalist world order. By now it is clear that democracy is not a one-country regime, not a characteristic of single states. Just as the ideology of the nation state implies a planet of nations, democracy implies a planet of democracies as well.

A democratic world order starts from the premise that only certain groups are a legitimate 'demos.' At any one time, therefore, there is a fixed number of legitimate regimes, each corresponding to a democratic state. For democrats, no other regime is legitimate. They claim that these non-democratic regimes may be converted (by military force or external pressure) into democracies. When this process is complete, and the fixed number of legitimate democratic states has been reached, no further change in the order of states would be legitimate. This corresponds to the claim made by nationalists, that only a world order of nation states is legitimate. This should be qualified by the recent trends in democratic interventionism. Although the number of cases is small so far (Bosnia, Kosovo, Timor), the democratizing protectorates are also considered part of 'global democracy.' A world order consisting of (mainly Western) full democracies, and their democratizing protectorates, cannot simply be accepted as 'global democracy.'

However, with or without protectorates, the pan-democratic world would have a fixed number of regimes, corresponding to a fixed number of states. In a world where democrats consider each state to correspond to a legitimate demos, democracy is an implicit prohibition of new state formation. Once again, the prohibition of secession appears to be a defining characteristic of democracy, far more than any of the characteristics listed in the polyarchy definitions.

There is also no place in democracy for any 'trans-demos' or 'extra-demos' political decision. Democracies can work together, but in the last instance each democratic state has its own democratic elections. In other words, no group can constitute a political unit comprising members of more than one demos. They can form associations, but not a regime or a government: that would require the formation of a new state. Since a cross-demos grouping is (by definition) not itself a demos, democrats would not allow it to form a state anyway. The emergence of a single global democracy would not help a cross-demos group since they would simply become an internal minority in a global demos.

The alternatives to democracy are alternatives to this emergent world order of stable democracies, a world in which there is literally no place for social and political innovation. From this perspective, it is possible to reformulate the definition of democracy. The most

206

helpful literature for this new definition was not the existing definitions, but a description of the eurosceptic No-Demos thesis. A democracy should therefore be a political regime in which political power is exercised by controlling the membership of a demos, a group within which political decisions are taken, in practice by a nation state. Control of territory and migration are preconditions for democracy.

A democracy claims political legitimacy from both the claimed legitimacy of the demos, and the claimed legitimacy of the decision-making procedures. Often, the procedures are claimed to legitimize the demos, and the demos is claimed to legitimize the procedures. A democratic world order is a world order with a fixed number of decision-making units (demos, plural demoi), and in which those units are considered legitimate, and those units only. In turn this world order is considered legitimate, and it should be the only legitimate basis for state formation. This definition implies that the most comprehensive alternatives to democracy can only be found at the level of the world order, and in state formation processes. Nevertheless there are also 'internal' alternatives to Western imposed democracy.

A Bahá'í Alternative to Western Political Competition

Winston Churchill once stated to the British House of Commons, 11 November 1947, that "democracy is the worst form of government—except for all the other forms that have been tried." More accurately, this statement describes competitive democracy because this is the only form of democracy that has been tried, to date, as a model of state governance. In keeping with Churchill's sentiment, apologists defend the prevailing system with the argument that it is the most rational alternative to political tyranny or anarchy. The problems inherent in the system of political competition are simply accepted as "necessary evils." All systems of government are imperfect, the argument goes, and competitive democracy is the best we can do.

This argument is premised, however, on the faulty assumption that processes of social innovation have come to an end. According to this "end of history" thesis, the social experiments that have characterized so much of human history have finally played themselves out and Western liberal models have emerged as the only viable models of social organization (Fukuyama, 1993). Yet this is an entirely unsupportable thesis. Indeed, it would be more plausible to say that the history of humankind as a single interdependent species, inhabiting a common homeland, is just beginning. Under conditions of increasing global interdependence, brought on by our reproductive and technological success as a species, we have barely begun to experiment with just and sustainable models of social organization.

Processes of social innovation have clearly not come to end. The example of the international Bahá'í community suffices to illustrate this point. The Bahá'í community is a vast social laboratory within which a new model of social organization is emerging. With a current membership of around six million people, drawn from over 2000 ethnic backgrounds and residing in every nation on the planet, the community is a microcosm of the entire human race. This diverse community has constructed a unique system of democratically-elected assemblies that govern Bahá'í (1998) affairs internationally, nationally, and locally in over 15,000 communities throughout the planet. Significantly, in many parts of the world, the first exercises in democratic activity have occurred within these Bahá'í communities.

The Bahá'í electoral system is entirely non-partisan and non-competitive. In brief, all adult community members are eligible for election and every member has the reciprocal duty to serve if elected. At the same time, nominations, campaigning, and all forms of solicitation are prohibited. Voters are guided only by their own consciences as they exercise real freedom of choice in voting for those they believe best embody the qualities of recognized ability, mature experience, and selfless service to others. Through a plurality count, the nine individuals that receive the most votes are called to serve as members of the governing assembly. For further details regarding Bahá'í electoral principles and practices, refer to the Universal House of Justice, ed., *Bahá'í Elections: A Compilation* (London: Bahá'í Publishing Trust, 1990).

Because no one seeks election, elections are not a pathway to power and privilege. On the contrary, elections are a call to service and the elected sacrifice their time and energy, and often their career aspirations, at the bidding of the community. As a matter of principle, and also because there is no incentive, no one calls attention to themselves or solicits votes in any way. In fact, Bahá'ís interpret solicitation of votes as an indicator of egoism and a lack of fitness to serve.

All decision-making within these assemblies is, in turn, guided by consultative principles that enable decision-making to be a unifying rather than a divisive process. These principles include striving to enter the process with no pre-conceived positions or platforms; regarding diversity as an asset and soliciting the perspectives, concerns, and expertise of others; striving to transcend the limitations of one's own ego and perspective; striving to express oneself with care and moderation; striving to raise the context of decision-making to the level of principle; and striving for consensus but settling for a majority when necessary. For details regarding Bahá'í consultative principles and practices, refer to the Universal House of Justice, ed., Consultation: A Compilation (Wilmette, IL: Bahá'í Publishing Trust, 1980).

Unlike competitive systems in which decision-makers must continually negotiate the demands of constituents, campaign contributors, lobbyists, and activists, the Bahá'í system is shielded from external lobbying and other pressures to influence decisions. This is accomplished in two ways. First, as discussed above, those who are elected to assemblies do not seek election and they have no interest in re-election. Elected members are not political entrepreneurs seeking to build or retain political capital and campaign financing opportunities do not exist because there are no campaigns.

Second, elected members decide matters through the application of principle, according to the promptings of their own consciences (one of the primary qualities for which they were elected), and not according to the dictates or pressures of competing interest groups. In this regard, elected members are expected to weigh all of their decisions in a principled manner, even if this means forgoing immediate local or short-term benefits out of consideration for the welfare of distant peoples or future generations. The instructive discussions of these themes are in the Bahá'í International Community, United Nations, *Prosperity—an Oral Statement Presented to the Plenary of the United Nations World Summit on Social Development* (Copenhagen, Denmark: 1995 as well as the BIC UN, *Statement on Nature* (New York: 1988).

In all of these ways, the Bahá'í electoral system embodies neither a contest nor the pursuit of power. Since no one seeks election, there is no concept of "winning." At the same time, the electoral process remains eminently democratic. This model has been used for more than three-quarters of a century within the Bahá'í community, which, as it grows in capacity and prominence, is increasingly attracting the attention of outside observers. For some insightful discussions on this topic I would like to refer our readers to the United Nations Institute for Namibia, *Comparative Electoral Systems & Political Consequences: Options for Namibia*, Namibia Studies Series No 14, ed. N. K. Duggal (Lusaka, Zambia: United Nations, 1989), pp. 6–7.

Beyond Western Hegemony of Political Competition

As the example of the Bahá'í community illustrates, processes of social innovation have clearly not come to an end. Given the problems inherent in partisan systems, along with their rising social and ecological costs, why are democratic populations not actively searching for alternatives to political competition? To answer this question, some historical context is helpful. Current forms of competitive democracy arose from the thinking of emerging political classes at the dawn of the industrial revolution. These emerging political classes were trying to wrestle absolute power away from the aristocracy. Competitive democracy advanced the interests of these classes because it ended absolute rule while, at the same time, it continued to privilege the exercise of wealth and power. This opened the arena of governance to merchants and lesser landowners and other people of means, while limiting the influence of the under-classes.

Although the transition to competitive democracy was marked by violent revolution and the threat of revolution in many countries, the force of ideas played a powerful role in fomenting these transitions, and an even more powerful role in buttressing and sustaining systems of political competition once they were established. This was possible because the same political classes that benefited most from the contest model were increasingly occupying positions of cultural leadership—as statesmen, writers, philosophers, educators, and so forth—through which, either consciously or unconsciously, they were able to cultivate and sustain assumptions regarding human nature and social organization that underlie the contest model.

The Italian theorist Antonio Gramsci described this form of cultural influence with remarkable insight in the first half of the twentieth century (Gramsci, 1971). His concept of *hegemony* has since entered the lexicon of cultural theorists around the world and it provides a useful framework for understanding the emergence and perpetuation of these contest models. In brief, Gramsci borrowed the term *hegemony*, which traditionally referred to the geo-political dominance of some states over others, and he reworked it to refer to the cultural dominance of some social classes over others. Gramsci pointed out that geo-political hegemony, which is achieved and maintained largely by force, is an obvious focus of resistance by oppressed populations and is therefore relatively difficult to maintain over time. Cultural hegemony, on the other hand, is achieved and maintained through the cultivation of "common sense" belief systems which are less visible and which therefore generate less resistance. In other words, if privileged social groups can naturalize the existing social order in the minds of subordinate groups, the latter will unconsciously consent to their own subordination.

An example of this can be seen in the traditional exclusion of women from many arenas of public life. This exclusion was reinforced by the cultivation of "common sense" notions regarding the "appropriate" role of women in society. Of course, not all women accepted these notions and many struggled against them. Yet, remarkably, many women did accept these notions, as demonstrated by women who organized in opposition to women's suffrage movements on the "common sense" conviction (among others) that the moral purity of women would be compromised by their entrance into public life and that the entire social fabric would thereby be weakened (Adams, 1995).

The theory of cultural hegemony is also useful in explaining the widespread consent given to prevailing systems of competitive democracy. Consider again the assumptions that this system rests upon: that human nature is essentially selfish and competitive; that different people develop conflicting interests; and that the best way to organize democratic governance is through a process of interest-group competition. These cultivated "common sense" assumptions have become part of the popular worldview—even though they do not serve the interests of most people. These assumptions are cultivated in civics classes and political science courses within our educational systems; they are cultivated in our mass media systems; and they are cultivated through institutionalized forms of competitive behavior that structure activity in our political, legal, and economic systems. All of these systems, however, are cultural constructs that embody the values, interests, and beliefs of the privileged political classes who constructed them.

This is not to suggest a conscious conspiracy on the part of those who benefit from the existing social order. This order often appears natural and inevitable to those who benefit from it because people tend to have an unconscious affinity for ideas that promote their own interests (Weber, 1946, pp. 62-63; Clement, 1975, pp. 92 and 283–284). When these people also happen to be from educated and affluent social groups who control the means of cultural production (i.e., education, media, and other social institutions), it is quite natural that they end up cultivating, within the wider population, beliefs for which they themselves have a natural and unconscious affinity. Indeed, members of these influential social groups may be acting out of the most sincere motives while contributing to this process of cultivation, because they may have come to believe that the existing social order benefits everyone in the same way it benefits themselves. The result, whether intentional or not, is a powerful form of cultural hegemony.

How then does a population transcend the constraints of its culturally-structured consciousness? Furthermore, how can this occur in a manner that does not result in further conflict—which would only reinforce the assumptions about human nature and social order that underlie and buttress the prevailing system of political competition? The metaphor of a game can be helpful to answer these questions. Cultural institutions—like our system of competitive democracy—can be understood as "games" that operate according to specific sets of "rules" (Wittgenstein, 1974; Cohen,1981). The rules of competitive democracy ensure not only that there will be winners and losers, but that the most powerful players are most likely to win. When less powerful players agree to join in this game they are consenting to play by rules that tend to promote their own defeat. Adversarial strategies of social change are consistent with these competitive rules. They simultaneously legitimize the old game while they ensure that the most powerful players continue to prevail within it (Karlberg,2004, pp. 329–351).

There is, however, another strategy. That strategy is to withdraw time and energy from the old game in order to construct a new one. The only thing perpetuating the old game is the fact that the majority of people consent to the rules. If an alternative game becomes more attractive (i.e., it demonstrates increased social justice and environmental sustainability), then it will begin to draw increasing numbers of people to it (i.e., the majority of people whose interests and values are not well served by the old game). If enough people stop playing by the old rules and start playing by new ones, the old game will come to an end not through protest and conflict but through attrition.

This strategy is one of *construction*, *attraction*, and *attrition*. It is entirely non adversarial and it reconciles the means of social change with the ends of a peaceful, just, and sustainable social order. Social change does not require defeating oppressors or attacking those who profit most from the old rules. Rather, it requires that we recognize the hegemonic nature of the old game, withdraw our time and energy from it, and invest that time and energy in the construction of a new one.

Increasing numbers of people are beginning to intuitively recognize this. Nonpartisan electoral and decision-making models are beginning to emerge in many sectors, through constructive experiments with social change. Most of these experiments are still below the radar of many political observers because non-governmental organizations, rather than states, have taken the lead in this regard. Yet these emerging models constitute important socio-political experiments.

Again, the example of the international Bahá'í community is instructive. Bahá'ís believe that partisan models of governance have become anachronistic and problematic in an age of increasing global interdependence. Yet Bahá'ís do not protest or attack existing partisan systems. On the contrary, Bahá'ís express loyalty and obedience to whatever governmental systems they live within and they may exercise their civic responsibilities to vote in those societies that afford the opportunity to do so. At the same time, Bahá'ís avoid active participation in partisan politics in order to focus their energy instead on the construction of an alternative system of governance which they offer as a model for others to study. Experiences such as these provide naturally occurring experiments that we would do well to monitor and learn from—if not participate in.

Rationale for the Decolonial/Delinking Theory

The "repressed" are returning and they do not need the "theory of some schools." Decolonial theories are not fighting for the return of the repressed and marginalized but are the ones returning in spite of who is fighting for their return. Notice that postmodern and poststructuralists were advanced mainly by white Euro/American intellectuals. In that sense, one should not be surprised that Chinese intellectuals fell into that illusion. It happened in other parts of the world too. And it was the last moment in history in which the Western right (neoliberalism) and the Western left (Marxism and its postmodern and poststructuralist versions), were producing the illusion that Eurocentered critiques of Europe and Eurocentrism was valid for the non-European world. Decolonial

214

thinkers did not swallow that pill. That is why Frantz Fanon, to name the better known, and for Latin Americans, Jose Carlos Mariategui, were the guiding lights. Both, in different ways, spell out the connections between racism, coloniality and capitalism. They did not use the word coloniality but colonialism. However, it was clear that they did not have yet a word to name what they were talking about.

In that regard, decoloniality is the thought of the repressed or of the barbarians themselves, and not about the barbarians and the repressed, and not of some avant guard Euro-US intellectual or anthropologist, journalist or Hollywood actor, who is "saving the oppressed." The barbarians and repressed are saving themselves: dewesternization and decoloniality are the ways they are doing it At that time, it was supposed that Third World intellectuals were not supposed to theorize by themselves: they were barbarians. That is why Chinese as well as other non-European intellectuals needed European theories to think. It was the same with the economy. Underdeveloped countries thought that the IMF and development theories of the West would save their life. In the same way, Third World progressive intellectuals were supposed (and they accepted to be epistemically and ontologically self-colonized) to comment and apply theories coming from the First world. Repressed and barbarians are scalar terms, not everyone repressed is in chains and not every barbarian is walking naked covered with animal furs.

Fanon was not just writing "about the wretched of the earth", he was himself one of the "wretched," and he was writing *as a wretched not just about the wretched*. His was theorizing as wretched, his was barbarian theorizing, that is why he received scant attention in the period of "high" postmodern and poststructuralist theories. His writing *was already the unmistakable sign of the return of the repressed*. We are trying to follow suit. But, we are not trying to theorize the subaltern, to save the repressed, but to fight the repressive logic of coloniality of which we are all victims, including the one who assumes himself to be beyond the colonial matrix and leading the world toward peace and prosperity. So it is necessary to accept that being a scholar and an intellectual is not being out of the "epistemically wretched" unless one thinks that once one reached a certain institutional level he is no longer target of the wide range of racial prejudice and you also think that the damnés shall always be where they are, until postmodern and poststructuralist intellectuals come to save them. That is also the discourse of Christianity, of liberalism and of Marxism — the Salvationist rhetoric of modernity, from the right, the left and the center.

If you reduce the wretched to a social class and to an extreme level of poverty, you will not understand that coloniality, or of what Fanon is talking about. Fanon offers us both an analytic of coloniality as a grammar of decoloniality. He focused on racial coloniality of knowledge and of being, in racial discrimination at all levels of social formation and at all levels of the social ladder. He, as a Black Caribbean, makes me understand that I am not black because I have a black skin and blue eyes, and I did not become "black" for being at a university as a professor. In the US, I am "African" in the official classification (passport, state forms) a "Black" in the civil society where "Black" has been rejected, as it is a State classification. "African" doesn't have much to do with Africa to which "African" refers. There are Africans in America who are not becoming "black" either.

One needs to think and conceptualize otherwise, to build decolonial horizons of life. That means, horizons of life that delink from coloniality, from the colonial matrix. I believe that many gays, lesbians, women of color who are scholars and intellectuals and that are fighting for their dignity are writing as wretched, as "repressed." So we have to stop thinking that the wretched and the repressed are "those" over there, the "others;" (gay, lesbian, women and men of color — black, yellow, brown); people from the Third World, underdeveloped and emerging countries; "yellow" people like East Asian according to Linnaeus and Kant. But it is precisely the situation one may find oneself in that demands and brings forward the ethics of scholarship and the politics of knowledge. How can one talk about "them and the other" if one knows and feels that one is seen as "them and the other." That is what Fanon defined as "sociogenetic principle." In the modern/colonial world we are all classified, but not all of us are in a position to enact institutional classifications. Classifications are not created by the wretched and the barbarians. Classifications are created by He who controls knowledge.

This is the bottom line: there is a circle in the sphere of the social where you find the States, the corporations, the universities and higher education as well as professional schools and the main stream media. And then there is another circle where you find the political society, the politicized civil society, the self-managing media, faculty in universities and professional schools that assume themselves as members of the politicized civil society and/or political society and not members of the first circle. Both circles are not separated, they are entangled and there are a lot of movements not only in the space where the circle intersects but also up and down left and right of the circles. The kind of dialogue we are entertaining here and much of the works of scholars concerned with these issues, belong to the second circle. We are not going to be invited to Davos, we are not going to be invited to the Summit on Climate Control. If we want to go to those places, we have to go by ourselves and be part of the "protesters." So, rewesternization and dewesternization is a struggle in the same circle, decoloniality in the second circle. Of course there are some points of encounters between dewesternization and decoloniality in that space where the two circles intersect but, in the long run, there is no possibility at this point of dewesternization and decoloniality merging in the same way that corporations merge. Once again, dewesternization and decoloniality, that forced rewesternization, are changing the ways in which we conceive ourselves, the world, and ourselves in the world order.

In sum, decolonial thinking always starts by calling into question existing structures and asking how they came to be. So if you ask how literary studies can benefit, it is not by taking decoloniality as a "new method" to analyze literary texts (a trap that postcolonial studies fell into), but by calling into question the very "raison d'être" of literary studies. Since when did literary studies acquire the status of a literary formation? Where did that happen, in Zimbabwe, in Bolivia, in China, in Uzbekistan or in Western Europe? In Western Europe, is the trivia answer. Now, why in Europe and not in Zimbabwe or Bolivia? And when? So there you have a set of questions for a couple of dissertations. And this is the first tip as to why decolonial thinking could be enormously be helpful in literary studies: to start by decolonizing them.

Secondly, and in relation to the previous question, the concept of "literature" in the sense it is understood today (fiction, aesthetics) is an invention of the eighteenth century. In the Middle Ages "literature" meant everything written in Latin alphabetic writing. I mean, Latin alphabet. So, "literature" derives from "letter." In the Middle Ages and through the Renaissance, "Poetry" and "Poetics" were the terms to refer to doing (poiesis) and analyzing a piece according to the rules (poetics). *Lessing's treatise Laocoon* (1767) is an essay on poetry and painting. "Literature" is not in sight. Briefly "literature," that in the sense of fiction, system of genre, aesthetics qualities, etc., doesn't exist before the end of eighteenth century neither in any part of the world nor in Europe itself. When "literature" emerges, contemporary of the imperial leadership of England and France, it expands all over the globe. And now we talk about "literature" as if it were a universal practice. This is another example where decolonial thinking could be useful: to decolonize the concept of literature and literary studies.

Third, and this is the most important, once literature reached colonized areas and became "written genres" local narrators and writers appropriated it and began to narrate infusing in their narratives the legacies of oral narratives, beliefs, non-European languages, etc. You can see this in any Chinese, African, and Latin America novel of the twentieth century on. At the same time, literary criticism and theory emerging from the experience, sensibilities and interests of ex-colonies or countries that were never colonized but that did not escape coloniality (like the case of China), began also to theorize decolonially. Traces can be found in the general decolonial thoughts of Présence Africaine, in Paris, since 1948. But most recently, the example of Ngugi wa Thiong'o's *Decolonizing the Mind: The Politics of Language in African Literature* (1986) is a case in point. Today, there are legions of articles, books, seminars, on decolonizing literary studies and Literature.

Fourth, there is recent unfolding of "decolonial aesthetics" that touches on all the arts as well as literature (http://www

.criticallegalthinking.com/?p=4455). "Decolonial aesthetics" began by pointing out that "aesthesis" is a Greek word meaning "sensing, affects, sensibilities." Once again, in the eighteenth century, and in Germany mainly, the concept of "aesthetic" mutates and means sensing and sensibilities but related to "taste." In that context, you have Kant's Observations on the Beautiful and the Sublime (1767) that remains one of the canonical texts in aesthetic as a branch of philosophy. Now, interestingly enough, even if aesthesis is a Greek concept, Aristotle did not pay too much attention to it in his Poetics. The key terms are poiesis, mimesis and catharsis. So that when in the eighteenth century aesthetics codified aiesthesis and restrict it to "taste" what aesthetics did was to colonize aiesthesis in such a way that aesthetics philosophy become also the regulator of good and bad taste and to decide what is literature and what is not, what is art and what is not. The rest of the world began to be subjected to the Western criteria of aesthetics. "Literature" was part of that movement. Last but not least, literature itself is a powerful medium of decolonial thinking and for decolonizing aesthetics. While literature, as we know, had a significant role in "colonizing the mind" it is also invaluable to "decolonize the mind" (Ngugi wa Thiongo, 1986).

The metaphor 'colonization of the mind', as I understand it, highlights the following characteristics of the phenomenon under scrutiny here: (a) the intervention of an external source – the 'colonizer' – in the mental sphere of a subject or group of subjects – the 'colonized'; (b) this intervention affects central aspects of the mind's structure, mode of operation, and contents; (c) its effects are long-lasting and not easily removable; (d) there is a marked asymmetry of power between the parties involved; (e) the parties can be aware or unaware of their role of colonizer or colonized; and (f) both can participate in the process voluntarily or involuntarily.

These characteristics are shared by a variety of processes of mind colonization, regardless of whether they occur in socio-political situations that are literally categorized as 'colonial'. Therefore, 'colonization of the mind' may take place through the transmission of mental habits and contents by means of social systems other than the colonial structure. For example, via the family, traditions, cultural practices, religion, science, language, fashion, ideology, political regimentation, the media, education, etc. These are pillars of the coloniality of power and must be decolonized to prepare freed minds of the repressed to carve out democratic systems responsive to their environments-not democratic import substitution.

Summary and Conclusion

The United Nations can take credit for having been the mid-wife of decolonization during the period 1945 to 1989. It was the greatest achievement of the United Nations during the era of the Cold War, which roughly coincided chronologically. Whether the Cold War between the United States and its allies, the West, the Capitalists, or the First World, versus the Soviet Union and its satellites, the East, the Communists, or the Second World, contributed to the end of Western Imperialism remains speculative. Certainly the Soviet Union found it expedient at times to act as champion of the colonial peoples. And the United States, remembering its own history as a British colony and struggle for independence, also championed decolonization in principle. In this pursuit the United States had mixed motives: it did so out of idealistic conviction; to clear the way for American influence in the former colonial territories of erstwhile trade rivals; and to prevent the Soviet Union from scoring points and emerging as the champion of the downtrodden. American support for anti-colonial movements was always hedged by its concern to safeguard private foreign investment in emerging countries and its concern about "communism" in developing countries. Too radical a movement, too strong an emphasis on socialism and land redistribution, and too close a tie to the Soviet Union brought with it American opposition.

The main reasons for the ending of five hundred years of European colonial exploration, exploitation, and domination are to be found in the rise of nationalism in colonial countries, the growth of democracy, and the weakening of the European metropolitan powers as a result of World Wars I and II. The United Kingdom of

Great Britain and Northern Ireland, the French Republic, the United Provinces of the Netherlands, the Kingdom of Belgium, Spain in the aftermath of the dictatorship of Generalissimo Franco, and Portugal after Salazar lacked the military power and political will to hang on to their colonial empires. One by one, almost in reverse order of their establishment, the Western European Powers surrendered their colonies. But, their dominant ideology, institutions and modes of knowledge about governance endured. To be sure, there were still contradictions among imperialist nations, but these were non-antagonistic and could be resolved without war. No longer would Western Europe devour itself in barbaric conflicts over colonial possessions; now, they would merge together and plunder the third world as one.

As the last standing capitalist superpower, the United States was charged with redesigning the imperial landscape after WWII. The former colonial empires of Western Europe were in shambles and no longer had the ability to manage their colonies. The United States adopted a comprehensive aid program to help rebuild Europe and Japan, investing some of its capital surplus into the devastated economies of the capitalist world. The Marshall Plan, as it was called, was no altruistic gesture stemming from America's noble spirit, but rather a way for American capital and products to penetrate European markets. In the end, the Marshall Plan pumped $13 billion into the reconstruction of Europe, reviving capitalism on a world scale.

The recovery of capitalism in fact began at the onset of WWII in the United States, with the war effort stimulating production on a massive scale. The New Deal government of Franklin D. Roosevelt also began implementing Keynesian economic policies, which would come to characterize the post-war capitalist economy. Keynesianism argued that capitalism, due to its inherent tendency towards underconsumption, required government intervention in the economy to stimulate aggregate consumption through government spending and progressive taxation. Similar measures were adopted in capitalist Europe after the war, resuscitating the economy and creating welfare states that limited the worse social consequences of capitalism, such as poverty, unemployment, and economic insecurity.

Along with the Marshall Plan, the U.S. pressured Britain and France to dismantle their colonial empires so that the whole third world could be opened up to American capital. Although the decolonized countries were seemingly independent, U.S. policy makers believed that these countries' only purpose was to "provide raw materials, investment opportunities, markets and cheap labor" to "complement the industrial countries of the West" (Chomsky, 1992). Thus, the primary threat to the U.S.-led order were "'nationalist regimes" that dared to use their national resources to attain the "immediate improvement of the low living standard of the masses'"(Chomsky, "On Foreign Policy). The so-called "Cold War," then, was conceived to be a war for U.S. control over the third world.

Formal colonies were no longer necessary to ensure the continuous transfer of wealth from the periphery to the metropolis and that is why the United States pushed for the abolition of colonialism. As one scholar of imperialism noted, "colonialism, considered as the direct application of military and political force, was essential to reshape the social and economic institutions of many of the dependent countries to the needs of the metropolitan centers. Once this reshaping had been accomplished economic forces – the international price, marketing, and financial systems – were by themselves sufficient to perpetuate and indeed intensify the relationship of dominance and exploitation between mother country and colony" (Magdoff, 139). Thus neo-colonialism was just as effective as colonialism.

The Cold War is often misinterpreted as a global conflict between the United States and the Soviet Union, the two contending world powers, with the U.S. working to contain Soviet ambitions of world domination. However, as declassified U.S. policy documents make clear, the primary threat posed by the Soviet Union was its willingness to supply military and economic support to third world regimes that were targets of U.S. aggression and subversion. The Soviet Union thus served to deter and restrain U.S. actions in the third world, which was unacceptable to U.S.

imperial ambitions. Further, the Soviet system with its "autarkic command economy interfered with U.S. plans to construct a global system based on (relatively) free trade and investment, which, under the conditions of mid-century, was expected to be dominated by U.S. corporations and highly beneficial to their interests, as indeed it was" (Chomsky, 1992). To be sure, the Soviet Union betrayed the cause of socialism after the death of Stalin, becoming a social imperialist power in its own right. However, its imperial aims were limited to the region allotted to it under the Malta agreements and the threat it posed to the U.S. was its willingness to support nationalist third world regimes resistant to U.S. imperial demands.

Throughout the Cold War, the military-industrial-complex became a major part of the U.S. economy, and thus a catalyst for sustained growth, albeit sluggish starting in the 1970's. For the Soviet Union, however, the "arms race" had the opposite effect of bleeding the Soviet economy and intensifying its internal contradictions until it imploded in 1989. With the collapse of the Soviet Union the Cold War came to an end, and with it, according to some, so did history. The triumph of the United States and Western Europe over the Soviet system proved to most people the superiority of free markets and capitalism. Free market euphoria swept the globe, giving birth to the new world order of neo-liberal capitalism.

Neo-liberalism, in stark contrast to Keynesianism, argued that economic growth required an end to government intervention in the economy (except in the military and prison sectors). Now the "invisible hand" of the market should rein unhindered, naturally allocating economic resources fairly and efficiently, creating a healthy equilibrium between supply and demand. Thus the era of Keynesianism and welfare capitalism came to an abrupt end, once again transforming the imperialist landscape.

The shift to neo-liberalism in the metropolis did not end neo-colonialism in the third world however. In fact, the neo-liberal onslaught began in the third world much earlier than it began in the developed world, starting with the U.S.-instigated coup in Chile in 1973. The third world was always encouraged to adopt trade liberalization and free market policies in order to facilitate the transfer of wealth from the third world to the U.S. and Europe. The shift to neo-liberalism in the metropolis only changed how neo-colonialism was enforced on the third world. Now international institutions, representing the collective economic will of the imperialist powers, emerged to impose neo-colonial policies on third world countries. The World Bank and International Monetary Fund gave third world countries "development loans" on the condition that they adopted "structural adjustment programs" designed to open their economies to western markets. Of course these policies did not lead to development, but only more intense underdevelopment for third world nations.

The neo-liberal empire of today is not the empire of one imperialist nation, but the empire of transnational corporations, based in the Triad, and enforced through U.S. and NATO military force. Neo-liberalism will not lead to the liberation or development of third world nations, but only their further underdevelopment and exploitation, as recent events in Iraq, Afghanistan and, most shamefully, Libya have proven. The empire of today is the most destructive and dangerous empire that has ever confronted the human race. In the name of freedom, democracy, and economic prosperity, it is pillaging the third world at an unprecedented rate, leading to devastating wars of terror and occupation. The failures of capitalism and its liberal democracy should be clear to everyone not on its payroll, and the choice facing humanity today should be even more clear: Socialism or barbarism.

The New World Democratic Order Questioned

New World Order as a concept was popular in a concrete historical momentum – precisely that when the Cold War ended (late 80's, Gorbatchev era) and the global cooperation between the USA and Soviet Union was considered near and very probable. The basis of NWO was presumably realization of the convergence theory predicting the synthesis of Soviet socialist and Western capitalist political forms and near cooperation of the Soviet Union and USA in the case of regional issues – for example first Gulf War in the beginning of 1991. Hence, as the Soviet Union split soon after, this project of NWO was naturally set aside and forgotten. After 1991 the other World Order was considered as something being created under our eyes – Unipolar World with open global hegemony of USA. It is described well in Fukuyama's political utopia "End of history".

This World Order ignored any other poles of power except the USA and its allies (first of all Europe and Japan) and was thought as universalization of free market economy, political democracy and human rights ideology as global pattern accepted by all countries in the world.

The skeptics thought that it was rather an illusion and the differences between the countries and people would reappear in other forms (for example, in the famous clash of civilizations of S. Huntington or ethnic or religious conflicts). Some experts regarded unipolarity not as the properly speaking World Order but as the unipolar momentum. In any case, what is questioned in all these projects is National Statehood. The Westphalian system did not correspond any more to the present global balance of powers. New actors of transnational or subnational scale affirm their growing importance and that was clear that the World was in need of new paradigm of International Relations.

So our actual contemporary world cannot be regarded as properly realized NWO. There is no definitive World Order of any kind at present. There is a Transition from the World Order we knew in XX century to the some other paradigm whose full features remains to be defined. Will the future be really global? Or the regionalist tendencies will win? Will there be a unique Order? Or will there be different local or regional Orders? Or maybe we are going to deal with World Chaos? It is not clear yet, the Transition is not accomplished. We are living in the middle of it.

If the global elite (first of all the United States political elite) has the clear vision of the desired future (that is rather doubtful), even so the circumstances can prevent the realization of it in practice. If the global elite lack the consensual project – the issue is much more complicated. So only the fact of Transition to some new paradigm is certain. The paradigm as such is on the contrary quite uncertain.

World Order from USA point of view

USA position in this shift is absolutely assured but the future of USA is under question. The USA undergoes now the test of global imperial rule and they have to deal with many challenges – some of them quite new and original. They could proceed in three different ways:

1) Creating an American Empire *sensu stricto* with a consolidated technically and socially developed central area (Imperial Core) while the outer spaces would keep divided and fragmentized in the state of permanent unrest (near the chaos); it seems the neo-cons are in favor of such a pattern.

2) Creating multilateral unipolarity where the USA would cooperate with other friendly powers (Canada, Europe, Australia, Japan, Israel – possibly other countries) in solving the regional problems and making pressure on the «rogue countries» (Iran, Venezuela, Belarus, Northern Korea) or on the hesitating countries striving to assure their own regional independence (China, Russia and so on); it seems that democrats and Obama are inclined to do so;

3) Promoting accelerated globalization with the creation of World Government and swift de-sovereignization of the National States in favor of the creation of United States of the World ruled by the global elite on the legal terms (that is the CFR project represented by the strategy of George Soros and his foundations; the colored revolutions are viewed here as the most effective weapon destabilizing and finally destroying States).

It seems that USA tries to go by these three ways simultaneously promoting all three strategies at the same time. This three directions strategy of USA creates the global context in International Relations, USA being the key actor on the global scale. Beyond the evident differences of these three images of future they have some essential points in common. In any case USA is interested in affirming its strategic, economic and political domination; in strengthening of the control or other global actors and in weakening them; in gradual or accelerated de-sovereignization of now more or less independent States; in the promotion of "universal" values reflecting the values of Western world (the liberal democracy, parliamentary system, free market, humans rights and so on).

So we are in the contemporary world in strong and permanent geopolitical field where in the Core is situated in the USA and where the rays of its influences (strategic, economic, political, technological, informational and so on) permeate all the rest of the World depending on the grade of the will to accept it in the case of different countries, ethnic or religious ambiances. It is a kind of "global imperial network" operating on a planetary scale.

This USA-centric global geopolitical field can be described on different levels:

Historically: The USA considers itself to be the logical conclusion and the peak of the Western civilization. In the ancient terms it was presented as the Manifest Destiny of USA. Now they speak in the terms of human rights, promotion of the democracy and of technology, free market institutions and so on. But in the essence, we deal with a new edition of the Western universalism that passed by Roman Empire, Medieval Christianity, the Modernity (with the Enlightenment and colonization) and up to present day postmodernism and ultra-individualism. The history is considered to be univocal (monotone) process of technological and social progress, the way of growing liberation of individuals from all kind of collective identities. The tradition and conservatism are regarded as the obstacles for the freedom and should be rejected. The USA is in vanguard of this historical progress and has the right and obligation (mission!) to move the history further and further. The historical existence of USA coincides with the course of the human history. So "American" means "universal". The other cultures have only an American future or no future at all.

Politically: there are very important trends in World politics that define the Transition. We watch the passage from the liberalism

227

becoming global and only possible political option (as the peak of the political thought of Modernity won the victory over alternative political doctrines – fascism and socialism) to the post-modern and post-individual concept of politics (generally described as post-humanism). The USA plays again here the key role. The politics promoted by USA globally is liberal democracy. So USA supports the globalization of the liberalism preparing thus the next step to the political post-modernity (described in the famous book of A. Negri and M. Hardt *Empire*). There is some distance between liberal ultra-individualism and properly postmodern post-humanism (promoting the cyborgs, genetic modification, cloning and the chimeras), but in the periphery of the World we have the common tendency – the accelerated destruction of any holistic social entities, the fragmentation and atomization of society included in the technology (internet, mobile phones and so on) where the principal actor is strictly individual and excerpt from the natural and social context.

There is important testimony of dual use of promotion of democracy explicitly described in the article of American military and political expert Stephen R. Mann (1992) who affirms that democracy can work as self-generating virus strengthening the existent and historically rife democratic societies but destroying and immersing in chaos the traditional societies not properly prepared for it. So democracy is thought to be an effective weapon to create the chaos and to govern the dissipating world cultures from the Core emulating and installing everywhere the democratic codes. We see how it works in the last events in the Arabic countries. After the accomplishing the full fragmentation of the societies to the individual atoms there will begin the second phase: the division of the individuals themselves on the parts and new (genetic, for example) combinations of the elements in the way of post-human creativity. That can be described as the post-politics as the last horizon of the political futurism.

Ideologically: There is the tendency in the case of the USA to link more the ideology and politics in the zone of the periphery. Before, USA acted on the basis of the pure realism: if the regimes were pro-USA they were tolerated with no regards of their ideological principles. Saudi Arabia represents the net example of that. So some features of the double morality were ideologically accepted. It seems that recently the USA have begun to try to deepen the democracy, supporting popular revolts in Egypt and Tunis whose chiefs were trustfully friends of USA being at the same time corrupted dictators. The double standards in the ideology is vanishing and the deepening of democracy progresses. The culminant point will be reached in the case of the probable unrest in Saudi Arabia. In this moment this trend of promoting the democracy on the ideological basis – including in the politically difficult circumstances – will be tested.

Economically: the USA economy is challenged by the Chinese growth, the energy issue, the critical disproportion between the financial sector and the zone of real industry. The overgrowth of American financial institutes and the delocalization of the industry have created the discontinuity between the sphere of the money and the sphere of the classical capitalist balance of the industry and demands. It was the main cause of the financial crisis of 2008. The Chinese economical politics tries to reaffirm its independence in front of the USA global strategy and once can become the main factor of the competition. The Russian, Iranian, Venezuelan and some other relatively independent (from USA) countries control over the huge amount of the natural resources puts the limits to the American economic influence.

The economy of European Community and the Japanese economic potential represent the two poles of competition inside the strategic partners and military allies of USA. So the USA tries to solve all these problems using not only purely economic instruments but also politics and sometimes military power. We could interpret in this manner the intrusion in Iraq and Afghanistan, the possible intervention in Libya, Iran and Syria. Indirectly promoting opposition in Russia, Iran and China and trying to cause some problems with Turkey and radical Islamism in general for Europe USA wants to reach the same goal. But these are only technical solutions. The main challenge is how to organize the post-modern and financially-centered economy with granted growth overcoming the more and more critical gap between the real sector and the financial instruments whose logic becomes more and more autonomous.

So we have observed the main and asymmetric actor USA situated in the center of the present Transition state of world affairs. This actor represents the true hyperpower and the strongest geopolitical field (that includes all the levels revised before) is structured around this American Core, representing its multilevel networks. The question can be raised here: is this actor fully conscious of what it does and whether it understand well what he will obtain in the end; which kind of Order it is going to get? It seems that the opinions on this most important point are divided: the neocons proclaim the New American Century being optimistic as to the future American Empire. But in their case it is obvious that they have clear (that doesn't mean necessary realistic) vision of the future (American, more precisely North-American future). In this case the World Order will be American Imperial Order based on the unipolar geopolitics. At least theoretically it has some positive point: it is clear and honest.

The multilateralists are more cautious and insist on the necessity to invite the other regional powers to share with the USA the burden of the planetary rule. It is obvious that only similar (regarding the USA) societies can be partners, so the success of promoting democracy becomes here the essential care. The multilateralists act not only in the name of USA but also in the name of the West, considered as something universal. The image of the future World Order is foggier. The fate of the global democracy is misty and not so clearly defined as the image of American Empire.

Yet hazier is the extreme version of promoters of accelerated globalization. It could effectively overthrow the existing national states but in some cases it will only open the way to much more archaic, local, religious or ethnic forces. So the earth-scale open society is such fantastic a perspective that it is much easier to imagine the total chaos and the war of everybody against everybody. So the image of the future World Order differs with regard to the group of American ideologists and decision makers. More consequent strategy is at the same time more ethnocentric, openly imperialistic and hegemonic. It is unipolar World Order. The other two versions are much more dim and uncertain. Up to certain point they can give way to world disorder. They are called summarily "non-polar." So the Transition in question, in any case, is Americano-centric by its nature and the global geopolitical field is structured so that main global processes would be moderated, orientated, directed and sometimes controlled by the unique actor performing its work lonely or with the help of the essentially pro-American Western (or at least pro-Western) allies.

The World Order from the Non-USA Point of View

The Americano-centric world perspective described above being the most important and central as global tendency is not the only one possible. There can be and there are the alternative visions of World architecture that can be taken into consideration. There are secondary and tertiary actors that are inevitable losers in the case of the success of USA-strategy: the countries, states, peoples, cultures that would lose all and gain nothing when the USA strategy realizes. They are multiple and heterogeneous. We could group them in the different categories.

The first category is composed by the more or less successful national States that are not happy to let their independence to the supranational exterior authority – not in the form of open American hegemony, nor in the Western-centered kind of World Government, nor in the chaotic dissolution. There many of such a countries – beginning from China, Russia, Iran, India, including many Southern American and Islamic States. They don't like the Transition at all, suspecting (with good reasons) the inevitable loss of the sovereignty. So they are inclined to resist the main trends of the planetary Americano-centric geopolitical field or adapt to it in such a manner that it would be possible to avoid the logical consequences of the success of American general strategy (it doesn't make difference whether imperialistic or globalist).

The will of the conservation of the sovereignty represents the natural contradiction and the point of resistance in front of the pro-American (or globalist) trends. These countries in general hardly possess the alternative vision of the future World Order. What they want - it is to preserve the status quo and national States in the present form adjusting and modernizing them if necessary. Between the members of this national Statehood clubs there are three kinds of actors: 1) those who try to adapt their societies to the Western standards and to keep friendly relations with the West and USA, but to avoid the direct de-sovereignization (India, Turkey, Brazil, up to the certain point Russia, Kazakhstan);

1) Those who are ready to cooperate with USA but under condition of the non-interference in their inner affairs (Arabia Saudi, Pakistan and so on);

2) Those who, cooperating with USA, strictly observe the particularity of their society making permanent filtration of what is compatible in Western culture with domestic culture or what is not, at the same time trying to use the dividends received by this cooperation to the strengthening of national independence (China);

3) Those who try to oppose the USA directly rejecting the Western values, the unipolarity and the USA hegemony (Iran, Venezuela, North Korea).

All these groups lack the global alternative strategy that could be symmetrically comparable with the American (there is not even a consensual or clear) vision of the future. Everybody acts by themselves and in their own direct interests. The difference consists only in the radicalism of the rejection of Americanization. We could define their position as reactive. This strategy of reactive opposition varying from the rejection to adaptation is sometimes effective, sometimes it is not. In sum it doesn't give any kind of future vision. The future of the World Order is considered as eternal conservation of status quo – Modernity, national Statehood, Westphalian systems, current ONU configuration and so on.

The Second category of actors who reject the Transition consists of subnational groups, movements and organizations that oppose Americanism as the structures of the global geopolitical field by ideological, religious or cultural reasons. These groups are quite different and vary from one concrete state to another. They are mostly based on the religious faith incompatible with the secular doctrine of Americanization, westernization and globalization. But they could be motivated by the ethnical or ideological (for example, socialist or communist) doctrines. Some other act on the regionalist grounds. The paradox is that in the globalization ambiance that aims to uniform all particularities and collective identities on the basis of purely individual identity, such subnational actors easily become transnational – the same religions and ideologies being present in different countries and national States. So in these circles we could find some alternative vision of the future World Order that can be opposed to the Transition and its structures.

We can roughly summarize the different ideas of some of the most important sub-national/trans-national groups:

1) The most famous one is the islamist world vision which represents the utopia of Islamic World State (Global Caliphate). This project is as opposed to the American architecture as to the *status quo* of the modern national States. Bin Laden is the symbol of such a trend of ideas and the two towers of New-York World Trade Center 9/11 are the prove of the importance and seriousness of such a network.

2) The other project can be defined as neo-socialist plan represented in the South American Left and personally by Hugo Chavez. This is roughly a new edition of Marxist critic of capitalism strengthened by nationalist emotion and in some cases (Bolivia, Zapatistas) ethnic sentiments. Some Arab regimes (as Libya of Kaddhafi until his assassination) could be considered in the same line. The next World Order here is presented as global socialist revolution preceded by the anti-USA liberation campaigns in every country. The Transition is identified by this group as the incarnation of classic imperialism criticized by Lenin.

3) The third example of such kind can be found in the Eurasian Project (aka "multipolar", aka "great spaces") proposing the

alternative model of World Order based on the principle of civilizations and great spaces. It presupposes the creation of different transnational political strategic and economic entities united by community of civilization and main (in some cases religious in some – secular and cultural) values. They should consist of integrated States and represent the poles of the multipolar world. European Union could be example of such a form. There can be also Eurasian Union (project of Kazakhstan's President N. Nazarbayev), Islamic Union, the South-American Union, Chinese Union, the Indian Union, Pan-Pacific Union and so on. The North-American great space can be regarded as one of the several other more or less equal poles, nothing more.

We could add some other theories but they are of smaller scale. There is, in the present state of affair, a serious gap between the national States and ideological movements mentioned above operating on the different levels. So the national States lack the vision, and movements lack sufficient infrastructure to put their ideas in practice. If we imagine that, in some circumstances, that gap could be bridged, the alternative to the Transition and to the Americano- or Western-centric tendencies (taken in consideration the demographical, economic and strategic weight of the Non-Western world) will obtain the realistic shape and can be regarded seriously as consequent and theoretically founded plan of concrete future Order.

We live in times characterized by some as an era of a rabid capitalist globalization in which the centers of the world power, while they try to minimize the role and the autonomy of the national states located in the South of the planet, use these as means to consolidate the devastating advance of the capitalist market with its negative consequences for two thirds of humanity. At the same time the thesis proliferates that the nation state loses its importance as there exist international regulatory agencies charged with designing the domestic policies.

Another element present in the analysis of this subject is tied to the multiple contradictions that exist in the contemporary world that are consequences derived from capitalism and from the myth that considers it the only legitimate mode of production for the entire planet, in spite of it having generalized social exclusion, poverty, the ruination of natural resources, violence and political corruption. These deformations caused by capitalist society have been joined by additional phenomena that affect the relations between countries, as there is, for example, terrorism.

This has become the fundamental pretext that the principal imperialist power of the world wields in order to exercise its influence in any country under the supposedly objective pretext of liberating the world from this sore which is deliberately attributed only to less developed countries. The nation-states of the South are also affected by the North American interventionism in their internal affairs exercised through a variety of means that include war as an instrument of coercion and domination, and declared legitimate. They are also affected because of the high rates of earnings by important oligarchical Yankee sectors. The military budget of the United States, that was already high, has grown in the last three years by more than 20%. The military rhetoric that accompanies the center of global imperialism turns even more cynical when the new North-American interventionism justifies itself in the name of civilization and as God's command. In our judgment, the nation-states, inclusive of the less developed ones, have the right to seek their own solutions to their existing democratic governance situations. These states continue to have a cardinal importance which, in many instances, is reinforced by the fact that they are territorial and cultural places where important searches for alternatives to capitalist democracy and struggles for a more just and equitable world are taking place.

Bibliography

Chapter I
Introduction: Framing the Global Democratic Dynamic

Ahluwalia, P. (2001). *Politics and Post-colonial Theory: African Inflections.* London: Routledge.

Ake , C. (1993), "The Unique Case of African Democracy", *International Affairs* (Royal Institute of International Affairs 1944-), Vol. 69, No. 2, pp.239-244.

Amin, Samir. (1996).. "The Challenge of Globalization." *Review of International Political Economy*, February 1996: 24-46.

Barnet, Richard J. and Cavanagh, John. (1994). *Global Dreams: Imperial Corporations and the New World Order.* New York: Simon and Schuster.

Barsun, J. Is Democratic Theory for Export?, in Sixth Morgenthau Memorial Lecture on Ethics & Foreign Policy (1986), pp. 25–26.

Bartelson, Jens. (2010). "Political Globalization." *Distinktion: Scandinavian Journal of Social Theory.* 2004. http://www.distinktion.dk/archive/d8.shtml (accessed March 12th, 2010).

Bell, Daniel. (1988). *The End of Ideology* .Cambridge, Mass: Harvard University Press.

Berger, M. T (1994), "The end of the 'Third World'?" Third World Quarterly, Vol. 15, No. 2, pp. 257-275.

Bratton, M. & Van de Walle, N. (1994), "Neopatrimonial Regimes and Political Transitions in Africa", World Politics, Vol. 46, No. 4, pp. 453-489.

Bratton, M. & Van de Walle, N. (1992), "Popular Protest and Political Reform in Africa", Comparative Politics, Vol. 24, No. 4, pp. 419-442

Brown, W. (2003), "Neo-Liberalism and the End of Liberal Democracy", Theory & Event, Vol. 7, pp. 37-59.

Cavanagh, John. (2002). *Alternatives to Economic Globalization.* San Francisco: Berrett-Koehler.

Chan, S. (2002), "Liberalism, Democracy and Development", Cambridge University Press, United Kingdom: Cambridge.

Chang, J. (2008). *Bad Samaritans: The Myth of Free Trade and the Secret History of Capitalism*. Bloomsbury: Cambridge University Press.

Cincotta, R. P. (2009), "Half a Chance: Youth Bulges and Transitions to Liberal Democracy", New Directions in Demographic Security, ECSP Report, Issue 13, pp. 10-18.

Clapham, C. (1999), "Sovereignty and the Third World State", Political Studies Association, pp.522-537.

Claxton, M. (2010), "A Flawed Analysis: The Inadequacies of Western Liberal Democracy", Agencia Latinoamericana de Informacíon, América Latina en Movimiento, pp. 1-19.

Cyllah, A. (2010), "Democracy and Elections in Africa: Recent Trends and the Role of the International Community", Available   at: http://www.ifes.org/Content/Publications/Testimony/2010/ Democracy-and-Elections-in-Africa.aspx [accessed 24th of April 2013].

Dahl. Robert A. (1998). On democracy. New Haven and London:Yale University Press.

Dalpino, Catharin E. "Does Globalization Promote Democracy?: An early assessment." *Brookings.* September 2001. http://www.brookings.edu/articles/2001/fall_democracy_dalpi no.aspx (accessed March 13th, 2010).

Dennett, D. (2007). Breaking the Spell: Religion as a Natural Phenomenon. New York : Penguin.

Dictionary.com Unabridged. Random House, Inc.Random House, Inc.   *Dictionary.com.* http://dictionary.reference.com/browse/democracy (accessed March 2010, 10).

Dirks, N. B. (2004), "Colonial and Postcolonial Histories: Comparative reflections on the legacies of empire", Global Background Paper for the Human Development Report 2004, Building   Inclusive   Societies,   pp.   1-32. Drucker, Peter F. "The Age of Social Transformation." *Atlantic Monthly*, November 1994: 53-80.

Edigheji, O. (2005), "A Democratic Developmental State in Africa: A concept paper", Centre for Policy Studies: Johannesburg . Enquist, Olov, P. (2003). The Visit of the Royal Physician. London : Vintage.

Exon, James. (1995). "Farewell Address," *Lessons and Legacies: Farewell Addresses from the Senate* (Reading, Mass: Addison-Wesley.

Fatton, R. (1990), "Liberal Democracy in Africa", Political Science Quarterly, Vol. 105, No. 3, pp. 455-473.

Fonte, J. (2002), "Liberal Democracy Vs. Transnational Progressivisim: The Future of the Ideological Civil War within the West", Hudson Institute, ORBIS, pp. 1-14.

Franck, T *(2006/1992). The Emerging Right to Democratic Governance. American* Journal of International Law *86* (1): *46-9*

Fredland, Richard.(2001). *Understanding Africa: A Political Economy Perspective.* Chicago: Burnham.

Frieden, Jeffry. (2006). *Global Capitalism.* New York: WW. Norton.

Fukuyama, F. (1989). The End of History?, *The National Interest,* Summer 1989.

General Globalization – Implications Of Globalization. http://science.jrank.org/pages/9546/General-Globalization-Implications-Globalization.html (accessed March 13th, 2010).

Glendon, M. A.(2001). *A World Made New: Eleanor Roosevelt and the Universal Declaration of Human Rights.* 3rd edn, Princeton: Princeton University Press.

Gray, John (2007).*Black Mass: Apocalyptic Religion and the Death of Utopia*, Allen Lane, London.

Hanen, Tatu Van.(1990). *The Process of Democratization: A Comparative Study of 147 States.* New York: Russak Publications.

Hardt, M. & Negri, A. (2000), "Empire", Harvard University Press, Cambridge MA. *Held D. (2006). Models of Democracy, 3rd edn.* Cambridge: Polity Press.

Habermas, Jürgen. (1996). Between Facts and Norms: Contributions to a Discourse Theory of Law and Democracy. Cambridge, Mass.: MIT Press.

Heflin, Howell. (1997). "Farewell Address," *Lessons and Legacies: Farewell Addresses from the Senate.* Reading, Mass: Addison-Wesley.

Hind, D.*(2007). The Threat to Reason*, Verso.

Hobson, C. (2009), "The Limits of Liberal Democracy Promotion", Institute for Sustainability and Peace, pp. 1-36.

Hudson, P. (1999), "Liberalism, Democracy and Transformation in South Africa", Department of Political Studies, University of the Witwatersrand, pp. 1-11.

Hughes, B. (2005), "The 'Fundamental' Threat of (Neo) Liberal Democracy: An Unlikely Source of Legitimation for Political Violence, Dialogue, pp. 43-85.

Huntington, S.(1993). The *Third Wave: Democratization in the Late 20th Century. University of Oklahoma Press.*

Huntington, Samuel. (1996). *The Clash of Civilizations and the Remaking of World Order.* New York: Simon & Schuster.

Ikenburry, M. Cox, G. John. (2006/2003). Takashi Inoguchi (eds), *American Democracy Promotion* (2006), p. 1). *American Democracy Promotion: Impulses, Strategies and Impacts 1*, No. 3 (Fall 2003

Jean-François Revel. (1976). *La Tentation totalitaire.*(Paris: Robert Laffont.

Joseph, R. (2008), "Progress and Retreat in Africa: Challenges of a 'Frontier' Region", Journal of Democracy, Vol. 19, pp. 94-108.

Kipling, Rudyard. (1995). "The White Man's Burden," *McClure's* 12, no. 4 (1899): 290–91, as reprinted in Dennis Sherman, *Western Civilization: Sources, Images, and Interpretations* (New York: McGraw-Hill, 1995), 271–72.

Klein, Naomi. (2002). No Logo. New York: Picador.

Korten, David. (1995). *When Corporations Rule the World.* Kumarian Press and Berrett-Koehler Publishers.

Knowlton, N. (2009), "Locking-in Liberal Democracy in South Africa, explaining democratisation through an alternative perspective", African Journal of Political Science and International Relations, Vol. 3, pp. 288-299.

Kura, Sulaiman Yusuf Balarabe. "Globalisation and Democracy: A Dialectical Framework for Understanding Democratisation." *Globalization* ICAAP. 2005. http://globalization.icaap.org/content/v5.1/kura.html (accessed March 12th, 2010).

O'Donnell, G. "The Browning of Latin America." *New Perspectives Quarterly*, October 1993: 50-53.

Leon, T. (2010), "The State of Liberal Democracy in Africa – Resurgence or Retreat?", Center for Global Liberty & Prosperity, Development Policy Analysis, Cato Institute, No. 12, pp. 1-31.

Mafeje, A. (2002), "Democratic governance and new democracy in Africa: agenda for the future", Prepared for presentation at the African Forum for Envisioning Africa, Nairobi, available at: http://www.worldsummit2002.org/texts/ArchieMafeje2.pdf [accessed 17th of April 2013].

Manuel, Castells. (1996, second edition, 2000). "The Rise of the Network Society*," The Information Age: Economy, Society and Culture Vol. I*. Cambridge, MA; Oxford, UK: Blackwell.

Mattes, R. & Gyimah-Boadi, E. (2003), "The Quality of Two Liberal Democracies in Africa: Ghana and South Africa", Centre on Democracy, Development and Rule of Law and European Forum Institute for International Studies, pp. 1-37.

Obeng, K. W. (2011), "Democracy in Africa's Post-Conflict States", available   at: http://www.pambazuka.org/aumonitor/comments/2356/ [accessed 20th April 2013].

Omotola, J. S. (2009), "Attractions and Limitations of Liberal Democracy in Africa", Africana, Vol. 3, No.1, pp. 5-30.

Orstein, Norman. (1997). "Introduction," *Lessons and Legacies: Farewell Addresses from the Senate*. Reading, Mass: Addison-Wesley.

Quan & Reuveny, Li & Rafael. "Economic Globalization and Democracy: An Empirical Analysis." *British Journal of Political Science*, January 2003: 29-54.

Pace, M. (2009), "Liberal of Social Democracy: Aspects of the EU's Democracy Promotion Agenda in the Middle East", International Institute for Democracy and Electoral Assistance (IDEA), European Research Institute: UK.

Pausewang, S. & Tronvoll, K. & Aalen, L. (2002), "Ethiopia since the Derg: a decade of democratic pretension and performance", London: Zed books.

Robertson, Roland. *Globalization: Social Theory and Global Culture.* London: Sage Publications, 1992.

Sachs, Jeffrey. (1994). *Shock Therapy in Poland: Perspectives of Five Years,* Tanner lectures (April 6 and 7, 1994), University of Utah.

Sankatsing, G. (2004), "People's Vote Compatible With People's Fate – A democratic alternative to liberal democracy", Political Democracy, Social Democracy and the Market in the Caribbean, pp. 1-27.

Saul, J. S. (1997), "Liberal Democracy vs. Popular Democracy in Southern Africa", Review of African Political Economy, Vol. 24, pp. 219-236.

Schattschneider, E. E. (1942), "Party government", New York: Rinehart

Schmitt, C. (1995). *The Concept of the Political,* University of Chicago Press.

Scholte, Jan Aart.(2005). *Globalization: A Critical Introduction.* New York, USA: Palgrave Macmillan.

Schumpeter, Joseph A.(1990). *Capitalism, Socialism and Democracy.* New York: Harper and Row.

Simon, Paul. (1997). "Farewell Address," *Lessons and Legacies: Farewell Addresses from the Senate* (Reading, Mass: Addison-Wesley.

Sklar, R. L. (1983), "Democracy in Africa", African Studies Review, Vol. 26, No. ¾, pp. 11-24.

Smith, P. H. & Ziegler, M. R. (2008), "Liberal and Illiberal Democracy in Latin America", Latin American Politics and Society, Vol. 50, No. 1, pp. 31-57.

Tar, U. & Shettima, A. G. (2010, "Hegemony and subordination: governing class, power politics and contested electoral democracy in Nigeria", Information, Society & Justice, Vol. 3, No 2, pp. 135-149.

Stiglitz, Joseph. (2002). *Globalization and its Discontents.* New York: W.W. Norton.

Tannen, Deborah. (1998). *The Argument Culture.* New York: Random House.

Tilly. Charles. (2007). *Democracy.* Cambridge, U.K.: Cambridge University Press.

Tully, J. (1999), "The agonic freedom of citizens", Economy and Society, pp. 161-182.

Uwizeyimana, D. E. (2009), "Democracy and pretend democracies in Africa: Myths of African democracies", Law Democracy & Development, Vol. 16, pp. 139-161.

Von Hippel, K. (2000), "Democracy by Force: US Military Intervention in the Post-Cold War World", Cambridge: Cambridge University Press.

WANG Changjiang, No Elections, No Democracy, China Elections & Governance, at www.chinaeletions.org, accessed 12/20/2014.

Zakaria, Fareed. (2003). The Future of Freedom. Illiberal Democracy at Home and Abroad,. Penguin Books India, New Delhi, June *2003*

Chapter II
Western Liberal Democracy as Cognitive Imperialism: A Theoretical Exploration

Ackerman, Frank. (2000). *The Political Economy of Inequality.* Washington DC: Island Press.

Amin, S. (1988) *Eurocentrism.* New York: Monthly Review Press.

Aronsson, Thomas and Karl-Gustaf Löfgren. (1997). *Green Accounting and Green Taxes in the Global Economy.* Umeå: University of Umeå.

Battiste, M.. (1986). Micmac Literacy and Cognitive Imperialism. In J. Barman, Y. Hébert, & D. McCaskill (Eds.), *Indian Education in Canada: The Legacy. Vol. 1* (pp.23-44). Vancouver, B.C.: University of British Columbia Press.

Blaut, J.M. (1993). *The Colonizer's Model of the World: Geographical Diffusionism and Eurocentric History.* New York: Guildford Press.

Blondel, Jean. (1978). *Political parties. A genuine case for discontent?.* London : Wildwood House.

Blumenthal, Sydney. (1980). *The Permanent Campaign.* Boston: Beacon.

Brown, Lester, Christopher Flavin and Hilary French, eds. (2000). *State of the World 2000: A Worldwatch Institute Report on Progress toward a Sustainable Society*. New York: W.W. Norton & Company.

Burchill, S. (2005) 'Liberalism', in S. L.-S. Burchill, Theories of International Relations, New York: Palgrave Macmillan.

Callari, Antonio, & Ruccio, David F., eds. 1996. *Postmodern Materialism and the Future of Marxist Theory*. Hanover, N.H.: University Press of New England.

Caporaso, James A. and David P. Levine. (1992). *Theories of Political Economy*. Cambridge: Cambridge University Press.

Chandler, D. (2006) 'Back to the Future? The Limits of Neo-Wilsonian Ideas of Exporting Democracy', Review of International Studies, 32 (3):475-494

Cheney, R. (2006) Vice Presidents Remarks at the 2006 Vilnius Conference, Reval Hotel Lietuva, Vilnius, Lithuania, 4 May [Online] Available at: www.whitehouse.gov/news/releases/2006/05/20060504-1.html [Accessed 22/01/2012]

Chorev, N. (2005) 'The Institutional Project of Neo-Liberal Globalism: The Case of the WTO', Theory and Society, 34 (3): 317-355.

Clift, Eleanor and Tom Brazaitis. (1997). *War without Bloodshed: The Art of Politics*. New York: Touchstone.

Cox, R. (1983) 'Gramsci, Hegemony and International Relations: An Essay in Method', Millennium: Journal of International Studies, 12 (2): 162-175

Cummins, J. (1989). *Empowering Minority Students*. Sacramento, CA: California Association for Bilingual Education.

Deudney, D. and Ikenberry, J. (1999) 'The Nature and Sources of Liberal International Order', Review of International Studies, 25 (2): 179-196

Deudney, D. and Ikenberry, J. (2009) 'The Myth of the Autocratic Revival: Why Liberal Democracy Will Prevail', Foreign Affairs, 88 (1): 77-93.

Downs, Anthony. (1965). *An Economic Theory of Democracy*. New York: Harper and Row.

Doyle, M. (1986) 'Liberalism and World Politics', American Political Science Review, 80 (4): 1151-1163

Dunne, T. (2006) 'Liberalism' in J. Baylis, and S. Smith, (eds) Globalisation of World Politics: An Introduction to International Relations, 3rd edn, Basingstoke: Palgrave, 185-204.

Esteva, Gustavo. (1992). "Development." In Wolfgang Sachs (ed.), *The Development Dictionary: A Guide to Knowledge as Power.* London: Zed Books.

Folmer, Henk ed. (2001). *Frontiers of Environmental Economics.* Cheltenham, UK: Edward Elgar.

Fraad, Harriet, Resnick, Stephen, & Wolff, Richard. 1994. *Bringing it All Back Home: Class, Gender, and Power in the Modern Household.* London: Pluto Press.

Gallagher, E. (2002) 'Reform and Openness: Why China's Economic Reform have delayed democracy', World Politics , 53(3): 338-372.

Germain, R. and Kenny, M. (1998) 'Engaging Gramsci: International Relations Theory and the New Gramscians', Review of International Studies, 24 (1): 3-21

Gibson-Graham, J.K. 1996. *The End of Capitalism.* Cambridge and Oxford: Blackwell.

Gibson-Graham, J.K., Resnick, Stephen, & Wolff, Richard, eds. 2000. *Class and Its Others.* Minneapolis and London: University of Minnesota Press.

_____. 2001. *Re/Presenting Class: Essays in Postmodern Political Economy.* Durham: Duke University Press.

Global Trade Negotiations (GTN), (2003) Washington Consensus, Harvard University [Online] Available at: http://www.cid.harvard.edu/cidtrade/issues/washington.ht ml , accessed on 23/01/2012]

Gramsci, A. (1971). Selections from the Prison Notebooks. London: International Publishers.

Heflin, Howell. (1997). "Farewell Address," *Lessons and Legacies: Farewell Addresses from the Senate.* Reading, Mass: Addison-Wesley.

Heiman, Michael. (1996). Race, Waste and Class: New Perspectives on Environmental Justice, (Editor's introduction for a special edition). Antipode, 28(2): 111-121.

Held, David. (1996). *Models of Democracy*, 2 ed. Stanford: Stanford University Press, 1996.

Hindess, Barry, & Hirst, Paul Q. 1975. *Pre-Capitalist Modes of Production*. London and New York: Routledge.

Huat, B. (2010) 'Disrupting Hegemonic Liberalism in East Asia', International Journal of Literature and Culture , 37(2): 199-216.

Hurrell, A. (2006) 'Hegemony, Liberalism and Global Order: What Space for Would-be Great Powers?', International Affairs, 82(1): 1-19

Ikenberry, J. (2002) 'America's Imperial Ambition', Foreign Affairs, 81(5): 44-60

Ikenberry, J. (2004) 'Liberalism and Empire: Logics of Order in the American Unipolar Age', Review of International Studies, 30 (4): 609-630

Ikenberry, J. (2008) 'The Rise of China and the Future of the West: Can the Liberal System Survive?', Foreign Affairs, 87 (1): 23-37

Ikenberry, J. (2011) 'The Future of the Liberal World Order: Internationalism After America', Foreign Affairs, 90 (3): 56-68

IMF, (2010) IMF Quota and Governance Reform- Elements of an Agreement, [Online] Available at: http://www.imf.org/external/np/pp/eng/2010/103110.pdf , accessed on 19/01/2012.

IMF, (2012) Reforming the IMF's Governance, International Monetary Fund, Online, available at: http://www.imf.org/external/np/exr/govern/index.htm, accessed on 19/01/2012.

Jones, T. and Hardstaff, P. (2005) Denying Democracy: How the IMF and the World Bank take Power from the People, World Development Movement, London, Online, available at: http://siteresources.worldbank.org/INTPRS1/Resources/P RSP-Review/WDMPRSPsdoc.pdf, accessed on 19/01/2012.

Kant, I. ([1795] 1970) 'Perpetual Peace: A Philosophical Sketch', in H. Reiss (eds), Kant's Political Writings, Cambridge: Cambridge University Press.

Latouche, Serge. (1993). *In the Wake of the Affluent Society: An Exploration of Post-Development*. London: Zed Books.

Lakoff, Robin. (1975). *Language and Woman's Place*. New York: Harper & Row.

246

Lindert and Williamson (2003) 'Does Globalization Make the World More Unequal?' in M. Bardo, A. Taylor and J. Williamson, Globalization in Historical Perspective, National Bureau of Economic Research: University of Chicago Press [Online] Available at: http://www.nber.org/chapters/c9590.pdf, accesses on 23/01/2012.

Lipset, S. (1959) 'Some Social Requisites of Democracy: Economic Development and Political Legitimacy', American Political Science Review, 53 (1): 69-105.

Lyon, Vaughan. (1992). "Green Politics: Parties, Elections, and Environmental Policy," *Canadian Environmental Policy: Ecosystems, Politics, and Process*, ed. Robert Boardman. Toronto: Oxford University Press.

Maggi, G. (1999) 'The role of Multilateral Institutions in International Trade Cooperation', The American Economic Review, 89 (1): 190-214.

Memmi, A. (1969). *Dominated Man: Notes toward a Portrait*. Boston, MA: Beacon Press.

Mies, Maria 1986. *Patriarchy and Accumulation on a World Scale*. London: Zed Books.

Minnick, E. (1990). *Transforming Knowledge*. Philadelphia, PA: Temple University Press.

Moulton, Janice. (1983). "A Paradigm of Philosophy: The Adversary Method," *Discovering Reality: Feminist Perspectives on Epistemology, Metaphysics, Methodology, and Philosophy of Science*, eds. Sandra Harding and Merrill Hintikka. Boston, MA: Kluwer Boston.

No&eumll, L. (1994). *Intolerance: A General Survey.*. (A. Bennet, Trans.). Montreal, QC and Kingston, Ont.: McGill - Queen's University Press.

Morozov, V. (2010) 'Global Democracy, Western Hegemony, and the Russian Challenge', in C. Browning and M. Lehti (eds), The Struggle for the West: A Divided and Contested Legacy, London, New York: Routledge, 185-200

Pieper, U. and Taylor, L. (1996, revised Jan 1998), The Revival of the liberal Creed: the IMF, the World Bank, and Inequality in a

Globalized Economy, CEPA Working Paper Series 1, No. 4 [Online] Available at: http://www.newschool.edu/scepa/publications/workingpapers /archive/cepa0104.pdf, accessed on 23/01/2012.

Planke, D. And Risse, T. (2007) 'Liberalism' in T. Dunne, M. Kurki, and S. Smith (eds), International Relations theories: Discipline and Diversity, 1ˢᵗ edn, Oxford: Oxford University Press

Poulantzas, Nicos. 1974. *Classes in Contemporary Capitalism.* (Trans. By David Fernbach). London: Verso.

Puchala, D. (2005) 'World Hegemony and the United Nations', International Studies Review, 7 (4): 571-584.

Raghavan, C. (1990): Recolonization: Gatt, the Uruguay Round and the Third World. London: Zed Books.

Resnick, Stephen, & Wolff, Richard. 1987. *Knowledge and Class: A Marxian Critique of Political Economy.* Chicago and London: University of Chicago Press.

_____. 1986. "Power, Property, and Class" *Socialist Review,* 86, pp. 97-124.

Rosaldo, R. (1989). *Culture and Truth: The Remaking of Social Analysis.* Boston, MA: Beacon Press.

Russet, B. (2010) 'Liberalism' in T. Dunne, M. Kurki, and S. Smith (eds), International Relations Theories: Discipline and Diversity, 2ⁿᵈ edn, Oxford: Oxford University Press, 95-115.

Said, E. (1992). *Culture and Imperialism.* Cambridge, MA: Harvard University Press.

SCO, (2012) Home Page, Shanghai Cooperation Organisation, [Online] Available at: http://www.sectsco.org/EN/, accessed on 23/01/2012.

Schumpeter, Joseph. (1976). *Capitalism, Socialism and Democracy.* New York: Harper.

Sterling- Folker, J. (2010) 'Neoliberalism' in T. Dunne, M. Kurki, and S. Smith (eds), International Relations theories: Discipline and Diversity, 2ⁿᵈ edn, Oxford: Oxford University Press, 116-134

Stiglitz, J. (2002) Globalization and its Discontents, London: Allen Lane.

Suzuki, David and Holly Jewell Dressel. (2004). *From Naked Ape to Superspecies: Humanity and the Global Eco-Crisis.* Vancouver: Greystone Books.

Wade, R. (2007) 'Globalisation, Growth, Poverty and Inequality', in J. Ravenhill (eds) Global Political Economy, Oxford: Oxford University Press

World Trade Organisation (WTO) (1995) International Trade: Trends and Statistics, Geneva: WTO.

Wright, Erik Olin. 1997. *Classes.* London and New York: Verso.

_____, ed. 1989. *The Debate on Classes.* London and New York: Verso.

Zamagni, Stefano ed.(1995). *The Economics of Altruism* (Aldershot, England: Edward Elgar Publishing.

Chapter III
Globalization and Democratization as Rewesternization

Amin, Samir, "The Challenge of Globalization." *Review of International Political Economy*, February 1996: 24-46.

ANGHIE, A. (1999), "Finding the Peripheries: Sovereignty and Colonialism in Nineteenth-Century International Law". *Harvard International Law Journal, vol. 40*, n. 1, pp.1 – 71.

Barro, Robert J.(2003). "A Democratic Iraq is not an Impossible Dream," *Business Week*, March 31, 2003.

Bartelson, Jens. "Political Globalization." *Distinktion: Scandinavian Journal of Social Theory.* 2004. http://www.distinktion.dk/archive/d8.shtml (accessed March 12th, 2010).

Bellin, Eva. (2004). "The Iraqi Intervention and Democracy in Comparative Perspective, *Political Science Quarterly*, vol. 119 (Winter 2004°05).

Berman, Sheri. (2003). "Islamism, Revolution and Civil Society," *Perspectives on Politics*, vol. 1 (June 2003).

Cappon, Lester J.(ed.). *The Adams-Jefferson Letters*, 2 volumes.(1959). Chapel Hill: The University of North Carolina Press.

Carothers, Thomas. (2003). "Promoting Democracy and Fighting Terrorism," *Foreign Affairs*, vol. 83 (January/February 2003).

Chambers, I. (eds), *The Post-colonial Question: Common Skies, Divided Horizons*. London: Routledge, pp. 242 – 260.

_____. (2007), "The West and the Rest: Discourse and Power". In: DAS GUPTA, T. et al. (eds), *Race and Racialization: Essential Readings*. Toronto: Canadian Scholars Press, pp. 56 – 64.

CHATTERJEE, P. (1998), "Community in the East". *Economic and Political Weekly*, vol. 33, n. 6, pp. 277 – 282.

CHIMNI, B. S. (2006), "Third World Approaches to International Law: A Manifesto". *International Community Law Review*, vol. 8, pp.3 – 27.

COSTA, S. (2003), "Democracia cosmopolita: déficits conceituais e equívocos políticos". *Revista Brasileira de Ciências Sociais*, vol. 18, n. 53, pp.19 – 32.

_____und BOATCĂ, M. (2009), "Postkoloniale Soziologie: ein Programm". In Reuter, J. e Villa, P. (Orgs.). *Postkoloniale Soziologie. Empirische Befunde, theoretische Anschlüsse, politische Intervention*. Bielefeld: Transcript, pp.69 – 90.

Dalpino, Catharin E. "Does Globalization Promote Democracy?: An early assessment." *Brookings*. September 2001. http://www.brookings.edu/articles/2001/fall_democracy_dalpino.aspx (accessed March 13th, 2010).

DE GIORGI, R. (2010), "Multiculturalismo, identidad y derecho". *XI Congreso Nacional y Latinoamericano de Sociología Jurídica*, Buenos Aires: Sociedad Argentina de Sociología Jurídica, pp.1 – 14.

Dictionary.com Unabridged. Random House, Inc.Random House, Inc. *Dictionary.com*. http://dictionary.reference.com/browse/democracy (accessed March 2010, 10).

Drake, Paul W. (1991). "From Good Men to Good Neighbors: 1912°1932," in *Exporting Democracy: The United States and Latin America*, ed. Abraham F. Lowenthal (Baltimore: Johns Hopkins University Press.

Drucker, Peter F. "The Age of Social Transformation." *Atlantic Monthly*, November 1994: 53-80.

DUSSEL, E. (2000), "Europa, modernidad y eurocentrismo," in Lander, Edgardo (Ed.), *La colonialidad del saber: eurocentrismo y ciencias sociales*, Caracas: Unesco/UCV, pp.41 – 53.

General Globalization – Implications Of Globalization. http://science.jrank.org/pages/9546/General-Globalization-Implications-Globalization.html (accessed March 13th, 2010).

Gerges, Fawaz A. (2003). "Can Democracy Take Root in the Islamic World? Empty Promises of Freedom," *New York Times*, July 18, 2003.

HALL, Stuart. (1996), "When was 'the Post-colonial'? Thinking at the Limit". In: Curti, L. and

Hanen, Tatu Van. *The Process of Democratization: A Comparative Study of 147 States.* New York: Russak Publications, 1990.

Hartlyn, Jonathan. (1991). "The Dominican Republic: The Legacy of Intermittent Engagement," in Lowenthal, ed., Lowenthal, Abraham F., ed. *Exporting Democracy: The United States and Latin America.* Baltimore: Johns Hopkins University Press, 1991.

Huntington, Samuel F.(1984). "Will More Countries Become Democratic?" *Political Science Quarterly*, vol. 99 (Summer 1984), p. 218.

Karlberg, M. (2007). "Western Liberal Democracy as New World Order?" In *The Bahá'í World: 2005-2006*, Robert Weinberg (ed.), Haifa, Israel: World Center Publications, 133-156.

Kura, Sulaiman Yusuf Balarabe.(2005). "Globalisation and Democracy: A Dialectical Framework for Understanding Democratisation." *Globalization ICAAP.* 2005. http://globalization.icaap.org/content/v5.1/kura.html (accessed March 12th, 2010).

Mansbridge, Jane. (1980). *Beyond Adversary Democracy.* Chicago: The University Of Chicago Press.

Makiya, Kanan. (1989). *Republic of Fear: The Politics of Modern Iraq.* Berkeley: University of California Press.

O'Donnell, G. "The Browning of Latin America." *New Perspectives Quarterly*, October 1993: 50-53.

Osborne, A.M.(1940). *Rousseau and Burke.* New York: Oxford University Press.

Przeworski Adam, Michael Alvarez, Josô Antonio Cheibub, and Fernando Limongi, *Democracy and Development: Political Institutions and Material Well-Being in the World, 1950°1990*. New York: Cambridge University Press.

Quan & Reuveny, Li & Rafael. "Economic Globalization and Democracy: An Empirical Analysis." *British Journal of Political Science*, January 2003: 29-54.

Rieff, David. (2003). "Blueprint for a Mess," *New York Times Magazine*, November 2, 2003.

Robertson, Roland. *Globalization: Social Theory and Global Culture*. London: Sage Publications, 1992.

Scholte, Jan Aart. *Globalization: A Critical Introduction*. New York, USA: Palgrave Macmillan.

Schumpeter, Joseph A.(1950). *Capitalism, Socialism and Democracy*. New York: Harper and Row, 1950.

SAID, Edward W. (2003) [1978], *Orientalism*. London: Penguin Books.

Smith, Peter H.(1996). *Talons of the Eagle: Dynamics of U.S.-Latin American Relations*. New York: Oxford University Press.

Schwartz, Thomas Alan. (1991). *America's Germany* (Cambridge, MA: Harvard University Press, 1991); and John W. Dower, *Embracing Defeat: Japan in the Wake of World War II* (Norton/Free Press, 1999).

Tierney, John. (2004). "The Hawks Loudly Express Their Second Thoughts," *New York Times*, May 16, 2004; and James Mann, "For Bush, Realpolitik Is No Longer a Dirty Word," *New York Times*, April 11, 2004.

Wong, Edward. (2005). "Top Iraq Shiites Pushing Religion in Constitution," *New York Times*, February 6, 2005.

Chapter IV
Toward Liberation from Western Democracy's Cognitive Imperialism

Adams, Diane L. (Ed.). (1995). Health issues for women of color: A cultural diversity perspective. Thousand Oaks: SAGE Publications.

Bahá'í World Centre. (1998). *The Bahá'í World 1996-97.*Haifa: World Centre Publications.

Bahá'u'lláh. (2005). *Gleanings from the Writings of Bahá'u'lláh.* Wilmette, Il: Bahá'í Publishing Trust.

Black, William K. (2013). "Blocking a Bad Idea That Enriches the Rich: Peterson, Austerity and the Washington Consensus." *Huffington Post* 17 Jan. 2013. Web. 16 April 2013.

Bowles, Samuel and Herbert Gintis. (1986). *Democracy and Capitalism: Poverty, Community, and the Contradictions of Modern Social Thought.* New York: Basic.

Césaire, Aimé. (1955). *Discourse on Colonialism.* Translated by Joan Pinkham. New York: Monthly Review.

Chatterjee, Partha. (1997). *Our Modernity..* Dakar : CODESRIA/SEPHIS.

Chomsky, Noam, "Deterring Democracy," (1992), retrieved online at http://books.zcommunications.org/chomsky/dd/dd-c01-s07.html.

Chomsky, Noam, "What Uncle Sam Really Wants," retrieved online at http://books.zcommunications.org/chomsky/dd/dd-c01-s07.html.

Dahl, Robert.(1989). *Democracy and Its Critics.*(New Haven, Conn.: Yale Univ. Press.

----------------(1971). Polyarchy*: Participation and Opposition* (New Haven, Conn.: Yale Univ. Press, 1971).

Clement, W. (1975). *The Canadian Corporate Elite: An Analysis of Economic Power* (Ottawa: McClelland and Stewart.

Cohen, Raymond. (1981). *International Politics: The Rules of the Game* .London: Longman.

Douzinas, Costas and Papaconstantinou, Petros. (2013). "Greece is standing up to EU neocolonialism: The usurious conditions of the Greek bailout reveals Brussels' colonial mindset – but Athens is showing citizens can resist." *The Guardian* 27 June 2011. Web. 10 April 2013.

Dussel, E. (2007), From Fraternity to Solidarity: Toward a Politics of Liberation. *Journal of Social Philosophy*, 38: 73–92

Fanon, Frantz.(2004). *The Wretched of the Earth*. Translated by Richard Philcox. New York: Grove.

Foucault, Michel (1997). *Society Must Be Defended: Lectures at the Collège de France, 1975-1976*. New York, NY: St. Martin's Press. p. 242.

Fukuyama, Francis . (1993). *The End of History and the Last Man*. New York: Avon Books.

Gramsci, Antonio (1971). *Selections from the Prison Notebooks*. International Publishers.

Grosfoguel, Ramón y Ana Margarita Cervantes-Rodríguez (2002). *The Modern/Colonial/Capitalist World-System in the Twentieth Century: Global Processes, Antisystemic Movements, and the Geopolitics of Knowledge*. Westport, Greenwood Press.

Grosfoguel, Ramón, Nelson Maldonado-Torres y José David Saldívar (2006). *Latin@s in the World-System. Decolonization Struggles in the 21st Century U.S. Empire*. Boulder: Paradigm Publishers.

Grosfoguel, Ramón y José Romero (2009). "Pensar Decolonial". Fondo Editorial La Urbana.

Hardt, M., and A. Negri.(2000). *Empire*. Cambridge, Mass.: Harvard University Press.

Juris, Jeffrey S. and Alex Khasnabish. (2013). Introduction. In *Insurgent Encounters: Transnational Activism, Ethnography, and the Political*. Jeffrey S. Juris and Alex Khasnabish, eds. pp. 1–38. Durham: Duke UP.

Karlberg, M. (2004). Beyond the Culture of Contest: From Adversarialism to Mutualism in an Age of Interdependence. Oxford: George Ronald.

Klein, Naomi. (2008). *The Shock Doctrine: The Rise of Disaster Capitalism*. Penguin Books, 2008. Print.

Lander, Edgardo (ed.).(2000). *La colonialidad del saber. Eurocentrismo y ciencias sociales. Perspectivas latinoamericanas*. Buenos Aires, CLACSO.

Magdoff, Harry. Imperialism: From the Colonial Age to the Present. Monthly Review Press (1978).

Mann, Stephen R. (1992). "Chaos Theory and Strategic Thought". *Parameters* 2U3, Autumn, 1992.

Mariátegui, José Carlos. (1971). *Seven Interpretive Essays on Peruvian Reality*. Texas Pan American Series. Translated by Marjory Urquidi. Austin: University of Texas Press.

Memmi, lbert. (1975). *Un entretien avec Robert Davies suivi de Itinéraire de l'expérience vécue à la théorie de la domination*. Montréal: Éditions L'Étincelle : distributeur, Réédition Québec.

Mignolo, Walter D. (2013). *Yes, we can: Non-European thinkers and philosophers*. Aljazeera 19 Feb 2013. Web. 10 April.

⸻. (2012). *The Darker Side of Western Modernity: Global futures, Decolonial Options*. Durham and London: Duke University Press.

Mignolo, Walter y Arturo Escobar (eds.). (2008). *Globalization and the Decolonial Option*. Nueva York: Routledge.

Mignolo, Walter. (2007). Delinking. Cultural Studies 21(2-3): 449-514.

Munoz-Pogossian, Betilde. (2008) Electoral Rules and the Transformation of Bolivian Politics: The Rise of Evo Morales. New York: Palgrave MacMillan.

Mignolo, Walter. (2000). (Post)Occidentalism, (Post)Coloniality, and (Post)Subaltern Rationality. In *The Pre-Occupation of Postcolonial Studies*. Fawzia Afzal-Khan and Kalpana Seshadri-Crooks, eds. pp. 86–118. Durham: Duke UP.

Walter Mignolo, Weihua He and Haiyan Xie. (2012), The Prospect of Harmony and the Decolonial View of the World, Marxism and Reality, no. 4, p.110 – 120.

Quijano, Aníbal. (2012). *'Live Well': Between the Development and the Decoloniality of Power*. In: Latin American Critical Thought: Theory and Practice. Ed. Alberto L. Bialakowsky. et al. 1st ed. Ciudad Autonoma de Buenos Aires: Clacso, 2012. Print.

⸻. (2007). *El Giro Decolonial: Reflexiones para una diversidad epistémica más allá del capitalismo global*. Ed. Ramón Grosfoguel. Pontificia Universidad Javeriana Bogotá: Siglo del Hombre Editores: 93-126.

Quijano, Aníbal. (2000). Coloniality of Power, Eurocentrism, and Latin America. Nepantla: Views from South 1(3): 533-580.

Quijano, Aníbal. (2007). Coloniality and Modernity/Rationality. Cultural Studies 21(2-3): 168-178.

Quijano, Aníbal and Immanuel Wallerstein. (1992). Americanity as Concept: Or the Americas in the Modern World-System. International Social Science Journal 131: 549-557.

Ribeiro, Gustavo, Lins.(2013). Why (post)colonialism and (de)coloniality are not enough: a post-imperialist perspective. *Postcolonial Studies*. 14. March (2011):285-297. Web. 12 April 2013.

Sader, Emir.(2011). *The New Mole: Paths of the Latin American Left.* London: Verso.

Said, Edward. (1981). *Covering Islam: How the Media and the Experts Determine How We See the Rest of the World.* London: Routledge & Kegan Paul.

Schumpeter, Joseph. (1976). *Capitalism, Socialism, and Democracy* (1943; repr., London: Allen and Unwin.

Thiong'o, Ngũgĩ wa. (1986). *Decolonising the Mind.* New York: Twayne Publishers.

Vivek, Chibber. (2013). *Postcolonial Theory and the Specter of Capital.* London: Verso.

Walsh, Catherine. (2000). *Pensamiento crítico y matriz (de)colonial. Reflexiones latinoamericanas.* Quito: Abya-Yala Editores.

Walsh, Catherine, Álvaro García Linero y Walter Mignolo (eds.).(2006). *Interculturalidad, descolonización del estado y del conocimiento.* Buenos Aires: Ediciones del Signo.

Weber, Max. (1946). *From Max Weber: Essays in Sociology,* trans. H.H. Girth and C. Wright Mills (Oxford: Oxford University Press.

Weihua He and Haiyan Xie. (2012, August 30), Decoloniality and its Re-imagination of the World Future: An Interview with Prof. Walter Mignolo, Social Sciences Weekly, p.5.

Wittgenstein, Ludwick. (1974). *Philosophical Investigations,* trans. G. Anscombe. Oxford: Basil Blackwell.

World Commission on Environment and Development. (1987). *Our Common Future.* Oxford: Oxford University Press.

Wright, Richard.(1956). *The Color Curtain: A Report on the Bandung Conference*. New York: World.

Žižek, Slavoj. (1998). *A Leftist Plea for Eurocentrism. Critical Inquiry*. 24. 4:988-1009.

www.ingramcontent.com/pod-product-compliance
Lightning Source LLC
Chambersburg PA
CBHW050636280326
41932CB00015B/2660